Unquiet Fronts

Unquiet Fronts
Two Personal Accounts of German Soldiers
During the First World War

A German Deserter's War Experience
Anonymous
Translated by J. Koettgen

The Diary of a German Soldier
Feldwebel C——.

Unquiet Fronts
Two Personal Accounts of German Soldiers During the First World War
A German Deserter's War Experience
by Anonymous
Translated by J. Koettgen
and
The Diary of a German Soldier
By Feldwebel C——.

First published under the titles
A German Deserter's War Experience
and
The Diary of a German Soldier

FIRST EDITION

Leonaur is an imprint
of Oakpast Ltd

Copyright in this form © 2013 Oakpast Ltd

ISBN: 978-1-78282-172-4 (hardcover)
ISBN: 978-1-78282-173-1 (softcover)

http://www.leonaur.com

Publisher's Notes
The views expressed in this book are not necessarily those of the publisher.

Contents

A German Deserter's War Experience 7
The Diary of a German Soldier 151

A German Deserter's War Experience

Contents

Translator's Preface	11
Marching Into Belgium	13
Fighting in Belgium	18
Shooting Civilians in Belgium	28
German Soldiers and Belgian Civilians	34
The Horrors of Street Fighting	38
Crossing the Meuse	43
In Pursuit	46
Nearly Buried Alive on the Battlefield	53
Soldiers Shooting Their Own Officers	58
Sacking Suippes	64
Marching to the Battle of the Marne—Into the Trap	71
At the Marne—In the Maw of Death	76
The Rout of the Marne	83
The Flight From the Marne	89
At the End of the Flight	97
The Beginning of Trench Warfare	104
Friendly Relations With the Enemy	113
Fighting in the Argonnes	117

Christmas in the Trenches	122
The "Itch"—A Saviour	128
In the Hell of Vauquois	134
Sent on Furlough	139
The Flight to Holland	143
America and Safety	147

Translator's Preface

The following narrative first appeared in German in the columns of the *New Yorker Volkszeitung*, the principal organ of the German speaking Socialists in the United States. Its author, who escaped from Germany and military service after 14 months of fighting in France, is an intelligent young miner. He does not wish to have his name made public, fearing that those who will be offended by his frankness might vent their wrath on his relatives. Since his arrival in this country his friends and acquaintances have come to know him as an upright and truthful man whose word can be relied upon.

The vivid description of the life of a common German soldier in the present war aroused great interest when the story presented in these pages to the English speaking reader was published in serial form. For here was an historian of the war who had been through the horrors of the carnage as one of the "Huns," one of the "Boches"; a soldier who had not abdicated his reason; a warrior against his will, who nevertheless had to conform to the etiquette of war; a hater of militarism for whom there was no romance in war, but only butchery and brutality, grime and vermin, inhuman toil and degradation. Moreover, he was found to be no mean observer of men and things. His technical training at a school of mining enabled him to obtain a much clearer understanding of the war of position than the average soldier possesses.

Most soldiers who have been in the war and have written down their experiences have done so in the customary way, never questioning for a moment the moral justification of war. Not so our author. He could not persuade his conscience to make a distinction between private and public morality, and the angle from which he views the events he describes is therefore entirely different from that of other actual observers of and participants in war. His story also contains the first German description of the retreat of the Teutonic armies after the Battle of the Marne. The chief value of this soldier's narrative lies, however, in his destructive, annihilating criticism of the romance and fabled virtues of war. If some of the incidents related in this book appear to be treated too curtly it is solely due to this author's limited literary powers. If, for instance, he does not dwell upon his inner experiences during his terrible voyage to America in the coal bunker of a Dutch ship it is because he is not a literary artist, but a simple workman.

The translator hopes that he has succeeded in reproducing faithfully the substance and the spirit of the story, and that this little book will contribute in combating one of the forces that make for war—popular ignorance of war's realities. Let each individual fully grasp and understand the misery, degradation, and destruction that await him in war, and the barbarous ordeal by carnage will quickly become the most unpopular institution on earth.

J. Koettgen.

1
Marching Into Belgium

At the end of July our garrison at Koblenz was feverishly agitated. Part of our men were seized by an indescribable enthusiasm, others became subject to a feeling of great depression. The declaration of war was in the air. I belonged to those who were depressed. For I was doing my second year of military service and was to leave the barracks in six weeks' time. Instead of the long wished-for return home war was facing me.

Also during my military service I had remained the anti-militarist I had been before. I could not imagine what interest I could have in the mass murder, and I also pointed out to my comrades that under all circumstances war was the greatest misfortune that could happen to humanity.

Our sapper battalion, No. 30, had been in feverish activity five days before the mobilization; work was being pushed on day and night so that we were fully prepared for war already on the 23rd of July, and on the 30th of July there was no person in our barracks who doubted that war would break out. Moreover, there was the suspicious amiability of the officers and sergeants, which excluded any doubt that any one might still have had. Officers who had never before replied to the salute of a private soldier now did so with the utmost attention. Cigars and beer were distributed in those days by the officers with great, uncommon liberality, so that it was not surprising that many soldiers were scarcely ever sober and did not realize the seriousness of the situation. But there were also others.

There were soldiers who also in those times of good-humour and the grinning comradeship of officer and soldier could not forget that in military service they had often been degraded to the level of brutes, and who now thought with bitter feelings that an opportunity might perhaps be offered in order to settle accounts.

The order of mobilization became known on the 1st of August, and the following day was decided upon as the real day of mobilization. But without awaiting the arrival of the reserves we left our garrison town on August 1st. Who was to be our "enemy" we did not know; Russia was for the present the only country against which war had been declared.

We marched through the streets of the town to the station between crowds of people numbering many thousands. Flowers were thrown at us from every window; everybody wanted to shake hands with the departing soldiers. All the people, even soldiers, were weeping. Many marched arm in arm with their wife or sweetheart. The music played songs of leave-taking. People cried and sang at the same time. Entire strangers, men and women, embraced and kissed each other; men embraced men and kissed each other. It was a real witches' Sabbath of emotion; like a wild torrent, that emotion carried away the whole assembled humanity. Nobody, not even the strongest and most determined spirit, could resist that ebullition of feeling.

But all that was surpassed by the taking leave at the station, which we reached after a short march. Here final *adieus* had to be said, here the separation had to take place. I shall never forget that leave-taking, however old I may grow to be. Desperately many women clung to their men; some had to be removed by force. Just as if they had suddenly had a vision of the fate of their beloved ones, as if they were beholding the silent graves in foreign lands in which those poor nameless ones were to be buried, they sought to cling fast to their possession, to retain what already no longer belonged to them.

Finally that, too, was over. We had entered a train that had been kept ready, and had made ourselves comfortable in our cattle-trucks. Darkness had come, and we had no light in our comfortable sixth-class carriages.

The train moved slowly down the Rhine, it went along without any great shaking, and some of us were seized by a worn-out feeling after those days of great excitement. Most of the soldiers lay with their heads on their knapsacks and slept. Others again tried to pierce the darkness as if attempting to look into the future; still others drew stealthily a photo out of their breast-pocket, and only a very small number of us spent the time by debating our point of destination. Where are we going to? Well, where? Nobody knew it. At last, after long, infinitely long hours the train came to a stop. After a night of quiet, slow riding we were at—Aix-la-Chapelle! At Aix-la-Chapelle! What were we doing at Aix-la-Chapelle? We did not know, and the officers only shrugged their shoulders when we asked them.

After a short interval the journey proceeded, and on the evening of the 2nd of August we reached a farm in the neighbourhood of the German and Belgian frontier, near Herbesthal. Here our company was quartered in a barn. Nobody knew what our business was at the Belgian frontier. In the afternoon of the 3rd of August reservists arrived, and our company was brought to its war strength. We had still no idea concerning the purpose of our being sent to the Belgian frontier, and that evening we lay down on our bed of straw with a forced tranquillity of mind. Something was sure to happen soon, to deliver us from that oppressive uncertainty. How few of us thought that for many it would be the last night to spend on German soil!

A subdued signal of alarm fetched us out of our "beds" at 3 o'clock in the morning. The company assembled, and the captain explained to us the war situation. He informed us that we had to keep ready to march, that he himself was not yet informed about the direction. Scarcely half an hour later fifty large traction motors arrived and stopped in the road before our quarters. But the drivers of these wagons, too, knew no particulars and had to wait for orders. The debate about our nearest goal was resumed. The orderlies, who had snapped up many remarks of the officers, ventured the opinion that we would march into Belgium the very same day; others contradicted them. None of us could know anything for certain. But the order to march did not arrive, and in the evening all of us could lie down again on our straw. But it was a short rest. At 1 o'clock in the morning an alarm aroused us again, and the captain honoured us with an address. He told us we were at war with Belgium, that we should acquit ourselves as brave soldiers, earn iron crosses, and do honour to our German name. Then he continued somewhat as follows:

> We are making war only against the armed forces, that is the Belgium army. The lives and property of civilians are under the protection of international treaties, international law, but you soldiers must not forget that it is your duty to defend your lives as long as possible for the protection of your Fatherland, and to sell them as dearly as possible. We want to prevent useless shedding of blood as far as the civilians are concerned, but I want to remind you that a too great considerateness borders

on cowardice, and cowardice in face of the enemy is punished very severely.

After that "humane" speech by our captain we were "laden" into the automobiles, and crossed the Belgian frontier on the morning of August 5th. In order to give special solemnity to that "historical" moment we had to give three cheers.

At no other moments the fruits of military education have presented themselves more clearly before my mind. The soldier is told, "The Belgian is your enemy," and he has to believe it. The soldier, the workman in uniform, had not known till then who was his enemy. If they had told us, "The Hollander is your enemy," we would have believed that, too; we would have been compelled to believe it, and would have shot him by order. We, the "German citizens in uniform," must not have an opinion of our own, must have no thoughts of our own, for they give us our enemy and our friend according to requirements, according to the requirements of their own interests. The Frenchman, the Belgian, the Italian, is your enemy. Never mind, shoot as we order, and do not bother your head about it. You have duties to perform, perform them, and for the rest—cut it out!

Those were the thoughts that tormented my brain when crossing the Belgian frontier. And to console myself, and so as to justify before my own conscience the murderous trade that had been thrust upon me, I tried to persuade myself that though I had no Fatherland to defend, I had to defend a home and protect it from devastation. But it was a weak consolation, and did not even outlast the first few days.

Travelling in the fairly quick motorcars we reached, towards 8 o'clock in the morning, our preliminary destination, a small but pretty village. The inhabitants of the villages which we had passed stared at us in speechless astonishment, so that we all had the impression that those peasants for the most part did not know why we had come to Belgium. They had been roused from their sleep and, half-dressed, they gazed from their windows after our automobiles. After we had stopped and alighted, the peasants of that village came up to us without any reluctance, offered us food, and brought us coffee, bread, meat, etc. As the field-kitchen had not arrived we were glad to receive those kindly gifts of the "enemy," the more so because those fine fellows absolutely refused any payment. They told us the Belgian soldiers had left, for where they did not know.

After a short rest we continued our march and the motor-cars went back. We had scarcely marched for an hour when cavalry, dragoons and huzzars, overtook us and informed us that the Germans were marching forward in the whole neighbourhood, and that cyclist companies were close on our heels. That was comforting news, for we no longer felt lonely and isolated in this strange country. Soon after the troop of cyclists really came along. It passed us quickly and left us by ourselves again. Words of anger were to be heard now; all the others were able to ride, but we had to walk. What we always had considered as a matter of course was now suddenly felt by us to be a great injustice. And though our scolding and anger did not help us in the least, it turned our thoughts from the heaviness of the "monkey" (knapsack) which rested like a leaden weight on our backs.

The heat was oppressive, the perspiration issued from every pore; the new and hard leather straps, the new stiff uniforms rubbed against many parts of the body and made them sore, especially round the waist. With great joy we therefore hailed the order that came at 2 o'clock in the afternoon, to halt before an isolated farm and rest in the grass.

2

Fighting in Belgium

About ten minutes we might have lain in the grass when we suddenly heard rifle shots in front of us. Electrified, all of us jumped up and hastened to our rifles. Then the firing of rifles that was going on at a distance of about a mile or a mile and a half began steadily to increase in volume. We set in motion immediately.

The expression and the behaviour of the soldiers betrayed that something was agitating their mind, that an emotion had taken possession of them which they could not master and had never experienced before. On myself I could observe a great restlessness. Fear and curiosity threw my thoughts into a wild jumble; my head was swimming, and everything seemed to press upon my heart. But I wished to conceal my fears from my comrades. I know I tried to with a will, but whether I succeeded better than my comrades, whose uneasiness I could read in their faces, I doubt very much.

Though I was aware that we should be in the firing line within half an hour, I endeavoured to convince myself that our participation in the fight would no longer be necessary. I clung obstinately, nay, almost convulsively to every idea that could strengthen that hope or give me consolation. That not every bullet finds its billet; that, as we had been told, most wounds in modern wars were afflicted by grazing shots which caused slight flesh-wounds; those were some of the reiterated self-deceptions indulged in against my better knowledge. And they proved effective. It was not only that they made me in fact feel more easy; deeply engaged in those thoughts I had scarcely observed that we were already quite near the firing line.

The bicycles at the side of the road revealed to us that the cyclist corps were engaged by the enemy. We did not know, of course, the strength of our opponents as we approached the firing line in leaps. In leaping forward every one bent down instinctively, whilst to our right and left and behind us the enemy's bullets could be heard striking; yet we reached the firing line without any casualties and were heartily welcomed by our hard-pressed friends. The cyclists, too, had not yet suffered any losses; some, it is true, had already been slightly wounded, but they could continue to participate in the fight.

We were lying flat on the ground, and fired in the direction indicated to us as fast as our rifles would allow. So far we had not seen our opponents. That, it seemed, was too little interesting to some of our soldiers; so they rose partly, and fired in a kneeling position. Two men of my company had to pay their curiosity with their lives. Almost at one and the same time they were shot through the head. The first victim of our group fell down forward without uttering a sound; the second threw up his arms and fell on his back. Both of them were dead instantly.

Who could describe the feelings that overcome a man in the first real hail of bullets he is in? When we were leaping forward to reach the firing line I felt no longer any fear and seemed only to try to reach the line as quickly as possible. But when looking at the first dead man I was seized by a terrible horror. For minutes I was perfectly stupefied, had completely lost command over myself and was absolutely incapable to think or act. I pressed my face and hands firmly against the ground, and then suddenly I was seized by an irrepressible excitement, took hold of my gun, and began to fire away blindly. Little after little I quieted down again somewhat, nay, I became almost quite confident as if everything was normal. Suddenly I found myself content with myself and my surroundings, and when a little later the whole line was commanded, "Leap forward! March, march!" I ran forward demented like the others, as if things could not be other than what they were. The order, "Position!" followed, and we flopped down like wet bags. Firing had begun again.

Our firing became more lively from minute to minute, and grew into a rolling deafening noise. If in such an infernal noise you want to make yourself understood by your neighbour, you have to shout at him so that it hurts your throat. The effect of our firing caused our opponent to grow unsteady; his fire became weaker; the line of the enemy began to waver. Being separated from the enemy by only about 500 yards, we could observe exactly what was happening there. We saw how about half of the men opposing us were drawn back. The movement is executed by taking back every second man whilst number one stays on until the retiring party has halted. We took advantage of that movement to inflict the severest losses possible on our retreating opponent. As far as we could survey the country to our right and left we observed that the Germans were pressing forward at several points. Our company, too, received the order to advance when the enemy took back all his forces.

Our task was to cling obstinately to the heels of the retreating enemy so as to leave him no time to collect his forces and occupy new positions. We therefore followed him in leaps with short breathing pauses so as to prevent him in the first place from establishing himself in the village before him. We knew that otherwise we should have to engage in costly street fighting. But the Belgians did not attempt to establish themselves, but disengaged themselves from us with astonishing skill.

Meanwhile we had been re-enforced. Our company had been somewhat dispersed, and everybody marched with the troop he chanced to find himself with. My troop had to stay in the village to search every house systematically for soldiers that had been dispersed or hidden. During that work we noticed that the Germans were marching forward from all directions. Field artillery, machine-gun sections, etc., arrived, and all of us wondered whence all of this came so quickly.

There was however no time for long reflections. With fixed bayonets we went from house to house, from door to door, and though the harvest was very meagre, we were not turned away quite empty-handed, as the inhabitants had to deliver up all privately owned fire-arms, ammunition, etc. The chief functionary of the village who accompanied us, had to explain to every citizen that the finding of arms after the search would lead to punishment by court-martial. And court-martial means—death.

After another hour had passed we were alarmed again by rifle and gun firing; a new battle had begun. Whether the artillery was in action on both sides could not be determined from the village, but the noise was loud enough, for the air was almost trembling with the rumbling, rolling, and growling of the guns which steadily increased in strength. The ambulance columns were bringing in the first wounded; orderly officers whizzed past us. War had begun with full intensity.

Darkness was falling before we had finished searching all the houses. We dragged mattresses, sacks of straw, feather beds, whatever we could get hold of, to the public school and the church where the wounded were to be accommodated. They were put to bed as well as it could be done. Those first victims of the horrible massacre of nations were treated with touching care. Later on, when we had grown more accustomed to those horrible sights, less attention was paid to the wounded.

The first fugitives now arrived from the neighbouring villages. They had probably walked for many an hour, for they looked tired, absolutely exhausted. There were women, old, white-haired men, and children, all mixed together, who had not been able to save anything but their poor lives. In a perambulator or a push-cart those unfortunate beings carried away all that the brutal force of war had left them. In marked contrast to the fugitives that we had hitherto met, these people were filled with the utmost fear, shivering with fright, terror-stricken in face of the hostile world. As soon as they beheld one of us soldiers they were seized with such a fear that they seemed to crumple up. How different they were from the inhabitants of the village in which we were, who showed themselves kind, friendly, and even obliging towards us.

We tried to find out the cause of that fear, and heard that those fugitives had witnessed bitter street fighting in their village. They had experienced war, had seen their houses burnt, their simple belongings perish, and had not yet been able to forget their streets filled with dead and wounded soldiers. It became clear to us that it was not fear alone that made these people look like the hunted quarry; it was hatred, hatred against us, the invaders who, as they had to suppose, had fallen upon them unawares, had driven them from their home. But their hatred was not only directed against us, the German soldiers, nay, their own, the Belgian soldiers, too, were not spared by it.

We marched away that very evening and tried to reach our section. When darkness fell the Belgians had concentrated still farther to the rear; they were already quite near the fortress of Liège. Many of the villages we passed were in flames; the inhabitants who had been driven away passed us in crowds; there were women whose husbands were perhaps also defending their "Fatherland," children, old men who were pushed hither and thither and seemed to be always in the way. Without any aim, any plan, any place in which they could rest, those processions of misery and unhappiness crept past us—the best illustration of man-murdering, nation-destroying war! Again we reached a village which to all appearances had once been inhabited by a well-to-do people, by a contented little humanity. There were nothing but ruins now, burnt, destroyed houses and farm buildings, dead soldiers, German and Belgian, and among them several civilians who had been shot by sentence of the court-martial.

Towards midnight we reached the German line which was trying to get possession of a village which was already within the fortifications of Liège, and was obstinately defended by the Belgians. Here we had to employ all our forces to wrench from our opponent house after house, street after street. It was not yet completely dark so that we had to go through that terrible struggle which developed with all our senses awake and receptive. It was a hand to hand fight; every kind of weapon had to be employed; the opponent was attacked with the butt-end of the rifle, the knife, the fist, and the teeth. One of my best friends fought with a gigantic Belgian; both had lost their rifle. They were pummelling each other with their fists. I had just finished with a Belgian who was about twenty-two years of age, and was going to assist my friend, as the Herculean Belgian was so much stronger than he. Suddenly my friend succeeded with a lightning motion in biting the Belgian in the chin. He bit so deeply that he tore away a piece of flesh with his teeth. The pain the Belgian felt must have been immense, for he let go his hold and ran off screaming with terrible pain.

All that happened in seconds. The blood of the Belgian ran out of my friend's mouth; he was seized by a horrible nausea, an indescribable terror, the taste of the warm blood nearly drove him insane. That young, gay, lively fellow of twenty-four had been cheated out of his youth in that night. He used to be the jolliest among us; after that we could never induce him even to smile.

Whilst fighting during the night I came for the first time in touch with the butt-end of a Belgian rifle. I had a hand to hand fight with a Belgian when another one from behind hit me with his rifle on the head with such force that it drove my head into the helmet up to my ears. I experienced a terrific pain all over my head, doubled up, and lost consciousness. When I revived I found myself with a bandaged head in a barn among other wounded.

I had not been severely wounded, but I felt as if my head was double its normal size, and there was a noise in my ears as of the wheels of an express engine.

The other wounded and the soldiers of the ambulance corps said that the Belgians had been pushed back to the fortress; we heard, however, that severe fighting was still going on. Wounded soldiers were being brought in continuously, and they told us that the Germans had already taken in the first assault several fortifications like outer-forts, but that they had not been able to maintain themselves because they had not been sufficiently provided with artillery. The defended places and works inside the forts were still practically completely intact, and so were their garrisons. The forts were not yet ripe for assault, so that the Germans had to retreat with downright enormous losses. The various reports were contradictory, and it was impossible to get a clear idea of what was happening.

Meanwhile the artillery had begun to bombard the fortress, and even the German soldiers were terror-stricken at that bombardment. The heaviest artillery was brought into action against the modern forts of concrete. Up to that time no soldier had been aware of the existence of the 42-centimetre mortars. Even when Liège had fallen into German hands we soldiers could not explain to ourselves how it was possible that those enormous fortifications, constructed partly of reinforced concrete of a thickness of one to six meters, could be turned into a heap of rubbish after only a few hours' bombardment. Having been wounded, I could of course not take part in those operations, but my comrades told me later on how the various forts were taken. Guns of all sizes were turned on the forts, but it was the 21- and 42-centimetre mortars that really did the work.

From afar one could hear already the approach of the 42-centimetre shell. The shell bored its way through the air with an uncanny, rushing and hissing sound that was like a long shrill whistling filling the whole atmosphere for seconds. Where it struck everything was destroyed within a radius of several hundred yards. Later I have often gazed in wonderment at those hecatombs which the 42-centimetre mortar erected for itself on all its journeys. The enormous air pressure caused by the bursting of its shells made it even difficult for us Germans in the most advanced positions to breathe for several seconds. To complete the infernal row the Zeppelins appeared at night in order to take part in the work of destruction. Suddenly the soldiers would hear above their heads the whirring of the propellers and the noise of the motors, well-known to most Germans.

The Zeppelins came nearer and nearer, but not until they were in the immediate neighbourhood of the forts were they discovered by our opponents, who immediately brought all available searchlights into play in order to search the sky for the dreaded flying enemies. The whirring of the propellers of the airships which had been distributed for work on the various forts suddenly ceased. Then, right up in the air, a blinding light appeared, the searchlight of the Zeppelin, which lit up the country beneath it for a short time. Just as suddenly it became dark and quiet until a few minutes later, powerful detonations brought the news that the Zeppelin had dropped its "ballast." That continued for quite a while, explosion followed explosion, interrupted only by small fiery clouds, shrapnel which the Belgian artillery sent up to the airships, exploding in the air. Then the whirring of the propellers began again, first loud and coming from near, from right above our heads, then softer and softer until the immense ship of the air had entirely disappeared from our view and hearing.

Thus the forts were made level with the ground; thousands of Belgians were lying dead and buried behind and beneath the ramparts and fortifications. General assault followed. Liège was in the hands of the Germans.

I was with the ambulance column until the 9th of August and by that time had been restored sufficiently to rejoin my section of the army. After searching for hours I found my company camping in a field. I missed many a good friend; my section had lost sixty-five men, dead and wounded, though it had not taken part in the pursuit of the enemy.

We had been attached to the newly-formed 18th Reserve Army Corps (Hessians) and belonged to the Fourth Army which was under the command of Duke Albrecht of Wurttemberg. Where that army, which had not yet been formed, was to operate was quite unknown to us private soldiers. We had but to follow to the place where the herd was to be slaughtered; what did it matter where that would be? On the 11th of August we began to march and covered 25-45 miles every day. We learned later on that we always kept close to the Luxemburg frontier so as to cross it immediately should necessity arise. Had it not been so oppressively hot we should have been quite content, for we enjoyed several days of rest which braced us up again.

On the 21st of August we came in contact with the first German troops belonging to the Fourth Army, about 15 miles to the east of the Belgian town of Neufchateau. The Battle of Neufchateau, which lasted from the 22nd to the 24th of August, had already begun. A French army here met with the Fourth German Army, and a murderous slaughter began. As is always the case it commenced with small skirmishes of advance guards and patrols; little after little ever-growing masses of soldiers took part and when, in the evening of the 22nd of August, we were led into the firing line, the battle had already developed to one of the most murderous of the world war. When we arrived the French were still in possession of nearly three-quarters of the town. The artillery had set fire to the greatest part of Neufchateau, and only the splendid villas in the western part of the town escaped destruction for the time being. The street fighting lasted the whole night.

It was only towards noon of the 23rd of August, when the town was in the hands of the Germans, that one could see the enormous losses that both sides had suffered. The dwelling-places, the cellars, the roads and side-walks were thickly covered with dead and horribly wounded soldiers; the houses were ruins, gutted, empty shells in which scarcely anything of real value had remained whole. Thousands had been made beggars in a night full of horrors. Women and children, soldiers and citizens were lying just where death had struck them down, mixed together just as the merciless shrapnel and shells had sent them out of life into the darkness beyond. There had been real impartiality. There lay a German soldier next to a white-haired French woman, a little Belgian stripling whom fear had driven out of the house into the street, lay huddled up against the "enemy," a German soldier, who might have been protection and safety for him.

Had we not been shooting and stabbing, murdering and clubbing as much and as vigorously as we could the whole night? And yet there was scarcely one amongst us who did not shed tears of grief and emotion at the spectacles presenting themselves. There was for instance a man whose age it was difficult to discover; he was lying dead before a burning house. Both his legs had been burnt up to the knees by the fire falling down upon him. The wife and daughter of the dead man were clinging to him, and were sobbing so piteously that one simply could not bear it. Many, many of the dead had been burnt entirely or partly; the cattle were burning in their stables, and the wild bellowing of those animals fighting against death by fire, intermingled with the crying, the moaning, the groaning and the shrieking of the wounded. But who had the time now to bother about that?

Everybody wanted help, everybody wanted to help himself, everybody was only thinking of himself and his little bit of life. "He who falls remains where he lies; only he who stands can win victories." That one learns from militarism and the average soldier acts upon that principle. And yet most soldiers are forced by circumstances to play the *rôle* of the good Samaritan. People who could formerly not look upon blood or a dead person, were now bandaging their comrades' arms and legs which had been amputated by shells. They did not do it because they were impelled by the command of their heart, but because they said to themselves that perhaps to-morrow already their turn might come and that they, too, might want assistance. It is a healthy egotism which makes men of mercy out of those hardened people.

The French had formed their lines again outside the town in the open. At the moment when the enemy evacuated the town an error was made by the Germans which cost many hundreds of German soldiers their lives. The Germans had occupied the rest of the town with such celerity that our artillery which was pounding that quarter had not been informed of the changed situation, and was raining shell upon shell into our own ranks. That failure of our intelligence department caused the death of many of our comrades. Compelled by the firing of the enemy and our own artillery we had finally to give up part of our gains, which later on we recovered, again with great sacrifice. Curiously enough, the residential quarter with the villas I mentioned before had not suffered seriously; the Red Cross flag was hoisted on the houses in which temporary hospitals were established.

It is here that the Belgian citizens are said to have mutilated some German wounded soldiers. Whether it was true, whether it was only rumoured, as was asserted also many times by German soldiers who had been in the hospitals, I do not know. But this I know, that on the 24th of August when the French had executed a general retreat, it was made known in an army order that German soldiers had been murdered there and that the German army could not leave the scenes of those shameful deeds without having first avenged their poor comrades. The order was therefore given—by the leader of the army—to raze the town without mercy. When later on (it was in the evening and we were pursuing the enemy) we were resting for a short time, clouds of smoke in the east showed that the judgment had been fulfilled. A battery of artillery that had remained behind had razed house after house. Revenge is sweet, also for Christian army leaders.

Outside the town the French had reformed their ranks, and were offering the utmost resistance. But they were no match for the German troops who consisted largely of young and active men. Frenchmen taken prisoner explained that it was simply impossible to withstand an assault of this war-machine, when the German columns attacked with the bayonet and the cry of "Hurrah! hurrah!" which penetrated to the very marrow. I can understand that, for we sometimes appeared to ourselves to be a good imitation of American Indians who, like us, rushed upon their enemies with shrill shouts. After a fight lasting three hours many Frenchmen surrendered, asking for quarter with raised hands. Whole battalions of the enemy were thus captured by us. Finally, in the night from the 23rd to the 24th of August, the ranks of the enemy were thrown into confusion and retreated, first slowly, then flying headlong. Our opponent left whole batteries, munition columns, ambulance columns, etc.

I found myself in the first pursuing section. The roads we used were again literally covered with corpses; knapsacks, rifles, dead horses and men were lying there in a wild jumble. The dead had been partly crushed and pounded to a pulp by the horses and vehicles, an indescribably terrible spectacle even for the most hardened mass-murderer. Dead and wounded were lying to the right and left of the road, in fields, in ditches; the red trousers of the French stood out distinctly against the ground; the field-gray trousers of the Germans were however scarcely to be noticed and difficult to discover.

The distance between ourselves and the fleeing Frenchmen became greater and greater, and the spirit of our soldiers, in spite of the hardships they had undergone, became better and gayer. They joked and sang, forgot the corpses which were still filling the roads and paths, and felt quite at ease. They had already accustomed themselves to the horrible to such a degree that they stepped over the corpses with unconcern, without even making the smallest detour. The experience of those first few weeks of the war had already brutalized us completely. What was to happen to us if this should continue for months—?

3

Shooting Civilians in Belgium

At 11 o'clock all further philosophizing was put a stop to; we were ordered to halt, and we were to receive our food from the field kitchen.

We were quite hungry and ate the tinned soup with the heartiest of appetites. Many of our soldiers were sitting with their dinner-pails on the dead horses that were lying about, and were eating with such pleasure and heartiness as if they were home at mother's. Nor did some corpses in the neighbourhood of our improvised camp disturb us. There was only a lack of water and after having eaten thirst began to torment us.

Soon afterwards we continued our march in the scorching midday sun; dust was covering our uniforms and skin to the depth of almost an inch. We tried in vain to be jolly, but thirst tormented us more and more, and we became weaker and weaker from one quarter of an hour to another. Many in our ranks fell down exhausted, and we were simply unable to move. So the commander of our section had no other choice but to let us halt again if he did not want every one of us to drop out. Thus it happened that we stayed behind a considerable distance, and were not amongst the first that were pursuing the French.

Finally, towards four o'clock, we saw a village in front of us; we began at once to march at a much brisker pace. Among other things we saw a farm-cart on which were several civilian prisoners, apparently snipers. There was also a Catholic priest among them who had, like the others, his hands tied behind his back with a rope. Curiosity prompted us to enquire what he had been up to, and we heard that he had incited the farmers of the village to poison the water.

We soon reached the village and the first well at which we hoped to quench our thirst thoroughly. But that was no easy matter, for a military guard had been placed before it who scared us off with the warning, "Poisoned"! Disappointed and terribly embittered the soldiers, half dead with thirst, gnashed their teeth; they hurried to the next well, but everywhere the same devilish thing occurred—the guard preventing them from drinking. In a square, in the middle of the village, there was a large village well which sent, through two tubes, water as clear as crystal into a large trough. Five soldiers were guarding it and had to watch that nobody drank of the poisoned water.

I was just going to march past it with my pal when suddenly the second, larger portion of our company rushed like madmen to the well. The guards were carried away by the rush, and every one now began to drink the water with the avidity of an animal. All quenched their thirst, and not one of us became ill or died. We heard later on that the priest had to pay for it with his death, as the military authorities "knew" that the water in all the wells of that village was poisoned and that the soldiers had only been saved by a lucky accident. Faithfully the God of the Germans had watched over us; the captured Belgians did not seem to be under his protection. They had to die.

In most places we passed at that time we were warned against drinking the water. The natural consequence was that the soldiers began to hate the population which they now had to consider to be their bitterest enemies. That again aroused the worst instincts in some soldiers. In every army one finds men with the disposition of barbarians. The many millions of inhabitants in Germany or France are not all civilized people, much as we like to convince ourselves of the contrary. Compulsory military service in those countries forces all without distinction into the army, men and monsters. I have often bitterly resented the wrong one did to our army in calling us all barbarians, only because among us—as, naturally also among the French and English—there were to be found elements that really ought to be in the penitentiary. I will only cite one example of how we soldiers ourselves punished a wretch whom we caught committing a crime.

One evening—it was dark already—we reached a small village to the east of the town of Bertrix, and there, too, found "poisoned" water. We halted in the middle of the village. I was standing before a house with a low window, through which one could see the interior. In the miserable poverty-stricken working man's dwelling we observed a woman who clung to her children as if afraid they would be torn from her. Though we felt very bitter on account of the want of water, every one of us would have liked to help the poor woman.

Some of us were just going to sacrifice our little store of victuals and to say a few comforting words to the woman, when all at once a stone as big as a fist was thrown through the window-pane into the room and hurt a little girl in the right hand. There were sincere cries of indignation, but at the same moment twenty hands at least laid hold of the wretch, a reservist of our company, and gave him such a hiding as to make him almost unconscious. If officers and other men had not interfered the fellow would have been lynched there and then. He was to be placed before a court-martial later on, but it never came to that. He was drowned in the river at the battle of the Meuse. Many soldiers believed he drowned himself, because he was not only shunned by his fellow soldiers, but was also openly despised by them.

We were quartered on that village and had to live in a barn. I went with some pals into the village to buy something to eat. At a farmer's house we got ham, bread, and wine, but not for money. The people positively refused to take our money as they regarded us as their guests, so they said; only we were not to harm them. Nevertheless we left them an adequate payment in German money. Later on we found the same situation in many other places. Everywhere people were terribly frightened of us; they began to tremble almost when a German soldier entered their house.

Four of us had formed a close alliance; we had promised each other to stick together and assist each other in every danger. We often also visited the citizens in their houses, and tried to the best of our ability to comfort the sorely tried people and talk them out of their fear of us. Without exception we found them to be lovable, kindly, and good people who soon became confidential and free of speech when they noticed that we were really their friends. But when, at leaving, we wrote with chalk on the door of their houses "*Bitte schonen, hier wohnen brave, gute, Leute!*" (Please spare, here live good and decent people) their joy and thankfulness knew no bounds. If so much bad blood was created, if so many incidents happened that led to the shooting by court-martial of innumerable Belgians, the difference of language and the mistakes arising therefrom were surely not the least important causes; of that I and many others of my comrades became convinced during that time in Belgium. But the at first systematically nourished suspicion against the "enemy," too, was partly responsible for it.

In the night we continued our march, after having been attached to the 21-centimetre mortar battery of the 9th Regiment of Foot Artillery which had just arrived; we were not only to serve as covering troops for that battery, but were also to help it place those giants in position when called upon. The gun is transported apart from the carriage on a special wagon. Gun-carriage and guns are drawn each by six horses. Those horses, which are only used by the foot artillery, are the best and strongest of the German army. And yet even those animals are often unable to do the work required of them, so that all available men, seventy or eighty at times, have to help transport the gun with ropes specially carried for that purpose. That help is chiefly resorted to when the guns leave the road to be placed in firing position. In order to prevent the wheels from sinking into the soil, other wheels, half a yard wide, are attached round them.

These guns are high-angle guns, *i.e.*, their shot rises into the air for several thousand yards, all according to the distance of the spot to be hit, and then drops at a great angle. That is the reason why neither hill nor mountain can protect an enemy battery placed behind those elevations. At first the French had almost no transportable heavy artillery so that it was quite impossible for them to fight successfully against our guns of large calibre. Under those conditions the German gunners, of course, felt themselves to be top-dog, and decorated their 21-centimetre guns with inscriptions like the following, "Here declarations of war are still being accepted."

We felt quite at ease with the artillery, and were still passably fresh when we halted at six o'clock in the morning, though we had been marching since two o'clock. Near our halting place we found a broken German howitzer, and next to it two dead soldiers. When firing, a shell had burst in the gun destroying it entirely. Two men of the crew had been killed instantly and some had been seriously wounded by the flying pieces. We utilised the pause to bury the two dead men, put both of them in one grave, placed both their helmets on the grave, and wrote on a board: "*Here rest two German artillerymen.*"

We had to proceed, and soon reached the town of Bertrix. Some few houses to the left and right of the road were burning fiercely; we soon got to know that they had been set alight because soldiers marching past were said to have been shot at from those houses. Before one of these houses a man and his wife and their son, a boy of 15 or 16, lay half burnt to cinders; all had been covered with straw. Three more civilians lay dead in the same street.

We had marched past some more houses when all at once shots rang out; they had been shooting from some house, and four of our soldiers had been wounded. For a short while there was confusion.

The house from which the shots must have come was soon surrounded, and hand grenades were thrown through all the windows into the interior. In an instant all the rooms were in flames. The exploding hand grenades caused such an enormous air pressure that all the doors were blown from their hinges and the inner walls torn to shreds. Almost at the same time, five men in civilian clothes rushed into the street and asked for quarter with uplifted hands. They were seized immediately and taken to the officers, who formed themselves into a tribunal within a few minutes. Ten minutes later sentence had already been executed; five strong men lay on the ground, blindfolded and their bodies riddled by bullets.

Six of us had in each of the five cases to execute the sentence, and unfortunately I, too, belonged to those thirty men. The condemned man whom my party of six had to shoot was a tall, lean man, about forty years of age. He did not wince for a moment when they blindfolded him. In a garden of a house nearby he was placed with his back against the house, and after our captain had told us that it was our duty to aim well so as to end the tragedy quickly, we took up our position six paces from the condemned one. The sergeant commanding us had told us before to shoot the condemned man through the chest. We then formed two lines, one behind the other. The command was given to load and secure, and we pushed five cartridges into the rifle.

Then the command rang out, "Get ready!" The first line knelt, the second stood up. We held our rifles in such a position that the barrel pointed in front of us whilst the butt-end rested somewhere near the hip. At the command, "Aim!" we slowly brought our rifles into shooting position, grasped them firmly, pressed the plate of the butt-end against the shoulder and, with our cheek on the butt-end, we clung convulsively to the neck of the rifle. Our right forefinger was on the trigger, the sergeant gave us about half a minute for aiming before commanding, "Fire!"

Even today I cannot say whether our victim fell dead on the spot or how many of the six bullets hit him. I ran about all day long like a drunken man, and reproached myself most bitterly with having played the executioner. For a long time I avoided speaking about it with fellow-soldiers, for I felt guilty. And yet—what else could we soldiers do but obey the order?

Already in the preceding night there had been encounters at Bertrix between the German military and the population. Houses were burning in every part of the town. In the market place there was a great heap of guns and revolvers of all makes. At the clergyman's house they had found a French machine-gun and ammunition, whereupon the clergyman and his female cook had been arrested and, I suppose, placed immediately before a court-martial.

Under those conditions we were very glad to get out of Bertrix again. We marched on in the afternoon. After a march of some 3 miles we halted, and received food from the field kitchen. But this time we felt no appetite. The recollection of the incidents of the morning made all of us feel so depressed that the meal turned out a real funeral repast. Silently we set in motion again, and camped in the open in the evening, as we were too tired to erect tents.

It was there that all discipline went to pieces for the first time. The officers' orders to put up tents were not heeded in the slightest degree. The men were dog-tired, and suffered the officers to command and chatter as much as they liked. Every one wrapped himself up in his cloak, lay down where he was, and as soon as one had laid down one was asleep. The officers ran about like mad shouting with redoubled energy their commands at the exhausted soldiers; in vain. The officers, of course had gone through the whole performance on horseback and, apparently, did not feel sufficiently tired to go to sleep.

When their calling and shouting had no effect they had to recourse to personal physical exertion and began to shake us up. But as soon as one of us was awake the one before had gone to sleep again. Thus for a while we heard the exhortation, "I say, you! Get up! Fall in line for putting up tents!" Whereupon one turned contentedly on the other side and snoozed on. They tried to shake me awake, too, but after having sent some vigorous curses after the lieutenant—there was no lack of cursing on either side that evening—I continued to sleep the sleep of the just.

For the first time blind discipline had failed. The human body was so exhausted that it was simply unable to play any longer the *rôle* of the obedient dog.

4

German Soldiers and Belgian Civilians

The march had made us very warm, and the night was cold. We shivered all over, and one after the other had to rise in order to warm himself by moving about. There was no straw to be had, and our thin cloaks offered but little protection. The officers slept in sleeping bags and woollen blankets.

Gradually all had got up, for the dew had wetted our clothing; things were very uncomfortable. The men stood about in groups and criticized the incidents of the preceding day. The great majority were of the opinion that we should tell the officers distinctly that in future it would not be so easy for them to work their deeds of oppression. One of the older reservists proposed that we should simply refuse in future to execute a command to shoot a condemned man; he thought that if all of us clung together nothing could happen to us. However, we begged him to be careful, for if such expressions were reported they would shoot him for sedition without much ado. Nevertheless all of us were probably agreed that the reservist had spoken exactly what was in our minds. The bitter feeling was general, but we would not and could not commit any imprudent action. We had learned enough in those few days of the war to know that war brutalises and that brutal force can no longer distinguish right from wrong; and with that force we had to reckon.

Meanwhile the time had come to march on. Before that we had to drink our coffee and arrange our baggage. When we were ready to march the captain gave us a speech in which he referred to the insubordination of the night before. "I take it," he said, "that it was the result of your stupidity. For if I were not convinced of that I should send you all before a court-martial, and all of you would be made unhappy for the rest of your lives. But in future," he continued after a short reflection, "I will draw the reins so tightly that incidents like these can never happen again, and the devil must be in it if I can not master you. An order is an order, even if one imagines himself too tired."

We joined the mortar battery again, and continued our march. The country we were passing was rather dreary and monotonous so that that part of our march offered few interesting changes. The few tiny villages we came through were all abandoned by their inhabitants, and the poverty-stricken dwellings were mostly devastated. However, we met long lines of refugees. These people had as a rule fled with the French army, and were returning now, only to find their homes destroyed by the brutal hand of war. After a lengthy march broken by rests and bivouacs we neared the fairly large village of Sugny on the Belgo-French frontier just inside Belgian territory.

It was about noon, and though the steadily increasing thunder of guns pointed to the development of another battle, we hoped to be able to stay at the place during the night. We entered it towards one o'clock, and were again quartered in a large barn. Most of the soldiers refused the food from the field-kitchen, and "requisitioned" eggs, chicken, geese, and even small pigs, and soon general cooking was in full swing. Everywhere the pots were steaming. Unfortunately most had taken the animals and foodstuffs from the inhabitants without paying for them.

Several soldiers arrived with barrels and bottles of wine, which were at once beheaded and emptied in spite of the warnings and admonitions of the wiser amongst us. It naturally followed that several sergeants and men were soon almost helplessly drunk. The proprietor of "our" barn had three medium-sized pigs left. One of those intoxicated sergeants attempted to kill one of the pigs with a blunt pocket-knife. He had tormented the poor beast almost to death when some sober soldiers caught him in the act. The animal was killed by a shot through the head, and the sergeant had to go to sleep at once. But that was only one incident of many, and not at all the worst one. The inhabitants of Sugny had to suffer much from the drunkenness of our men. The open and secret plundering of gardens, stables and houses was quite a common thing, and as the soldiers were practically left to do what they pleased, no matter what happened or how many complaints were made, matters could naturally not improve.

The people of Sugny were to be pitied. First they had been plundered by the flying French soldiers, the allies of the Belgians, who had taken along with them everything they could get together in a hurry, and now the Germans were acting in no better way.

In a family of seven we were told that the French had taken away all the bread and meat. They had gone through all the cupboards and shelves, and had even stolen the gold watches belonging to the daughters of the house. These and similar tales we heard from several families of the place, and what at first we did not think possible on our side we now beheld with our own eyes—even our well-trained soldiers robbed, pillaged, and stole. War makes no difference between friend and foe.

The roaring of the guns, which could be heard very distinctly, kept the inhabitants in constant fear and excitement, so that we were finally quite able to understand why those people prayed to God to be so kind as to give victory to the Germans. An old inn-keeper explained to me in fairly fluent German: "You see it is not that we are for Germany. Heaven forbid! We are just Belgians and are so accustomed to it that we would rather remain Belgians to the end of our lives. But if the Germans had to retreat now, the French would come again and our village would again become the scene of battle. The little left to us would then be a prey to the flames. Therefore the Germans must win." And then he began praying again.

That part of the country had twice harboured the French, and now we Germans were there. That the population suffered from want and hunger was not to be wondered at, and often we divided our rations with the severely tried people. Myself and two mates had given our "iron ration" (preserved meat and vegetables and a bag of biscuits) to a woman "blessed" with eight children. At the call we could not show our "iron one," so we each of us had to mount guard twice as a punishment for that feeble proof of our charity. Our half-file leader, Lieutenant Spahn, expressed the opinion that pity was idiocy, and if the woman had eight children it was her own concern. Then he concluded literally with great emphasis, "In war everybody is his own nearest neighbour, even if all around us die in a ditch."

Another soldier got fourteen days' close confinement. He was on his way with bread for a hungry poor family, and had in his arms six of those little army loaves which he had begged from the soldiers. He was met by that same Lieutenant Spahn who was in company of some sergeants. When Spahn asked him where he was taking the bread the sapper replied that he was on his way to a poor family that was really starving. The lieutenant then ordered him to take the bread immediately to the company. Thereupon he overwhelmed the soldier with all the "military" expressions he could think of, like, "Are you mad?" "Donkey!" "Silly ass?" "Duffer!" "Idiot!" etc. When the soldier showed nevertheless no sign of confusion, but started to proceed on his way, the lieutenant roared out the order again, whereupon the soldier turned round, threw the bread before the feet of Lieutenant Spahn, and said quietly: "The duffers and idiots have to shed their blood to preserve also your junker family from the misery that has been brought upon this poor population."

That the sapper got only two weeks of close confinement for "unmannerly conduct towards a superior" with aggravating circumstances, was a wonder; he had indeed got off cheaply.

According to martial law he had to work off his punishment in the following manner: When his company went to rest in the evening, or after a fight or a march, the man had to report himself every day for two weeks at the local or camp guard. While the company was resting and the men could move about freely, he had to be in the guard room which he could only leave to do his needs, and then only by permission of the sergeant on guard, and in company of a soldier belonging to the guard. He was not allowed to smoke or read or converse or speak, received his rations from the guard, and had to stay in the guard-room until his company marched off. Besides that he was tied to a tree or some other object for fully two hours every day. He was fettered with ropes and had to spend those two hours standing, even if he had marched 30 miles or had risked his life in a fight for the same "Fatherland" that bound him in fetters.

The resentment continued to grow and, in consequence of the many severe punishments that were inflicted, had reached such a height that most soldiers refused to fetter their comrades. I, too, refused, and when I continued my refusals in spite of repeated orders I was likewise condemned to two weeks of close confinement as an "entirely impenitent sinner," for "not obeying an order given" and for "persistent disobedience."

5

The Horrors of Street Fighting

We left Sugny the next morning, and an hour later we crossed the Belgo-French frontier. Here, too, we had to give three cheers. The frontier there runs through a wood, and on the other side of the wood we placed the 21-cm. mortars in position.

Our troops were engaged with the rear-guard of the enemy near the French village of Vivier-au-Court. We were brought in to reinforce them, and after a five hours' fight the last opponents had retired as far as the Meuse. Vivier-au-Court had hardly suffered at all when we occupied it towards noon. Our company halted again here to wait for the mortar battery.

Meanwhile we walked through the village to find some eatables. After visiting several houses we came upon the family of a teacher. Father and son were both soldiers; two daughters of about twenty and twenty-two were alone with their mother. The mother was extremely shy, and all the three women were crying when we entered the home. The eldest daughter received us with great friendliness and, to our surprise, in faultless German. We endeavoured to pacify the women, begging them not to cry; we assured them again and again that we would not harm them, and told them all kinds of merry stories to turn their thoughts to other things.

One of my mates related that in a fight in the morning, we had lost seven men and that several on our side had been wounded. That only increased the women's excitement, a thing we really could not understand. At last one of the girls, who had been the first one to compose herself, explained to us why they were so much excited. The girl had been at a boarding school at Charlottenburg (Germany) for more than two years, and her brother, who worked in Berlin as a civil engineer, had taken a holiday for three months after her graduation in order to accompany his sister home. Both had liked living in Germany, it was only the sudden outbreak of war that had prevented the young engineer from returning to Berlin. He had to enter the French army, and belonged to the same company in which his father was an officer of the reserve.

After a short interval the girl continued: "My father and brother were here only this morning. They have fought against you. It may have been one of their bullets which struck your comrades down. O, how terrible it is! Now they are away—they who had only feelings of respect and friendship for the Germans—and as long as the Germans are between them and us we shall not be able to know whether they are dead or alive. Who is it that has this terrible war, this barbaric crime on his conscience?" Tears were choking her speech, and our own eyes did not remain dry. All desire to eat had gone; after a silent pressing of hands we slunk away.

We remained in the village till the evening, meanwhile moving about freely. In the afternoon nine men of my company were arrested; it was alleged against them that they had laid hands on a woman. They were disarmed and kept at the local guard-house; the same thing happened to some men of the infantry. Seven men of my company returned in the evening; what became of the other two I have not been able to find out.

At that time a great tobacco famine reigned amongst us soldiers. I know that one mark and more was paid for a single cigarette, if any could be got at all. At Vivier-au-Court there was only one tobacco store run by a man employed by the state. I have seen that man being forced by sergeants at the point of the pistol to deliver his whole store of tobacco for a worthless order of requisition. The "gentlemen" later on sold that tobacco for half a mark a packet.

Towards the evening we marched off, and got the mortar battery in a new position from where the enemy's positions on the Meuse were bombarded.

After a short march we engaged the French to the northeast of Donchéry. On this side of the Meuse the enemy had only his rearguard, whose task was to cover the crossing of the main French armies, a movement which was almost exclusively effected at Sédan and Donchéry. We stuck close to the heels of our opponents, who did not retreat completely till darkness began to fall. The few bridges left did not allow him to withdraw his forces altogether as quickly as his interest demanded. Thus it came about that an uncommonly murderous nocturnal street fight took place in Donchéry which was burning at every corner. The French fought with immense energy; an awful slaughter was the result. Man against man! That "man against man" is the most terrible thing I have experienced in war. Nobody can tell afterwards how many he has killed. You have gripped your opponent, who is sometimes weaker, sometimes stronger than yourself. In the light of the burning houses you observe that the white of his eyes has turned red; his mouth is covered with a thick froth. With head uncovered, with dishevelled hair, the uniform unbuttoned and mostly ragged, you stab, hew, scratch, bite and strike about you like a wild animal. It means life or death.

You fight for your life. No quarter is given. You only hear the gasping, groaning, jerky breathing. You only think of your own life, of death, of home. In feverish haste, as in a whirlwind, old memories are rushing through your mind. Yet you get more excited from minute to minute, for exhaustion tries to master you; but that must not be—not now! And again the fight is renewed; again there is hewing, stabbing, biting. Without rifle, without any weapon in a life and death struggle. You or I. I? I?—Never! you! The exertion becomes superhuman. Now a thrust, a vicious bite, and you are the victor. Victor for the moment, for already the next man, who has just finished off one of your mates, is upon you—. You suddenly remember that you have a dagger about you. After a hasty fumbling you find it in the prescribed place. A swift movement and the dagger buries itself deeply in the body of the other man.

Onward! onward! new enemies are coming up, real enemies. How clearly the thought suddenly flashes on you that that man is your enemy, that he is seeking to take your life, that he bites, strikes, and scratches, tries to force you down and plant his dagger in your heart. Again you use your dagger. Thank heavens! He is down. Saved!—Still, you must have that dagger back! You pull it out of his chest. A jet of warm blood rushes out of the gaping wound and strikes your face. Human blood, warm human blood! You shake yourself, horror strikes you for only a few seconds. The next one approaches; again you have to defend your skin. Again and again the mad murdering is repeated, all night long—

Finally, towards four o'clock in the morning, the rest of the French surrendered after some companies of infantry had occupied two roads leading to the bridges. When the French on the other side became aware of this they blew up the bridges without considering their own troops who were still on them. Germans and Frenchmen were tossed in the air, men and human limbs were sent to the sky, friend and foe found a watery grave in the Meuse.

One could now survey with some calm the scene of the mighty slaughter. Dead lay upon dead, it was misery to behold them, and above and around them all there were flames and a thick, choking smoke. But one was already too brutalized to feel pity at the spectacle; the feeling of humanity had been blown to all the winds. The groaning and crying, the pleading of the wounded did not touch one. Some Catholic nuns were lying dead before their convent. You saw it and passed on.

The only building that had escaped destruction was the barracks of the 25th regiment of French Dragoons. However, we had not much time to inspect things, for at seven o'clock the French artillery began already sending shell after shell into the village. We entrenched behind a thick garden wall, immediately behind the Meuse. Our side of the Meuse was flat, the opposite one went up steeply. There the French infantry had entrenched themselves, having built three positions on the slope, one tier above the other. As the enemy's artillery overshot the mark we remained outside their fire. We had however an opportunity to observe the effects of the shots sent by our own artillery into the enemy's infantry position on the slope in front of us. The shells (21-cm. shells) whizzed above our heads and burst with a tremendous noise, each time causing horrible devastation in the enemy's trenches.

The French were unable to resist long such a hail of shells. They retreated and abandoned all the heights of the Meuse. They had evacuated the town of Sédan without a struggle. In fact, that town remained completely intact, in contrast to the completely demolished Donchéry. Not a house in Sédan had suffered. When the rallying-call was sounded at Donchéry it turned out that my company had lost thirty men in that fight. We mustered behind the barracks of the dragoons, and our company, which had shrunk to ninety men, was ordered to try and build a pontoon-bridge across the Meuse at a place as yet unknown to us. Having been reinforced by eighty men of the second company we marched away in small groups so as not to draw the enemy's attention to us. After an hour's march we halted in a small wood, about 200 yards away from the Meuse, and were allowed to rest until darkness began to fall.

When it had become dark the bridge transportation column—it was that belonging to our division—came up across the fields, to be followed soon after by that of the army corps. All preparations having been made and the chief preliminaries, like the placing of the trestle and the landing boards, gone through, the various pontoon-wagons drove up noiselessly, in order to be unloaded just as noiselessly and with lightning speed. We had already finished four pontoons, *i.e.*, twenty yards of bridge, without being observed by our opponent. Everything went on all right. Suddenly the transportable search-lights of the enemy went into action, and swept up and down the river. Though we had thrown ourselves flat upon the ground wherever we stood, our opponents had observed us, for the search-lights kept moving a little to and fro and finally kept our spot under continual illumination. We were discovered. We scarcely had time to consider, for an artillery volley almost immediately struck the water to our left and right. We were still lying flat on the ground when four more shots came along. That time a little nearer to the bridge, and one shot struck the bank of the river.

Immediately another volley followed, and two shells struck the bridge. Some sappers fell into the water and two fell dead on the bridge; those in the water swam ashore and escaped with a cold ducking. One only was drowned. It was the man of whom I told before that he was despised by his fellow-soldiers because he had hurt the child of a poor woman with a stone he had thrown through the window into her room.

6

Crossing the Meuse

In spite of the continual and severe cannonading of the artillery we succeeded in fetching away the two dead soldiers and bringing them on land. The bridge had been much damaged so that we could do nothing but replace the ruined pontoons by new ones. When the firing of the artillery had died down somewhat we began the difficult task for the second time. But we had scarcely begun when another salvo found its mark and damaged the bridge severely; fortunately no losses were inflicted upon us that time. We were now ordered to retire, only to begin afresh after half an hour.

The enemy's searchlights had been extinguished, and we were able to take some ten pontoons into line without being molested. Then, suddenly, we were again overwhelmed by the fire of the artillery; the enemy's patrols had noticed us. Several batteries had opened fire on us at the same time, and in ten minutes' time all our work was nothing but a heap of sinking pontoons; twelve men were killed.

We now were ordered to march away. Only eight of our party were left behind to look after the dead and wounded. We set out to get out of the danger zone. After having marched upstream for a distance of about a mile and a quarter we halted and observed that the bridge-building section of the army corps was present again. We were told that we should complete the individual links of the bridge on land. Those bridge-links, consisting each of two pontoons, were firmly tied together, provided with anchors and all accessories, completed on land, and then let down into the water. The site of the bridge, which had meanwhile been determined upon, was made known to us, and we rowed with all our might down the river towards that spot.

Our opponent, who had gained no knowledge of that ruse, did not molest us, and in quick succession all the bridge-links reached the determined place. The various links were rowed into their proper position with tremendous speed, and joined together. It did not take quite twenty minutes to get everything just sufficiently in shape. The infantry, who had kept in readiness, then rushed across the bridge which had been thickly strewn with straw so as to deaden the noise.

At the same time we had begun to cross the river by pontoon at various points, and before the French were properly aware of what was going on, the other side of the river had been occupied by our troops and was soon firmly held by them.

The French artillery and infantry now began to pour a terrific fire on the pontoons. We, the sappers, who were occupying the pontoons of the bridge, were now for the greater part relieved and replaced by infantry, but were distributed among the rowing pontoons to serve as crews. I was placed at the helm of one of the pontoons. With four sappers at the oars and eighteen infantrymen as our passengers we began our first trip in an infernal rain of missiles. We were lucky enough to reach the other side of the river with only one slightly wounded sapper. I relieved that man, who then took the steering part. On the return trip our pontoon was hit by some rifle bullets, but happily only above the water-line. To our right and left the pontoons were crossing the river, some of them in a sinking condition.

The sappers, who are all able to swim, sought to reach the bank of the river and simply jumped into the water, whilst the infantrymen were drowned in crowds. Having landed and manned another pontoon we pushed off once more and, pulling the oars through the water with superhuman strength, we made the trip a second time. That time we reached the other side with two dead men and a wounded infantryman. We had not yet reached the other side when all the infantry jumped into the shallow water and waded ashore. We turned our boat to row back with the two dead men on board. Our hands began to hurt much from the continual rowing and were soon covered with blisters and blood blisters. Still, we had to row, however much our hands might swell and hurt; there was no resting on your oars then.

We were about twenty yards from shore when our pontoon was hit below the water-line by several rifle-bullets at the same time. A shot entering a pontoon leaves a hole no bigger that the shot itself, but its exit on the other side of the pontoon may be as big as a fist or a plate. Our pontoon then began to sink rapidly so that we sappers had no choice but to jump into the icy water. Scarcely had we left the boat when it disappeared; but all of us reached the river-bank safely.

We were saved—for the moment. In spite of our wet clothes we had to man another boat immediately, and without properly regaining breath we placed our torn hands again on the oars.

We had scarcely reached the middle of the river when we collided with another boat. That other boat, which had lost her helmsman, and two oarsmen, rammed us with such force that our pontoon turned turtle immediately and took down with her all the eighteen infantrymen besides one of the sappers. Four of us saved ourselves in another pontoon and, thoroughly wet, we steered her to the left bank. We had just landed when we were commanded to bring over a pontoon laden with ammunition, and the "joy-ride" was renewed. We crossed the Meuse about another five times after that.

Meanwhile day had come. On the left bank a terrible fight had begun between the German troops that had been landed, and the French. The Germans enjoyed the advantage that they were no longer exposed to the French artillery.

We got a short rest, and lay wet to the skin in an old trench shivering all over with cold. Our hands were swollen to more than double their ordinary size; they hurt us so much that we could not even lift our water-bottle to our mouths. It must have been a harrowing sight to watch us young, strong fellows lying on the ground helpless and broken.

7

In Pursuit

After a short rest we were commanded to search the burning houses for wounded men. We did not find many of them, for most of the severely wounded soldiers who had not been able to seek safety unaided had been miserably burnt to death, and one could only judge by the buttons and weapons of the poor wretches for what "fatherland" they had suffered their terrible death by fire. With many it was even impossible to find out the nationality they belonged to; a little heap of ashes, a ruined house were all that was left of whole families, whole streets of families.

It was only the wine cellars, which were mostly of strong construction, that had generally withstood the flames. The piping hot wine in bottles and barrels, proved a welcome refreshment for the soldiers who were wet to their skins and stiff with cold. Even at the risk of their lives (for many of the cellars threatened to collapse) the soldiers would fetch out the wine and drink it greedily, however hot the wine might be.

And strangely enough, former scenes were repeated. After the hot wine had taken effect, after again feeling refreshed and physically well, that same brutality which had become our second nature in war showed itself again in the most shameful manner. Most of us behaved as if we had not taken part in the unheard-of events of the last hours, as if we did not see the horrible reminders of the awful slaughter, as if we had entirely forgotten the danger of extinction which we had so narrowly escaped. No effort was made to do honour to the dead though every one had been taught that duty by his mother from the earliest infancy; there was nothing left of that natural shyness which the average man feels in the presence of death. The pen refuses even to attempt a reproduction of the expressions used by officers and soldiers or a description of their actions, when they set about to establish the nationality or sex of the dead. Circumstances were stronger than we men, and I convinced myself again that it was only natural that all feelings of humanity should disappear after the daily routine of murdering and that only the instinct of self-preservation should survive in all its strength. The longer the war lasted the more murderous and bestial the men became.

Meanwhile the fight between our troops that had crossed the river and the French on the other side of the Meuse had reached its greatest fury. Our troops had suffered great losses; now our turn came. While we were crossing, the German artillery pounded the enemy's position with unheard-of violence. Scarcely had we landed and taken our places when our section proceeded to the assault. The artillery became silent, and running forward we tried to storm the slope leading to the enemy positions. We got as near as 200 yards when the French machine-guns came into action; we were driven back with considerable losses. Ten minutes later we attempted again to storm the positions, but had only to go back again exactly as before. Again we took up positions in our trenches, but all desire for fighting had left us; every one stared stupidly in front of him. Of course we were not allowed to lose courage, though the victims of our useless assaults were covering the field, and our dead mates were constantly before our eyes.

The artillery opened fire again; reinforcements arrived. Half an hour later we stormed for the third time over the bodies of our dead comrades. That time we went forward in rushes, and when we halted before the enemy's trench for the last time, some twenty yards away from it, our opponent withdrew his whole first line. The riddle of that sudden retreat we were able to solve some time later. It turned out that the main portions of the French army had retreated long ago; we had merely been engaged in rear-guard actions which, however, had proved very costly to us.

During the next hour the enemy evacuated all the heights of the Meuse. When we reached the ridge of those heights we were able to witness a horrifying sight with our naked eyes. The roads which the retreating enemy was using could be easily surveyed. In close marching formation the French were drawing off. The heaviest of our artillery (21-cm.) was pounding the retreating columns, and shell after shell fell among the French infantry and other troops. Hundreds of French soldiers were literally torn to pieces. One could see bodies and limbs being tossed in the air and being caught in the trees bordering the roads.

We sappers were ordered to rally and we were soon going after the fleeing enemy. It was our task to make again passable for our troops the roads which had been pounded and dug up by the shells; that was all the more difficult in the mid-day sun, as we had first to remove the dead and wounded. Two men would take a dead soldier by his head and feet and fling him in a ditch. Human corpses were here treated and used exactly as a board in bridge building. Severed arms and legs were flung through the air into the ditch in the same manner. How often since have I not thought of these and similar incidents, asking myself whether I thought those things improper or immoral at the time? Again and again I had to return a negative answer, and I am therefore fully convinced of how little the soldiers can be held responsible for the brutalities which all of them commit, to whatever nation they belong. They are no longer civilized human beings, they are simply bloodthirsty brutes, for otherwise they would be bad, very bad soldiers.

When, during the first months of the war a Social-Democratic member of parliament announced that he had resolved to take voluntary service in the army because he believed that in that manner he could further the cause of humanity on the battle-field, many a one began to laugh, and it was exactly our Socialist comrades in our company who made pointed remarks. For all of us were agreed that that representative of the people must either be very simple-minded or insincere.

The dead horses and shattered batteries had also to be removed. We were not strong enough to get the bodies of the horses out of the way so we procured some horse roaming about without a master, and fastened it to a dead one to whose leg we had attached a noose, and thus we cleared the carcass out of the road. The portions of human bodies hanging in the trees we left, however, undisturbed. For who was there to care about such "trifles"?

We searched the bottles and knapsacks of the dead for eatable and drinkable things, and enjoyed the things found with the heartiest appetite imaginable. Hunger and thirst are pitiless customers that cannot be turned away by fits of sentimentality.

Proceeding on our march we found the line of retreat of the enemy thickly strewn with discarded rifles, knapsacks, and other accoutrements. French soldiers that had died of sunstroke were covering the roads in masses. Others had crawled into the fields to the left and right, where they were expecting help or death. But we could not assist them for we judged ourselves happy if we could keep our worn-out bodies from collapsing altogether. But even if we had wanted to help them we should not have been allowed to do so, for the order was "Forward!"

At that time I began to notice in many soldiers what I had never observed before—they felt envious. Many of my mates envied the dead soldiers and wished to be in their place in order to be at least through with all their misery. Yet all of us were afraid of dying—afraid of dying, be it noted, not of death. All of us often longed for death, but we were horrified at the slow dying lasting hours which is the rule on the battle-field, that process which makes the wounded, abandoned soldier die piecemeal. I have witnessed the death of hundreds of young men in their prime, but I know of none among them who died willingly.

A young sapper of the name of Kellner, whose home was at Cologne, had his whole abdomen ripped open by a shell splinter so that his entrails were hanging to the ground. Maddened by pain he begged me to assure him that he would not have to die. Of course, I assured him that his wounds were by no means severe and that the doctor would be there immediately to help him. Though I was a layman who had never had the slightest acquaintance with the treatment of patients I was perfectly aware that the poor fellow could only live through a few hours of pain. But my words comforted him. He died ten minutes later.

We had to march on and on. The captain told us we had been ordered to press the fleeing enemy as hard as possible. He was answered by a disapproving murmur from the whole section. For long days and nights we had been on our legs, had murdered like savages, had had neither opportunity nor possibility to eat or rest, and now they asked us worn-out men to conduct an obstinate pursuit. The captain knew very well what we were feeling, and tried to pacify us with kind words.

The cavalry divisions had not been able to cross the Meuse for want of apparatus and bridges. For the present the pursuit had to be carried out by infantry and comparatively small bodies of artillery. Thus we had to press on in any case, at least until the cavalry and machine-gun sections had crossed the bridges that had remained intact farther down stream near Sédan. Round Sommepy the French rear-guard faced us again. When four batteries of our artillery went into action at that place our company and two companies of infantry with machine guns were told off to cover the artillery.

The artillery officers thought that the covering troops were insufficient, because aeroplanes had established the presence of large masses of hostile cavalry an attack from whom was feared. But reinforcements could not be had as there was a lack of troops for the moment. So we had to take up positions as well as we could. We dug shallow trenches to the left and right of the battery in a nursery of fir trees which were about a yard high. The machine-guns were built in and got ready, and ammunition was made ready for use in large quantities. We had not yet finished our preparations when the shells of our artillery began to whizz above our heads and pound the ranks of our opponent. The fir nursery concealed us from the enemy, but a little wood, some 500 yards in front of us, effectively shut out our view.

We were now instructed in what we were to do in case of an attack by cavalry. An old white-haired major of the infantry had taken command. We sappers were distributed among the infantry, but those brave "gentlemen," our officers, had suddenly disappeared. Probably the defence of the fatherland is in their opinion only the duty of the common soldier. As those "gentlemen" are only there to command and as we had been placed under the orders of infantry officers for that undertaking, they had become superfluous and had taken French leave.

Our instructions were to keep quiet in case of an attack by cavalry, to take aim, and not allow ourselves to be seen. We were not to fire until a machine-gun, commanded by the major in person, went into action, and then we were to fire as rapidly as the rifle could be worked; we were not to forget to aim quietly, but quickly.

Our batteries fired with great violence, their aiming being regulated by a biplane, soaring high up in the air, by means of signals which were given by rockets whose signification experts only could understand.

One quarter of an hour followed the other, and we were almost convinced that we should be lucky enough that time to be spared going into action. Suddenly things became lively. One man nudged the other, and all eyes were turned to the edge of the little wood some five hundred yards in front of us. A vast mass of horsemen emerged from both sides of the little wood and, uniting in front of it, rushed towards us. That immense lump of living beings approached our line in a mad gallop. Glancing back involuntarily I observed that our artillery had completely ceased firing and that its crews were getting their carbines ready to defend their guns.

But quicker than I can relate it misfortune came thundering up. Without being quite aware of what I was doing I felt all over my body to find some place struck by a horse's hoof. The cavalry came nearer and nearer in their wild career. Already one could see the hoofs of the horses which scarcely touched the ground and seemed to fly over the few hundred yards of ground. We recognized the riders in their solid uniforms, we even thought we could notice the excited faces of the horsemen who were expecting a sudden hail of bullets to mow them down. Meanwhile they had approached to a distance of some 350 yards. The snorting of the horses was every moment becoming more distinct. No machine-gun firing was yet to be heard.

Three hundred yards—250. My neighbor poked me in the ribs rather indelicately, saying, "Has the old mass murderer (I did not doubt for a moment that he meant the major) gone mad! It's all up with us, to be sure!" I paid no attention to his talk. Every nerve in my body was hammering away; convulsively I clung to my rifle, and awaited the calamity. Two hundred yards! Nothing as yet. Was the old chap blind or—? One hundred and eighty yards! I felt a cold sweat running down my back and trembled as if my last hour had struck. One hundred and fifty! My neighbour pressed close to me. The situation became unbearable. One hundred and thirty—an infernal noise had started. *Rrrrrrr*—An overwhelming hail of bullets met the attacking party and scarcely a bullet missed the lump of humanity and beasts.

The first ranks were struck down. Men and beasts formed a wall on which rolled the waves of succeeding horses, only to be smashed by that terrible hail of bullets. "Continue firing!" rang out the command which was not needed. "More lively!" The murderous work was carried out more rapidly and with more crushing effect. Hundreds of volleys were sent straight into the heap of living beings struggling against death. Hundreds were laid low every second. Scarcely a hundred yards in front of us lay more than six hundred men and horses, on top of each other, beside each other, apart, in every imaginable position. What five minutes ago had been a picture of strength, proud horsemen, joyful youth, was now a bloody, shapeless, miserable lump of bleeding flesh.

And what about ourselves? We laughed about our heroic deed and cracked jokes. When danger was over we lost that anxious feeling which had taken possession of us. Was it fear? It is, of course, supposed that a German soldier knows no fear—at the most he fears God, but nothing else in the world—and yet it was fear, low vulgar fear that we feel just as much as the French, the English, or the Turks, and he who dares to contradict this and talk of bravery and the fearless courage of the warrior, has either never been in war, or is a vulgar liar and hypocrite.

Why were we joyful and why did we crack jokes? Because it was the others and not ourselves who had to lose their lives that time. Because it was a life and death struggle. It was either we or they. We had a right to be glad and chase all sentimentality to the devil. Were we not soldiers, mass murderers, barbarians?

8
Nearly Buried Alive on the Battlefield

The commander of the artillery smilingly came up to the major of the infantry and thanked and congratulated him.

We then went after the rest of our attackers who were in full flight. The machine guns kept them under fire. Some two hundred might have escaped; they fled in all directions. The artillery thereupon began again to fire, whilst we set about to care for our wounded enemies. It was no easy job, for we had to draw the wounded from beneath the horses some of which were still alive. The animals kicked wildly about them, and whenever they succeeded in getting free they rushed off like demented however severely they had been hurt. Many a wounded man who otherwise might have recovered was thus killed by the hoofs of the horses.

With the little packet of bandaging material which we all had on us we bandaged the men, who were mostly severely wounded, but a good many died in our hands while we were trying to put on a temporary dressing. As far as they were still able to speak they talked to us with extreme vivacity. Though we did not understand their language we knew what they wanted to express, for their gestures and facial expressions were very eloquent. They desired to express their gratitude for the charitable service we were rendering them, and like ourselves they did not seem to be able to understand how men could first kill each other, could inflict pain on each other, and then assist each other to the utmost of their ability. To them as well as to us this world seemed to stand on its head; it was a world in which they were mere marionettes, guided and controlled by a superior power. How often were we not made aware in that manner of the uselessness of all this human slaughter!

We common soldiers were here handling the dead and wounded as if we had never done anything else, and yet in our civilian lives most of us had an abhorrence and fear of the dead and the horribly mangled. War is a hard schoolmaster who bends and reshapes his pupils.

One section was busy with digging a common grave for the dead. We took away the papers and valuables of the dead, took possession of the eatable and drinkable stores to be found in the saddle bags attached to the horses and, when the grave was ready, we began to place the dead bodies in it. They were laid close together in order to utilize fully the available space. I, too, had been ordered to "bring in" the dead. The bottom of the grave was large enough for twenty-three bodies if the space was well utilized. When two layers of twenty-three had already been buried a sergeant of the artillery, who was standing near, observed that one of the "dead" was still alive. He had seen the "corpse" move the fingers of his right hand.

On closer examination it turned out that we came near burying a living man, for after an attempt lasting two hours we succeeded in restoring him to consciousness. The officer of the infantry who supervised the work now turned to the two soldiers charged with getting the corpses ready and asked them whether they were sure that all the men buried were really dead. "Yes," the two replied, "we suppose they are all dead." That seemed to be quite sufficient for that humane officer, for he ordered the interments to proceed. Nobody doubted that there were several more among the 138 men whom we alone buried in one grave (two other, still bigger, graves had been dug by different burial parties) from whose bodies life had not entirely flown. To be buried alive is just one of those horrors of the battlefield which your bar-room patriot at home (or in America) does not even dream of in his philosophy.

Nothing was to be seen of the enemy's infantry. It seemed that our opponent had sent only artillery and cavalry to face us. Meanwhile the main portions of our army came up in vast columns. Cavalry divisions with mounted artillery and machine-gun sections left all the other troops behind them. The enemy had succeeded in disengaging himself almost completely from us, wherefor our cavalry accelerated their movements with the intention of getting close to the enemy and as quickly as possible in order to prevent his demoralized troops from resting at night. We, too, got ready to march, and were just going to march off when we received orders to form camp. The camping ground was exactly mapped out, as was always the case, by the superior command, so that they would know where we were to be found in case of emergency.

We had scarcely reached our camping grounds when our field kitchen, which we thought had lost us, appeared before our eyes as if risen from out of the ground. The men of the field kitchen, who had no idea of the losses we had suffered during the last days, had cooked for the old number of heads. They were therefore not a little surprised when they found in the place of a brave company of sturdy sappers only a crowd of ragged men, the shadows of their former selves, broken and tired to their very bones. We were given canned soup, bread, meat, coffee, and a cigarette each. At last we were able to eat once again to our hearts' content. We could drink as much coffee as we liked. And then that cigarette, which appeared to most of us more important than eating and drinking!

All those fine things and the expectation of a few hours of rest in some potato field aroused in us an almost childish joy. We were as merry as boys and as noisy as street urchins. "Oh, what a joy to be a soldier lad!"—that song rang out, subdued at first, then louder and louder. It died away quickly enough as one after the other laid down his tired head. We slept like the dead.

We could sleep till six o'clock the next morning. Though all of us lay on the bare ground it was with no little trouble that they succeeded in waking us up. That morning breakfast was excellent. We received requisitioned mutton, vegetables, bread, coffee, a cupful of wine, and some ham. The captain admonished us to stuff in well, for we had a hard day's march before us. At seven o'clock we struck camp. At the beginning of that march we were in fairly good humor. Whilst conversing we discovered that we had completely lost all reckoning of time. Nobody knew whether it was Monday or Wednesday, whether it was the fifth or the tenth of the month. Subsequently, the same phenomenon could be observed only in a still more noticeable way.

A soldier in war never knows the date or day of the week. One day is like another. Whether it is Saturday, Thursday or Sunday, it means always the same routine of murdering. "Remember *the Sabbath day to keep it holy!*" "*Six days shalt thou labor and do all thy work. But the seventh day—thou shalt not do any work.*" These, to our Christian rulers, are empty phrases. "*Six days shalt thou murder and on the seventh day, too.*"

When we halted towards noon near a large farm we had again to wait in vain for our field kitchen. So we helped ourselves. We shot one of the cows grazing in the meadows, slit its skin without first letting off the blood, and each one cut himself a piece of meat. The meat, which was still warm, was roasted a little in our cooking pots. By many it was also eaten raw with pepper and salt. That killing of cattle on our own hook was repeated almost daily. The consequence was that all suffered with their stomachs, for the meat was mostly still warm, and eating it without bread or other food did not agree with us. Still, the practice was continued. If a soldier was hungry and if he found a pig, cow, or lamb during his period of rest, he would simply shoot the beast and cut off a piece for his own use, leaving the rest to perish.

On our march we passed a little town, between Attigny and Sommepy, crowded with refugees. Many of the refugees were ill, and among their children an epidemic was raging which was infecting the little ones of the town. A German medical column had arrived a short time before us. They asked for ten sappers—the maids of all work in war time—to assist them in their labours. I was one of the ten drafted off for that duty.

We were first taken by the doctors to a wonderfully arranged park in the centre of which stood a castle-like house, a French manor-house. The owner, a very rich Frenchman, lived there with his wife and an excessive number of servants. Though there was room enough in the palace for more than a hundred patients and refugees, that humane patriot refused to admit any one, and had locked and bolted the house and all entrances to the park. It did not take us long to force all the doors and make all the locks useless. The lady of the house had to take up quarters in two large rooms, but that beauty of a male aristocrat had to live in the garage and had to put up with a bed of straw. In that way the high and mighty gentleman got a taste of the refugee life which so many of his countrymen had to go through. He was given his food by one of the soldiers of the medical corps; it was nourishing food, most certainly too nourishing for our gentleman. One of my mates, a Socialist comrade, observed drily,

"It's at least a consolation that our own gang of junkers isn't any worse than that mob of French aristocrats; they are all of a kidney. If only the people were to get rid of the whole pack they wouldn't then have to tear each other to pieces any longer like wild beasts."

In the meantime our mates had roamed through the country and captured a large barrel full of honey. Each one had filled his cooking pot with honey to the very brim and buckled it to his knapsack. The ten of us did likewise, and then we went off to find our section with which we caught up in a short time. But we had scarcely marched a few hundred yards when we were pursued by bees whose numbers increased by hundreds every minute. However much we tried to shake off the little pests their attentions grew worse and worse. Every one of us was stung; many had their faces swollen to such an extent that they were no longer able to see. The officers who were riding some twenty yards in front of us began to notice our slow movements. The "old man" came along, saw the bees and the swollen faces but could, of course, not grasp the meaning of it all until a sergeant proffered the necessary information. "Who's got honey in his cooking pot?" the old chap cried angrily.

"All of us," the sergeant replied.

"You, too?"

"Yes, captain."

The old man was very wild, for he was not even able to deal out punishments. We had to halt and throw away the "accursed things," as our severe master called them. We helped each other to unbuckle the cooking pots, and our sweet provisions were flung far away into the fields on both sides of the road. With the honey we lost our cooking utensils, which was certainly not a very disagreeable relief.

We continued our march in the burning noon-day sun. The ammunition columns and other army sections which occupied the road gave the whirled-up dust no time to settle. All around us in the field refugees were camping, living there like poor, homeless gypsies. Many came up to us and begged for a piece of dry bread.

Without halting we marched till late at night. Towards nine o'clock in the evening we found ourselves quite close to the town hall of Sommepy. Here, in and about Sommepy, fighting had started again, and we had received orders to take part in it to the northwest of Sommepy.

9

Soldiers Shooting Their Own Officers

It was dark already, and we halted once more. The ground around us was strewn with dead. In the middle of the road were some French batteries and munition wagons, with the horses still attached; but horses and men were dead. After a ten minutes' rest we started again. Marching more quickly, we now approached a small wood in which dismounted cavalry and infantry were waging a desperate hand-to-hand struggle with the enemy. So as to astonish the latter we had to rush in with a mighty yell. Under cover of darkness we had succeeded in getting to the enemy's rear. Taken by surprise by the unexpected attack and our war whoop, most of the Frenchmen lifted their hands and begged for quarter, which was, however, not granted by the infuriated cavalrymen and infantry. When, on our side, now and then the murdering of defenceless men seemed to slacken it was encouraged again by the loud commands of the officers. "No quarter!" "Cut them all down!" Such were the orders of those estimable gentlemen, the officers.

We sappers, too, had to participate in the cold-blooded slaughtering of defenceless men. The French were defenceless because they threw away their arms and asked for quarter the moment that they recognized the futility of further resistance. But the officers then saw to it, as on many earlier and later occasions, that "too many prisoners were not made." The sapper carries a bayonet which must not be fixed to the rifle according to international agreement, because the back of that bayonet is an extremely sharp steel saw, three millimetres in thickness. In times of peace the sapper never does bayonet practice, the bayonet being exclusively reserved for mechanical purposes. But what does militarism care for international law! We here had to fix the saw, as had always been done since the beginning of the war. Humanity was a jest when one saw an opponent with the toothed saw in his chest and the victim, who had long given up all resistance, endeavouring to remove the deadly steel from the wound. Often that terrible tool of murder had fastened itself so firmly in the victim's chest that the attacker, in order to get his bayonet back, had to place his foot on the chest of the miserable man and try with all his might to remove the weapon.

The dead and wounded lay everywhere covered with terrible injuries, and the crying of the wounded, which might soften a stone, but not a soldier's heart, told of the awful pain which those "defenders of their country" had to suffer.

However, not all the soldiers approved of that senseless, that criminal murdering. Some of the "gentlemen" who had ordered us to massacre our French comrades were killed "by mistake" in the darkness of the night, by their own people, of course. Such "mistakes" repeat themselves almost daily, and if I keep silence with regard to many such mistakes which I could relate, giving the exact name and place, the reader will know why.

During that night it was a captain and first lieutenant who met his fate. An infantryman who was serving his second year stabbed the captain through the stomach with his bayonet, and almost at the same time the first lieutenant got a stab in the back. Both men were dead in a few minutes. Those that did the deeds showed not the slightest signs of repentance, and not one of us felt inclined to reproach them; on the contrary, every one knew that despicable, brutal murderers had met their doom.

In this connection I must mention a certain incident which necessitates my jumping a little ahead of events. When on the following day I conversed with a mate from my company and asked him for the loan of his pocket knife he drew from his pocket three cartridges besides his knife. I was surprised to find him carrying cartridges in his trousers' pockets and asked him whether he had no room for them in his cartridge case. "There's room enough," he replied, "but those three are meant for a particular purpose; there's a name inscribed on each of them." Some time after—we had meanwhile become fast friends—I inquired again after the three bullets. He had one of them left. I reflected and remembered two sergeants who had treated us like brutes in times of peace, whom we had hated as one could only hate slave-drivers. They had found their grave in French soil.

The murder did not cease as long as an opponent was alive. We were then ordered to see whether all the enemies lying on the ground were really dead or unable to fight. "Should you find one who pretends to be dead, he must be killed without mercy." That was the order we received for that tour of inspection. However, the soldiers who had meanwhile quieted down a little and who had thus regained their senses took no trouble to execute the shameful command. What the soldiers thought of it is shown by the remark of a man belonging to my company who said, "Let's rather look if the two officers are quite dead; if not, we shall have to kill them, too, without mercy." An order was an order, he added.

We now advanced quickly, but our participation was no longer necessary, for the whole line of the enemy retired and then faced us again, a mile and a quarter southwest of Sommepy. Sommepy itself was burning for the greater part, and its streets were practically covered with the dead. The enemy's artillery was still bombarding the place, and shells were falling all around us. Several hundred prisoners were gathered in the market-place. A few shells fell at the same time among the prisoners, but they had to stay where they were.

An officer of my company, lieutenant of the reserve Neesen, observed humanely that that could not do any harm, for thus the French got a taste of their own shells. He was rewarded with some cries of shame. A Socialist comrade, a reservist, had the pluck to cry aloud, "Do you hear that, comrades? That's the noble sentiment of an exploiter; that fellow is the son of an Elberfeld capitalist and his father is a sweating-den keeper of the worst sort. When you get home again do not forget what this capitalist massacre has taught you. Those prisoners are proletarians, are our brethren, and what we are doing here in the interest of that gang of capitalist crooks is a crime against our own body; it is murdering our own brothers!" He was going to continue talking, but the sleuths were soon upon him, and he was arrested. He threw down his gun with great force; then he quietly suffered himself to be led away.

All of us were electrified. Not one spoke a word. One suddenly beheld quite a different world. We had a vision which kept our imagination prisoner. Was it true what we had heard—that those prisoners were not our enemies at all, that they were our brothers? That which formerly—O how long ago might that have been!—in times of peace, had appeared to us as a matter of course had been forgotten; in war we had regarded our enemies as our friends and our friends as our enemies. Those words of the Elberfeld comrade had lifted the fog from our brains and from before our eyes. We had again a clear view; we could recognize things again.

One looked at the other and nodded without speaking; each one felt that the brave words of our friend had been a boon to us, and none could refrain from inwardly thanking and appreciating the bold man. The man in front of me, who had been a patriot all along as far as I knew, but who was aware of my views, pressed my hand, saying, "Those few words have opened my eyes; I was blind; we are friends. Those words came at the proper time." Others again I heard remark: "You can't surpass Schotes; such a thing requires more courage than all of us together possess. For he knew exactly the consequences that follow when one tells the truth. Did you see the last look he gave us? That meant as much as, 'Don't be concerned about me; I shall fight my way through to the end. Be faithful workers; remain faithful to your class!'"

The place, overcrowded with wounded soldiers, was almost entirely occupied by the Germans. The medical corps could not attend to all the work, for the wounded kept streaming in in enormous numbers. So we had to lend a helping hand, and bandaged friend and enemy to the best of our ability. But contrary to earlier times when the wounded were treated considerately, things were now done more roughly.

The fighting to the south of the place had reached its greatest violence towards one o'clock in the afternoon, and when the Germans began to storm at all points, the French retired from their positions in the direction of Suippes.

Whether our ragged company was no longer considered able to fight or whether we were no longer required, I do not know; but we got orders to seek quarters. We could find neither barn nor stable, so we had to camp in the open; the houses were all crowded with wounded men.

On that day I was commanded to mount guard and was stationed with the camp guard. At that place arrested soldiers had to call to submit to the punishment inflicted on them. Among them were seven soldiers who had been sentenced to severe confinement which consisted in being tied up for two hours.

The officer on guard ordered us to tie the "criminals" to trees in the neighborhood. Every arrested soldier had to furnish for that purpose the rope with which he cleaned his rifle. The victim I had to attend to was Sapper Lohmer, a good Socialist. I was to tie his hands behind his back, wind the loose end of the rope round his chest, and tie him with his back towards the tree. In that position my comrade was to stand for two hours, exposed to the mockery of officers and sergeants. But comrade Lohmer had been marching with the rest of us in a broiling sun for a whole day, had all night fought and murdered for the dear Fatherland which was now giving him thanks by tying him up with a rope.

I went up to him and told him that I would not tie him to the tree.

"Do it, man," he tried to persuade me; "if you don't do it another one will. I shan't be cross with you, you know."

"Let others do it; I won't fetter you."

The officer, our old friend Lieutenant Spahn, who was getting impatient, came up to us. "Can't you see that all the others have been seen to? How long do you expect me to wait?" I gave him a sharp look, but did not answer. Again he bellowed out the command to tie my comrade to the tree. I looked at him for a long time and did not deign him worthy of an answer. He then turned to the "criminal" who told him that I could not get myself to do the job as we were old comrades and friends. Besides, I did not want to fetter a man who was exhausted and dead tired.

"So you won't do it?" he thundered at me, and when again he received no reply—for I was resolved not to speak another word to the fellow—he hissed, "That b—— is a Red to the marrow!"

I shall never in my life forget the look of thankfulness that Lohmer gave me; it rewarded me for the unpleasantness I had in consequence of my refusal. Of course others did what I refused to do; I got two weeks' confinement. Naturally I was proud at having been a man for once at least. As a comrade I had remained faithful to my mate. Yet I had gained a point. They never ordered me again to perform such duty, and I was excluded from the guard that day. I could move about freely and be again a free man for a few hours.

The evening I had got off I employed to undertake a reconnoitring expedition through the surrounding country in the company of several soldiers. We spoke about the various incidents of the day and the night, and, to the surprise, I daresay, of every one of us, we discovered that very little was left of the overflowing enthusiasm and patriotism that had seized so many during the first days of the war. Most of the soldiers made no attempt to conceal the feeling that we poor devils had absolutely nothing to gain in this war, that we had only to lose our lives or, which was still worse, that we should sit at some street corner as crippled "war veterans" trying to arouse the pity of passers-by by means of some squeaking organ.

At that moment it was already clear to us in view of the enormous losses that no state, no public benevolent societies would be able after the war to help the many hundreds of thousands who had sacrificed their health for their "beloved country." The number of the unfortunate wrecks is too great to be helped even with the best of intentions.

Those thoughts which occupied our minds to an ever increasing extent did not acquire a more cheerful aspect on our walk. The wounded were lying everywhere, in stables, in barns, wherever there was room for them. If the wounds were not too severe the wounded men were quite cheerful. They felt glad at having got off so cheaply, and thought the war would long be over when they should be well again. They lived by hopes just as the rest of us.

10

Sacking Suippes

The inhabitants of the place who had not fled were all quartered in a large wooden shed. Their dwelling places had almost all been destroyed, so that they had no other choice but live in the shed that was offered them. Only one little, old woman sat, bitterly crying, on the ruins of her destroyed home, and nobody could induce her to leave that place.

In the wooden shed one could see women and men, youths, children and old people, all in a great jumble. Many had been wounded by bits of shell or bullets; others had been burned by the fire. Everywhere one could observe the same terrible misery—sick mothers with half-starved babies for whom there was no milk on hand and who had to perish there; old people who were dying from the excitement and terrors of the last few days; men and women in the prime of their life who were slowly succumbing to their wounds because there was nobody present to care for them.

A soldier of the *landwehr*, an infantryman, was standing close to me and looked horror-struck at some young mothers who were trying to satisfy the hunger of their babes. "I, too," he said reflectively, "have a good wife and two dear children at home. I can therefore feel how terrible it must be for the fathers of these poor families to know their dear ones are in the grip of a hostile army. The French soldiers think us to be still worse barbarians than we really are, and spread that impression through their letters among those left at home. I can imagine the fear in which they are of us everywhere. During the Boxer rebellion I was in China as a soldier, but the slaughter in Asia was child's play in comparison to the barbarism of civilized European nations that I have had occasion to witness in this war in friend and foe."

After a short while he continued: "I belong to the second muster of the *landwehr*, and thought that at my age of 37 it would take a long time before my turn came. But we old ones were no better off than you of the active army divisions—sometimes even worse. Just like you we were sent into action right from the beginning, and the heavy equipment, the long marches in the scorching sun meant much hardship to our worn-out proletarian bodies so that many amongst us thought they would not be able to live through it all.

"How often have I not wished that at least one of my children were a boy? But today I am glad and happy that they are girls; for, if they were boys, they would have to shed their blood one day or spill that of others, only because our rulers demand it."

We now became well acquainted with each other. Conversing with him I got to know that dissatisfaction was still more general in his company than in mine and that it was only the ruthless infliction of punishment, the iron discipline, that kept the men of the *landwehr*, who had to think of wife and children, from committing acts of insubordination. Just as we were treated they treated those older men for the slightest breach of discipline; they were tied with ropes to trees and telegraph poles.

Dear Fatherland, may peace be thine;
Fast stands and firm the Watch on the Rhine.

A company of the Hessian *landwehr*, all of them old soldiers, were marching past with sore feet and drooping heads. They had probably marched for a long while. Officers were attempting to liven them up. They were to sing a song, but the Hessians, fond of singing and good-natured as they certainly are known to be, were by no means in a mood to sing. "I tell you to sing, you swine!" the officer cried, and the pitifully helpless-looking "swine" endeavoured to obey the command. Here and there a thin voice from the ranks of the overtired men could be heard to sing, "*Deutschland, Deutschland über alles, über alles in der Welt.*" With sore feet and broken energy, full of disgust with their "glorious" trade of warriors, they sang that symphony of supergermanism that sounded then like blasphemy, nay, like a travesty—"*Deutschland, Deutschland über alles, über alles in der Welt.*"

Some of my mates who had watched the procession like myself came up to me saying, "Come, let's go to the bivouac. Let's sleep, forget, and think no more."

We were hungry and, going "home," we caught some chicken, "candidates for the cooking pot," as we used to call them. They were eaten half cooked. Then we lay down in the open and slept till four o'clock in the morning when we had to be ready to march off. Our goal for that day was Suippes. Before starting on the march an army order was read out to us

> Soldiers, His Majesty, the Emperor, our Supreme War Lord, thanks the soldiers of the Fourth Army, and expresses to all his imperial thankfulness and appreciation. You have protected our dear Germany from the invasion of hostile hordes. We shall not rest until the last opponent lies beaten on the ground, and before the leaves fall from the trees we shall be at home again as victors. The enemy is in full retreat, and the Almighty will continue to bless our arms.

Having duly acknowledged receipt of the message by giving those three cheers for the "Supreme War Lord" which had become almost a matter of daily routine, we started on our march and had now plenty of time and opportunity to talk over the imperial "thankfulness." We were not quite clear as to the "fatherland" we had to "defend" here in France. One of the soldiers thought the chief thing was that God had blessed our arms, whereupon another one, who had been president of a freethinking religious community in his native city for many a long year, replied that a religious man who babbled such stuff was committing blasphemy if he had ever taken religion seriously.

All over the fields and in the ditches lay the dead bodies of soldiers whose often sickening wounds were terrible to behold. Thousands of big flies, of which that part of the country harbours great swarms, were covering the human corpses which had partly begun to decompose and were spreading a stench that took away one's breath. In between these corpses, in the burning sun, the poor, helpless refugees were camping, because they were not allowed to use the road as long as the troops were occupying it. But when were the roads not occupied by troops!

Once, when resting, we chanced to observe a fight between three French and four German aeroplanes. We heard above us the well-known hum of a motor and saw three French and two German machines approach one another. All of them were at a great altitude when all at once we heard the firing of machine-guns high up in the air. The two Germans were screwing themselves higher up, unceasingly peppered by their opponents, and were trying to get above the Frenchmen. But the French, too, rose in great spirals in order to frustrate the intentions of the Germans. Suddenly one of the German flying-men threw a bomb and set alight a French machine which at the same time was enveloped in flames and, toppling over, fell headlong to the ground a few seconds after. Burning rags came slowly fluttering to the ground after it.

Unexpectedly two more strong German machines appeared on the scene, and then the Frenchmen took to flight immediately, but not before they had succeeded in disabling a German Rumpler-Taube by machine-gun fire to such an extent that the damaged aeroplane had to land in a steep glide. The other undamaged machines disappeared on the horizon.

That terrible and beautiful spectacle had taken a few minutes. It was a small, unimportant episode, which had orphaned a few children, widowed a woman—somewhere in France.

In the evening we reached the little town of Suippes after a long march. The captain said to us, "Here in Suippes there are swarms of *franctireurs*. We shall therefore not take quarters but camp in the open. Anybody going to the place has to take his rifle and ammunition with him." After recuperating a little we went to the place in order to find something to eat. Fifteen dead civilians were lying in the middle of the road. They were inhabitants of the place. Why they had been shot we could not learn. A shrugging of the shoulders was the only answer one could get from anybody. The place itself, the houses, showed no external damage.

I have never in war witnessed a greater general pillaging than here in Suippes. It was plain that we had to live and had to have food. The inhabitants and storekeepers having fled, it was often impossible to pay for the things one needed. Men simply went into some store, put on socks and underwear, and left their old things; they then went to some other store, took the food they fancied, and hied themselves to a wine-cellar to provide themselves to their hearts' content. The men of the ammunition trains who had their quarters in the town, as also the men of the transport and ambulance corps and troopers went by the hundred to search the homes and took whatsoever pleased them most.

The finest and largest stores—Suippes supplied a large tract of country and had comparatively extensive stores of all descriptions—were empty shells in a few hours. Whilst men were looking for one thing others were ruined and broken. The drivers of the munition and transport trains dragged away whole sacks full of the finest silk, ladies' garments, linen, boots, and shoved them in their shot-case. Children's shoes, ladies' shoes, everything was taken along, even if it had to be thrown away again soon after. Later on, when the field-post was running regularly, many things acquired in that manner were sent home. But all parcels did not reach their destination on account of the unreliable service of the field-post, and the maximum weight that could be sent proved another obstacle. Thus a pair of boots had to be divided and each sent in a separate parcel if they were to be dispatched by field-post. One of our sappers had for weeks carried about with him a pair of handsome boots for his *fiancée* and then had them sent to her in two parcels. However, the field-post did not guarantee delivery; and thus the war bride got the left boot, and not the right one.

An important chocolate factory was completely sacked, chocolates and candy lay about in heaps trodden under foot. Private dwellings that had been left by their inhabitants were broken into, the wine-cellars were cleared of their contents, and the windows were smashed—a speciality of the cavalry.

As we had to spend the night in the open we tried to procure some blankets, and entered a grocer's store in the market-place. The store had been already partly demolished. The living-rooms above it had remained, however, untouched, and all the rooms had been left unlocked. It could be seen that a woman had had charge of that house; everything was arranged in such a neat and comfortable way that one was immediately seized by the desire to become also possessed of such a lovely little nest. But all was surpassed by a room of medium size where a young lady had apparently lived. Only with great reluctance we entered that *sanctum*.

To our surprise we found hanging on the wall facing the door a caustic drawing on wood bearing the legend in German: "*Ehret die Frauen, sie flechten und weben himmlische Rosen ins irdische Leben.*" (Honor the women, they work and they weave heavenly roses in life's short reprieve.) The occupant was evidently a young bride, for the various pieces of the *trousseau*, trimmed with dainty blue ribbons, could be seen in the wardrobes in a painfully spick and span condition. All the wardrobes were unlocked. We did not touch a thing. We were again reminded of the cruelty of war. Millions it turned into beggars in one night; the fondest hopes and desires were destroyed. When, the next morning, we entered the house again, driven by a presentiment of misfortune, we found everything completely destroyed.

Real barbarians had been raging here, who had lost that thin varnish with which civilization covers the brute in man. The whole trousseau of the young bride had been dragged from the shelves and was still partly covering the floor. Portraits, photographs, looking-glasses, all lay broken on the floor. Three of us had entered the room, and all three of us clenched our fists in helpless rage.

Having received the command to remain in Suippes till further orders we could observe the return of many refugees the next day. They came back in crowds from the direction of Châlons-sur-Marne, and found a wretched, dreary waste in the place of their peaceful homes. The owner of a dry-goods store was just returning as we stood before his house. He collapsed before the door of his house, for nothing remained of his business. We went up to the man. He was a Hebrew and spoke German. After having somewhat recovered his self-possession he told us that his business had contained goods to the value of more than 8000 *francs*, and said: "If the soldiers had only taken what they needed I should have been content, for I expected nothing less; but I should have never believed of the Germans that they would destroy all of my possessions." In his living-rooms there was not even a cup to be found. The man had a wife and five children, but did not know where they were at that time. And his fate was shared by uncounted others, here and elsewhere.

I should tell an untruth if I were to pretend that his misery touched me very deeply. It is true that the best among us—and those were almost always the men who had been active in the labour movement at home, who hated war and the warrior's trade from the depth of their soul—were shaken out of their lethargy and indifference by some especially harrowing incident, but the mass was no longer touched even by great tragedies. When a man is accustomed to step over corpses with a cold smile on his lips, when he has to face death every minute day and night, he gradually loses that finer feeling for human things and humanity. Thus it must not surprise one that soldiers could laugh and joke in the midst of awful devastation, that they brought wine to a concert room in which there was a piano and an electric organ, and had a joyful time with music and wine. They drank till they were unconscious; they drank with sergeants and corporals, pledging "brotherhood"; and they rolled arm in arm through the streets with their new "comrades."

The officers would see nothing of this, for they did not behave much better themselves, even if they knew how to arrange things in such a manner that their "honour" did not entirely go to the devil.

The "gentleman" of an officer sends his orderly out to buy him twenty bottles of wine, but as he does not give his servant any money wherewith to "buy," the orderly obeys the command the best he can. He knows that at any rate he must not come back without the wine. In that manner the officers provide themselves with all possible comforts without losing their "honour." We had five officers in our company who for themselves alone needed a wagon with four horses for transporting their baggage. As for ourselves, the soldiers, our knapsack was still too large for the objects we needed for our daily life.

11
Marching to the Battle of the Marne—Into the Trap

A large proportion of the "gentlemen," our officers, regarded war as a pleasant change to their enchanting social life in the garrison towns, and knew exactly (at least as far as the officers of my company were concerned) how to preserve their lives as long as possible "in the interest of the Fatherland." When I buried the hatchet, fourteen months after, our company had lost three times its original strength, but no fresh supply of officers had as yet become necessary; we had not lost a single officer. In Holland I got to know, some months later, that after having taken my "leave" they were still very well preserved. One day at Rotterdam, I saw a photo in the magazine, *Die Woche*, showing "Six members of the 1st Company of the Sapper Regiment No. 30 with the Iron Cross of the 1st Class." The picture had been taken at the front, and showed the five officers and Corporal Bock with the Iron Cross of the 1st Class. Unfortunately Scherl[1] did not betray whether those gentlemen had got the distinction for having preserved their lives for further service.

We spent the following night at the place, and then had to camp again in the open, "because the place swarmed with *franctireurs*." In reality no *franctireurs* could be observed, so that it was quite clear to us that it was merely an attempt to arouse again our resentment against the enemy which was dying down. They knew very well that a soldier is far more tractable and pliant when animated by hatred against the "enemy."

The next day Châlons-sur-Marne was indicated as the next goal of our march. That day was one of the most fatiguing we experienced.

---
1. A proprietor of many German sensational newspapers.

Early in the morning already, when we started, the sun was sending down its fiery shafts. Suippes is about 21 miles distant from Châlons-sur-Marne. The distance would not have been the worst thing, in spite of the heat. We had marched longer distances before. But that splendid road from Suippes to Châlons does not deviate an inch to the right or left, so that the straight, almost endless seeming road lies before one like an immense white snake. However far we marched that white ribbon showed no ending, and when one looked round, the view was exactly the same. During the whole march we only passed one little village; otherwise all was bare and uncultivated.

Many of us fainted or got a heatstroke and had to be taken along by the following transport column. We could see by the many dead soldiers, French and German, whose corpses were lying about all along the road, that the troops who had passed here before us had met with a still worse fate.

We had finished half of our march without being allowed to take a rest. I suppose the "old man" was afraid the machine could not be set going again if once our section had got a chance to rest their tired limbs on the ground, and thus we crawled along dispirited like a lot of snails, carrying the leaden weight of the "monkey" in the place of a house. The monotony of the march was only somewhat relieved when we reached the immense camp of Châlons. It is one of the greatest military camps in France. Towards three o'clock in the afternoon we beheld Châlons in the distance, and when we halted towards four o'clock in an orchard outside the town, all of us, without an exception, fell down exhausted.

The field kitchen, too, arrived, but nobody stirred for a time to fetch food. We ate later on, and then desired to go to the town to buy several things, chiefly, I daresay, tobacco which we missed terribly. Nobody was allowed however, to leave camp. We were told that it was strictly forbidden to enter the town. "Châlons," so the tale went, had paid a war contribution, and nobody could enter the town. With money you can do everything, even in war. Mammon had saved Châlons from pillage.

Far away could be heard the muffled roar of the guns. We had the presentiment that our rest would not be of long duration. The rolling of the gun firing became louder and louder, but we did not know yet that a battle had started here that should turn out a very unfortunate one for the Germans—the five days' battle of the Marne.

At midnight we were aroused by an alarm, and half an hour later we were on the move already. The cool air of the night refreshed us, and we got along fairly rapidly in spite of our exhaustion. At about four o'clock in the morning we reached the village of Chepy. At that place friend Mammon had evidently not been so merciful as at Châlons, for Chepy had been thoroughly sacked. We rested for a short time, and noticed with a rapid glance that preparations were just being made to shoot two *franctireurs*. They were little peasants who were alleged to have hidden from the Germans a French machine-gun and its crew. The sentence was carried out. One was never at a loss in finding reasons for a verdict. And the population had been shown who their "master" was.

The little village of Pogny half-way between Châlons-sur-Marne and Vitry-le-François, had fared no better than Chepy, as we observed when we entered it at nine o'clock in the morning. We had now got considerably nearer to the roaring guns. The slightly wounded who were coming back and the men of the ammunition columns told us that a terrible battle was raging to the west of Vitry-le-François. At four o'clock in the afternoon we reached Vitry-le-François, after a veritable forced march. The whole town was crowded with wounded; every building, church, and school was full of wounded soldiers. The town itself was not damaged.

Here things must have looked very bad for the Germans for, without allowing us a respite, we were ordered to enter the battle to the west of Vitry-le-François. We had approached the firing line a little more than two miles when we got within reach of the enemy's curtain of fire. A terrific hail of shells was ploughing up every foot of ground. Thousands of corpses of German soldiers were witnesses of the immense losses the Germans had suffered in bringing up all available reserves. The French tried their utmost to prevent the Germans from bringing in their reserves, and increased their artillery fire to an unheard-of violence.

It seemed impossible for us to break through that barricade of fire. Hundreds of shells were bursting very minute. We were ordered to pass that hell singly and at a running pace. We were lying on the ground and observed how the first of our men tried to get through. Some ran forward like mad, not heeding the shells that were bursting around them, and got through. Others were entirely buried by the dirt dug up by the shells or were torn to pieces by shell splinters. Two men had scarcely reached the line when they were struck by a bull's-eye, *i.e.*, the heavy shell exploded at their feet leaving nothing of them.

Who can imagine what we were feeling during those harrowing minutes as we lay crouching on the ground not quite a hundred feet away, seeing everything, and only waiting for our turn to come? One had entangled oneself in a maze of thoughts. Suddenly one of the officers would cry, "The next one!" That was I! Just as if roused out of a bad dream, I jump up and race away like mad, holding the rifle in my right hand and the bayonet in my left. I jumped aside a few steps in front of two bursting shells and run into two others which are bursting at the same time. I leap back several times, run forward again, race about wildly to find a gap through which to escape. But—fire and iron everywhere. Like a hunted beast one seeks some opening to save oneself. Hell is in front of me and behind me the officer's revolver, kept ready to shoot.—The lumps of steel fall down like a heavy shower from high above. Hell and damnation! I blindly run and run and run, until somebody gets me by my coat.

"We're there!" somebody roars into my ear. "Stop! Are you wounded? Have a look; perhaps you are and don't know it?" Here I am trembling all over. "Sit down; you will feel better; we trembled too." Slowly I became more quiet. One after the other arrived; many were wounded. We were about forty when the sergeants took over the command. Nothing was again to be seen of the officers.

We proceeded and passed several German batteries. Many had suffered great losses. The crews were lying dead or wounded around their demolished guns. Others again could not fire as they had no more ammunition. We rested. Some men of the artillery who had "nothing to do" for lack of ammunition came up to us. A sergeant asked why they did not fire.

"Because we have used up all our ammunition," a gunner replied.

"O yes, it would be quite impossible to bring up ammunition through that curtain of fire."

"It's not that," announced the gunner; "it's because there isn't any more that they can't bring it up!" And then he went on:

"We started at Neufchâteau to drive the French before us like hunted beasts; we rushed headlong after them like savages. Men and beasts were used up in the heat; all the destroyed railroads and means of transportation could not be repaired in those few days; everything was left in the condition we found it; and in a wild intoxication of victory we ventured to penetrate into the heart of France. We rushed on without thinking or caring, all the lines of communication in our rear were interrupted—we confidently marched into the traps the

French set for us. Before the first ammunition and the other accessories, which had all to be transported by wagon, have reached us we shall be all done for."

Up to that time we had had blind confidence in the invincible strategy of our "Great General Staff," and now they told us this. We simply did not believe it. And yet it struck us that the French (as was made clear by everything around us) were in their own country, in the closest proximity of their largest depot, Paris, and were in possession of excellent railroad communications. The French were, besides, maintaining a terrible artillery fire with guns of such a large size as had never yet been used by them. All that led to the conclusion that they had taken up positions prepared long before, and that the French guns had been placed in such a manner that we could not reach them.

In spite of all we continued to believe that the gunner had seen things in too dark a light. We were soon to be taught better.

12
At the Marne—In the Maw of Death

We got in the neighbourhood of the line of defence, and were received by a rolling fire from the machine-guns. We went up to the improvised trenches that were to protect us, at the double-quick. It was raining hard. The fields around were covered with dead and wounded men who impeded the work of the defenders. Many of the wounded contracted tetanus in consequence of contact with the clayey soil, for most of them had not been bandaged. They all begged for water and bread, but we had none ourselves. In fact, they implored us to give them a bit of bread. They had been in that hell for two days without having eaten a mouthful.

We had scarcely been shown our places when the French began to attack in mass formation. The occupants of those trenches, who had already beaten back several of those attacks, spurred us on to shoot and then began to fire themselves into the on-rushing crowd as if demented. Amidst the shouting and the noise one could hear the cries of the officers of the infantry: "Fire! Fire! More lively!" We fired until the barrels of our rifles became quite hot. The enemy turned to flee. The heap of victims lying between us and our opponents had again been augmented by hundreds. The attack had been beaten back.

It was dark, and it rained and rained. From all directions one heard in the darkness the wounded calling, crying, and moaning. The wounded we had with us were likewise moaning and crying. All wanted to have their wounds dressed, but we had no more bandages. We tore off pieces of our dirty shirts and placed the rags on those sickening wounds. Men were dying one after the other. There were no doctors, no bandages; we had nothing whatever. You had to help the wounded and keep the French off at the same time. It was an unbearable, impossible state of things. It rained harder and harder. We were wet to our skins. We fired blindly into the darkness. The rolling fire of rifles increased, then died away, then increased again. We sappers were placed among the infantry. My neighbour gave me a dig in the ribs. "I say," he called out.

"What do you want?" I asked.

"Who are you?"

"A sapper."

"Come here," he hissed. "It gives you an uncanny feeling to be alone in this hell of a night. Why are you here too?—They'll soon come again, those over there; then there'll be fine fun again. Do you hear the others cry?"

He laughed. Suddenly he began again: "I always shoot at those until they leave off crying—that's great fun."

Again he laughed, that time more shrilly than before.

I knew what was the matter. He had become insane. A man passed with ammunition. I begged him to go at once and fetch the section leader. The leader, a lieutenant of the infantry, came up. I went to meet him and told him that my neighbour was continually firing at the wounded, was talking nonsense, and was probably insane. The lieutenant placed himself between us.

"Can you see anything?" he asked the other man.

"What? See? No; but I hear them moaning and crying, and as soon as I hit one—well, he is quiet, he goes to sleep—"

The lieutenant nodded at me. He took the gun away from the man. But the latter snatched it quickly away again and jumped out of the trench. From there he fired into the crowd of wounded men until, a few seconds after, he dropped down riddled by several bullets.

The drama had only a few spectators. It was scarcely over when it was forgotten again. That was no place to become sentimental. We continued shooting without any aim. The crying of the wounded became louder and louder. Why was that so? Those wounded men, lying between the two fighting lines, were exposed to the aimless fire of both sides. Nobody could help them, for it would have been madness to venture between the lines. Louder and more imploring became the voices that were calling out, "Stretcher-bearer! Help! Help! Water!" For an answer they got at most a curse or a malediction.

Our trench was filled with water for about a foot—water and mud. The dead and wounded lay in that mire where they had dropped. We had to make room. So we threw the dead out of the trench. At one o'clock in the night people came with stretchers and took away part of the wounded. But there was no help at all for the poor fellows between the lines.

To fill the cup of misery we received orders, in the course of the night, to attack the enemy's lines at 4:15 o'clock in the morning. At the time fixed, in a pouring rain, we got ready for storming. Received by a terrible fire from the machine-guns we had to turn back half-way. Again we had sacrificed uselessly a great number of men. Scarcely had we arranged ourselves again in our trench when the French began a new attack. They got as far as three yards from our trenches when their attack broke down under our fire. They, too, had to go back with enormous losses. Three times more the French attacked within two hours, each time suffering great losses and achieving not the slightest success.

We did not know what to do. If help did not arrive soon it would be impossible for us to maintain our position. We were tormented by hunger and thirst, were wet to the skin, and tired enough to drop down. At ten o'clock the French attacked a fourth time. They came up in immense masses. Our leaders recognized at last the danger in which we were and withdrew us. We retreated in waves abandoning the wounded and our material. By exerting our whole strength we succeeded in saving the machine-guns and ammunition. We went back a thousand yards and established ourselves again in old trenches. The officers called to us that we should have to stay there whatever happened; reinforcements would soon come up. The machine-guns were in their emplacements in a jiffy.

Our opponents, who were following us, were immediately treated to a hail of bullets. Their advance stopped at once. Encouraged by that success we continued firing more wildly than ever so that the French were obliged to seek cover. The reinforcements we had been promised did not arrive. Some 800 yards behind us were six German batteries which, however, maintained but a feeble fire.

An officer of the artillery appeared in our midst and asked the commander of our section whether it would not be wise to withdraw the batteries. He said he had been informed by telephone that the whole German line was wavering. Before the commander had time to answer another attack in mass formation took place, the enemy being five or seven times as numerous as we were. As if by command, we quitted our position without having been told to do so, completely demoralized; we retired in full flight, leaving the six batteries (36 guns) to the enemy. Our opponent had ceased his curtain of fire fearing to endanger his own advancing troops. The Germans used that moment to bring into battle reinforcements composed of a medley of all arms. Portions of scattered infantry, dismounted cavalry, sappers without a lord and master, all had been drummed together to fill the ranks. Apparently there were no longer any proper complete reserve formations on that day of battle.

Again we got the order, "Turn! Attention!" The unequal fight started again. We observed how the enemy made preparations to carry off the captured guns. We saw him advance to the assault. He received us with the bayonet. We fought like wild animals. For minutes there was bayonet fighting of a ferocity that defies description. We stabbed and hit like madmen—through the chest, the abdomen, no matter where. There was no semblance of regular bayonet fighting: that, by the way, can only be practised in the barracks yard. The butt-ends of our rifles swished through the air. Every skull that came in our way was smashed in. We had lost helmets and knapsacks. In spite of his great numerical superiority the enemy could not make headway against our little barrier of raving humanity. We forgot all around us and fought bloodthirstily without any calculation. A portion of our fellows had broken through the ranks of the enemy, and fought for the possession of the guns.

Our opponent recognized the danger that was threatening him and retired, seeking with all his might to retain the captured guns. We did not allow ourselves to be shaken off, and bayoneted the retiring foes one after the other. But the whole mass of the enemy gathered again round the guns. Every gun was surrounded by corpses, every minute registered numerous victims. The artillery who took part in the fight attempted to remove the breech-blocks of the guns. To my right, around the third gun, three Germans were still struggling with four Frenchmen; all the others were lying on the ground dead or wounded. Near that one gun were about seventy dead or wounded men. A sapper could be seen before the mouth of the gun. With astonishing coolness he was stuffing into the mouth of that gun one hand grenade after another. He then lit the fuse and ran away. Friends and enemies were torn into a thousand shreds by the terrible explosion that followed. The gun was entirely demolished. Seventy or eighty men had slaughtered each other for nothing—absolutely nothing.

After a struggle lasting nearly one hour all the guns were again in our possession. Who can imagine the enormous loss of human lives with which those lost guns had been recaptured! The dead and wounded, infantry, cavalry, sappers and artillery, together with the Frenchmen, hundreds and hundreds of them, were covering the narrow space, that comparatively small spot which had been the scene of the tragedy.

We were again reinforced, that time by four regular companies of infantry, which had been taken from another section of the battlefield. Though one takes part in everything, one's view as an individual is very limited, and one has no means of informing oneself about the situation in general. Here, too, we found ourselves in a similar situation. But those reinforcements composed of all arms, and the later arrivals, who had been taken from a section just as severely threatened as our own, gave us the presentiment that we could only resist further attacks if fresh troops arrived soon. If only we could get something to quiet the pangs of hunger and that atrocious thirst!

The horses of the guns now arrived at a mad gallop to take away the guns. At the same moment the enemy's artillery opened a murderous fire, with all sizes of guns, on that column of more than thirty teams that were racing along. Confusion arose. The six horses of the various teams reared and fled in all directions, drawing the overturned limbers behind them with wheels uppermost. Some of the maddest animals ran straight into the hottest fire to be torn to pieces together with their drivers. Then our opponent directed his fire on the battery positions which were also our positions. We had no other choice—we had either to advance or retire. Retire? No! The order was different. We were to recapture our lost first positions, now occupied by the French, who were now probably getting ready for another attack. Had we not received fresh food for cannon so that the mad dance could begin again? We advanced across a field covered with thousands upon thousands of torn and bleeding human bodies.

No shot was fired. Only the enemy's artillery was still bombarding the battery positions. We were still receiving no fire from the artillery; neither did the enemy's infantry fire upon us. That looked suspicious; we knew what was coming. We advanced farther and farther without being molested. Suddenly we found ourselves attacked by an army of machine-guns. An indescribable hail of bullets was poured into us. We threw ourselves to the ground and sought cover as well as we could. "Jump forward! March, march!"

Again we ran to meet our fate. We had lost already more than a third of our men. We halted again, exhausted. Scarcely had we had time to take up a position when we were attacked both in front and the flank. We had no longer strength enough to withstand successfully a simultaneous frontal and flank attack. Besides, we were being almost crushed by superior numbers. Our left wing had been completely cut off, and we observed our people on that wing raising their hands to indicate that they considered themselves prisoners of war. However, the French gave no quarter—exactly as we had acted on a former occasion. Not a man of our left wing was spared; every one was cut down.

We in the center could give them no help. We were getting less from minute to minute. "Revenge for Sommepy!" I heard it ringing in my ears. The right wing turned, drew us along, and a wild stampede began. Our direct retreat being cut off, we ran backwards across the open field, every one for himself, with beating hearts that seemed ready to burst, all the time under the enemy's fire.

After a long run we reached a small village to the northeast of Vitry-le-François. There we arrived without rifles, helmets or knapsacks; one after the other. But only a small portion could save themselves. The French took plenty of booty. All the guns we fought for were lost, besides several others. Of the hundreds of soldiers there remained scarcely one hundred. All the others were dead, wounded or missing. Who knew?

Was that the terrible German war machine? Were those the cowardly, degenerate Frenchmen whom we had driven before us for days? No; it was war, terrible, horrid war, in which fortune is fickle. Today it smiles upon you; tomorrow the other fellow's turn comes.

We sought to form up again in companies. There were just twelve men left of our company. Little by little more came up from all directions until at last we counted twenty. Then every one began to ask questions eagerly; every one wanted to know about his friend, mate, or acquaintance. Nobody could give an answer, for every one of us had been thinking merely of himself and of nobody else. Driven by hunger we roamed about the place. But our first action was drinking water, and that in such quantities as if we wanted to drink enough for a lifetime. We found nothing to eat. Only here and there in a garden we discovered a few turnips which we swallowed with a ravenous appetite without washing or even cleaning them superficially.

But where was our company? Nobody knew. We were the company, the twenty of us. And the officers? "Somewhere," a soldier observed, "somewhere in a bomb-proof shelter." What were we to do? We did not know. Soon after a sergeant-major of the field *gendarmes* came up sitting proudly on his steed. Those "defenders of the Fatherland" have to see to it that too many "shirkers" do not "loiter" behind the front. "You are sappers, aren't you?" he roared out. "What are you doing here? 30th. Regiment?" He put a great many questions which we answered as well as we were able to. "Where are the others?" "Over there," said a young Berliner, and pointed to the battle-field, "dead or prisoners; maybe some have saved themselves and are elsewhere!" "It doesn't matter," roared out our fierce sergeant-major for whom the conversation began to become unpleasant. "Wait till I come back." "Where are the officers?" Again nobody could answer him. "What are their names? I daresay I shall find them. Maybe they are at Vitry?"

We gave him their names—Captain Menke, First Lieutenant Maier, Lieutenants of the Reserves Spahn, Neesen and Heimbach. He gave us a certificate with which to prove the purpose of our "loitering" to other overseers and disappeared. "Let's hope the horse stumbles and the fellow breaks his neck." That was our pious wish which one of our chaps sent after him.

We went into one of the houses that had been pillaged like all the rest, lay down on mattresses that were lying about the rooms and slept—slept like dormice.

13

The Rout of the Marne

None of us knew how long we had slept; we only knew that it was night. Some men of our company had waked us up. They had been looking for us for a long time. "Come along," they said; "the old man is outside and making a hell of a row. He has got seventeen men together and is swearing like a trooper because he can't find you." Drowsily and completely bereft of any will-power of our own we trudged after them. We knew we were again being sent forward. But we did not care; we had lost all balance. Never before had I noticed such indifference on our part as on that night.

There the old man was standing. He saw us coming up, without headgear, the uniforms all torn to tatters, and minus our knapsacks. He received us with the greeting, "Where have you been, you boobies?" Nobody answered. What did we care? Things could not get any worse than they were. Though all of us resented the wrong done to us we all remained silent.

"Where is your equipment?—Lost?—Lost? That's a fine story. You rag-tag miserable vagabonds. If they were all like you—" For a while he went on in that style. That pretty fellow had suffered the "miserable vagabonds" to go forward while he himself had been defending his "Fatherland" at Vitry, three or four miles behind the front. We picked out the best from among the rifles that were lying about, and soon we were again "ready for battle."

We were standing half-asleep, leaning on the barrel of our rifles and waiting to be led forth again to slaughter, when a shot was fired right in our midst. The bullet had shattered the entire right hand of a "spoiled ensign," as the officers express themselves. His hand was bandaged. "How did that happen?" asked the officers. An eyewitness related the incident saying: "Like all of us he put his hand on the mouth of the barrel when it happened; I did not see any more." "Had he secured the gun? Don't you know that it is forbidden to lean with your hand on the mouth of your rifle and that you have been ordered to secure your rifle when it is loaded?" Then turning to the "spoiled ensign," who was writhing with pain, he bawled at him: "I shall report you for punishment on account of gross negligence and self-mutilation on the battle-field!"

We all knew what was the matter. The ensign was a sergeant, but a poor devil. He was fully aware that he had no career before him. We soldiers liked him because we knew that military life disgusted him. Though he was a sergeant he chose his companions solely among the common soldiers. We would have divided with him our last crust of bread, because to us especially, he behaved like a fellow-man. We also knew how harshly he was treated by his superiors, and wondered that the "accident" had not happened before. I do not know whether he was placed before a court-martial later on. Punishments for self-mutilation are the order of the day, and innumerable men are being severely punished. Now and then the verdicts are made known to the soldiers at the front to serve as a deterrent. The people at home, however, will get to hear very little of them.

The captain passed on the command to an officer's representative, and then the old man disappeared again in the direction of Vitry. He spurred on his steed, and away he flew. One of the soldiers thought that the captain's horse was a thousand times better off than we were. We knew it. We knew that we were far below the beast and were being treated accordingly.

We marched off and halted at the north-western exit of the village. There we met sappers gathered from other companies and battalions, and our company was brought up to 85 men. The officer's representative then explained to us that we should not be led into the firing line that day; our only task was to watch that German troops fighting on the other side of the Marne should find the existing temporary bridges in order in case they had to retreat. We marched to the place where the Saulx enters the Marne.

So we marched off and reached our destination towards six o'clock in the morning. The dead were lying in heaps around us in every field; death had gathered in a terrible harvest. We were lying on a wooded height on our side of the Marne, and were able to overlook the country for many miles in front of us. One could see the explosions of the shells that were raining down by the thousand. Little, almost nothing was to be seen of the men, and yet there were thousands in front of us who were fighting a desperate battle. Little by little we could make out the faint outline of the struggle. The Germans were about a mile and a half behind the Marne in front of us. Near the banks of the Marne large bodies of German cavalry were stationed. There were only two tumble-down bridges constructed of make-shift materials. They stood ready to be blown up, and had plenty of explosive matter (dynamite) attached to them. The electrical priming wires led to our position; we were in charge of the firing apparatus. Connected by telephone we were able to blow up the bridges in an instant.

On the other side things began to get lively. We saw the French at various places pressing forward and flowing back again. The rifle fire increased continually in violence, and the attacks became more frequent. Two hours passed in that way. We saw the French bringing up reinforcement after reinforcement, in spite of the German artillery which was maintaining but a feeble fire. After a long pause the enemy began to attack again. The French came up in several lines. They attacked several times, and each time they had to go back again; each time they suffered great losses. At about three o'clock in the afternoon our troops attacked by the enemy with all his strength, began to give ground, slowly at first, then in a sort of flight.

Our exhausted men could no longer withstand the blow dealt with enormous force. In a wild stampede all of them tried at the same time to reach safety across the bridges. The cavalry, too, who were in cover near the banks of the river, rushed madly to the bridges. An enormous crowd of men and beasts got wedged before the bridges. In a trice the bridge before us was thickly covered with human beings all of whom were trying to reach the opposite side in a mad rush. We thought we could notice the temporary bridge sway under its enormous burden. Like ourselves the officer's representative could overlook the whole country. He pressed the receiver of the telephone convulsively to his left ear, his right hand being on the firing apparatus after which another man was looking. With bated breath he gazed fixedly into the fleeing crowds. "Let's hope the telephone is in order," he said to himself at intervals. He knew as well as we did that he had to act as soon as the sharp order was transmitted by telephone. It was not much he had to do. Directed by a movement of the hand the man in charge of the apparatus would turn a key that looked like a winged screw—and all would be over.

The crowds were still rushing across the bridge, but nearly half of our men, almost the whole of the cavalry, were still on the other side. The bridge farther up was not being used so much and nearly all had reached safety in that portion of the battlefield. We observed the foremost French cross that bridge, but the bridge remained intact. The sergeant-major who was in charge of the other apparatus was perplexed as he received no order; so he blew up that bridge on his own responsibility sending hundreds of Frenchmen to their watery grave in the River Marne.

At the same moment the officer's representative next to me received the command to blow up the second and last bridge. He was confused and hesitated to pass on the order. He saw that a great crowd of Germans were still on the other side, he saw the struggles of that mass of men in which every one was trying to be the first one to reach the bridge and safety beyond. A terrible panic ensued. Many soldiers threw themselves into the river and tried to swim across. The mass of soldiers on the other side, still numbering several thousands, were pressed harder and harder; the telephone messages were becoming ever more urgent. All at once the officer's representative jumped up, pushed aside the sapper in charge of the apparatus, and in the next second a mighty explosion was heard. Bridge and men were blown into the air for hundreds of yards. Like a river at times of inundations the Marne was carrying away wood and men, tattered uniforms and horses. Swimming across it was of no earthly use, and yet soldiers kept throwing themselves into the river.

On the other side the French began to disarm completely the German soldiers who could be seen standing there with hands uplifted. Thousands of prisoners, innumerable horses and machine guns had fallen into the hands of the enemy. Some of us were just going to return with the firing apparatus which was now superfluous when we heard the tale of the significance of the incident, confirming the suspicions of many a one amongst us. An error had been committed, that could not be undone! When the bridge higher up, that was being used to a smaller degree by the soldiers, had been crossed by the German troops and the enemy had immediately begun his pursuit, the staff of officers in command at that passage intended to let a certain number of enemies cross the bridge, *i.e.*, a number that could not be dangerous to the German troops who were in temporary safety. Those hasty troops of the enemy could not have received any assistance after the bridge had been blown up, and would have been annihilated or taken prisoners. For that reason it was intended to postpone the blowing up of the bridge.

However, the sergeant-major in charge of the firing apparatus imagined, as his thoughts kept whirling through his head, that the telephone wires must have been destroyed, and blew up on his own initiative the bridge that was densely crowded with Frenchmen, before our opponent succeeded in interrupting the wires. But at the same time the officer's representative in charge of the firing apparatus of the second bridge received an order, the words of which (as he later himself confessed) were not at all clear to him, threw aside the receiver, lost the absolutely necessary assurance, killed all the people on the bridge, and delivered hundreds upon hundreds into the hands of the enemy.

We had no time to gather any more detailed impressions, for we received the order that all the men of our company were to gather at Vitry before the cathedral. We began to sling our hook with a sigh of relief, that time a little more quickly than ordinarily, for the enemy's artillery was already beginning to sweep the country systematically. We heard from wounded men of other sections, whom we met on the way, that the French had crossed the Marne[1] already at various places. We discussed the situation among us, and found that we were all of the same opinion.

Even on Belgian territory we had suffered heavy losses; every day had demanded its victims; our ranks had become thinner and thinner; many companies had been used up entirely and, generally speaking, all companies had suffered severely. These companies, furnished and reduced to a minimum strength, now found themselves opposed to an enemy excellently provided with all necessaries. Our opponent was continually bringing up fresh troops, and we were becoming fewer every hour. We began to see that it was impossible for us to make a stand at that place. Soldiers of the various arms confirmed again and again that things were looking just as bad with them as with us, that the losses in men and material were truly enormous. I found myself thinking of the "God of the Germans." Had He cast them aside? I "thought" it so loudly that the others could hear me. "Well," one of them remarked, "whom God wants to punish He first strikes with blindness. Perhaps He thought of Belgium, of Drucharz, of Sommepy, of Suippes, and of so many other things, and suffered us to rush into

---

1. *1914: the Marne and the Aisne* by H. W. Carless-Davis and A. Neville Hilditch, Two Accounts of the Early Battles of the First Year of the First World War, *The Battles of the Marne and the Aisne* by H. W. Carless-Davis and T*royon—an Engagement in the Battle of the Aisne* by A. Neville Hilditch is also published by Leonaur.

this ruin in our blind rage."

We reached Vitry. There the general misery seemed to us to be greater than outside. There was not a single house in the whole town that was not overcrowded with wounded men. Amidst all that misery pillaging had not been forgotten. To make room for the wounded all the warehouses had been cleared and their contents thrown into the streets. The soldiers of the ambulance corps walked about, and everything that was of value and that pleased them they annexed. But the worst "hyenas" of the battlefield are to be found in the ammunition and transport trains. The men of these two branches of the army have sufficient room in their wagons to store things away. The assertion is, moreover, proved by the innumerable confiscations, by the German Imperial Post Office, of soldiers' parcels, all of them containing gold rings, chains, watches, precious stones, etc. The cases discovered in that or any other way are closely gone into and the criminals are severely punished, but it is well known that only a small percentage of the crimes see the light of day. What are a thousand convictions or so for a hundred thousand crimes!

In Vitry the marauders' business was again flourishing. The soldiers of the transport trains, above all, are in no direct danger in war. Compared with the soldiers fighting at the front it is easy for them to find food; besides, it is they who transport the provisions of the troops. They know that their lives are not endangered directly and that they have every reason to suppose that they will return unscathed. To them war is a business, because they largely take possession of all that is of any value. We could therefore comprehend that they were enthusiastic patriots and said quite frankly that they hoped the war would continue for years. Later on we knew what had happened when the emperor had made one of his "rousing" speeches somewhere in the west and had found the "troops" in an "excellent" mood and "full of fight." Among that sort of troops there were besides the transport soldiers numerous cavalry distributed among the various divisions, army corps staffs, and general staffs.

14

The Flight From the Marne

We soon reached the cathedral and reported to Lieutenant Spahn whom we found there. He, too, had defended his "Fatherland" in that town. Clean shaven and faultlessly dressed, he showed up to great advantage contrasted with us. There we stood in ragged, dirty, blood-stained uniforms, our hair dishevelled, with a growing beard covered with clay and mud. We were to wait. That was all. We sat down and gazed at the misery around us. The church was filled with wounded men. Many died in the hands of the medical men. The dead were carried out to make room for others. The bodies were taken to one side where whole rows of them were lying already. We took the trouble to count the dead, who had been mostly placed in straight rows, and counted more than sixty. Some of them were in uniforms that were still quite good, whilst our uniforms were nothing but rags hanging from our backs. There were some sappers among them, but their coats were not any better than our own.

"Let us take some infantry coats," somebody ventured; "what's the difference? A coat is a coat." So we went and took the coats from several bodies and tried them on. Taking off their clothes was no easy job, for the corpses were already rigid like a piece of wood. But what was to be done? We could not run about in our shirt-sleeves! All did not find something to fit them, and the disappointed ones had to wait for another chance to turn up. We also needed boots, of course; but the corpses lying before our eyes had boots on that were not much better than our own. They had worn theirs as long as we had worn ours, but we thought we might just inspect them all the same.

We looked and found a pair of fairly good ones. They were very small, but we guessed they might fit one or the other amongst us. Two of us tried to remove them. "But they are a tight fit," one of the two remarked. Two more came up to help. Two were holding the leg of the dead man while the two others tugged at the boot. It was of no use; the leg and the foot were so rigid that it was found impossible to get the boot off. "Let it go," one of those holding the leg remarked, "you will sooner pull off his leg than remove that boot." We let go just as the doctor passed.

"What are you doing there?" he asked us.

"We want to get some boots."

"Then you will have to cut them open; don't waste your time, the rigid leg will not release the boot." He passed on.

The situation was not complete without a brutal joke. An infantryman standing near said, pointing to the dead, "Now you know it; let them keep their old boots, they don't want to walk on their bare feet." The joke was laughed at. And why not? Here we were out of danger. What were the others to us? We were still alive and those lying there could hear no longer. We saw no other things in war, and better things we had not been taught.

It is true that on the way we had got some bread by begging for it, but we were still quite hungry. Nothing was to be seen of our field kitchen. The crew of our field kitchen and the foraging officer and sergeant always preferred to defend their Fatherland several tens of miles behind the front. What were others to them? What were we to them? As long as they did not need to go within firing range of the artillery they were content. Comradeship ceases where the field kitchen begins.

There were, however, some field kitchens belonging to other parts of the army. They had prepared meals, but could not get rid of the food; even if their company, *i.e.*, the rest of their company, should have arrived they would have had far too much food. Many a one for whom they had prepared a meal was no longer in need of one. Thus we were most willingly given as much to eat as we wanted. We had scarcely finished eating when we had to form up again. Gradually several men of our company had come together. We lined up in a manner one is used to in war. The "old man" arrived. One of the officers reported the company to him, but evidently did not report the number of the missing. Perhaps the old man did not care, for he did not even ask whether we knew anything about the one or the other. He stepped in front of the company and said (a sign of his good temper), "Good morning, men!" (It was seven o'clock in the evening!)

As an answer he got a grunting noise such as is sometimes made by a certain animal, and a sneering grin. Without much ado we were ordered to go to the tool wagons which were standing near the northern exit of the town, and provide ourselves with rifle ammunition and three hand grenades each. "At half past nine tonight you have to line up here; each man must have 500 cartridges, three hand grenades, and fuses for igniting them; step aside!"

On our way to the implement wagons we noticed that everywhere soldiers that had lost their companies were being drawn together and that new formations were being gotten together with the greatest speed. We felt that something was in the air, but could not tell what it might be. The rain had started again and was coming down in torrents. When we were at the appointed place at half past nine in the evening we saw all the principal streets filled with troops, all of them in storming outfit like ourselves. A storming outfit consists of a suit made of cloth, a cap, light marching baggage, tent canvas, cooking utensils, tent-pegs, the iron ration, and, in the case of sappers, trench tools also. During the day we got our "*Klamotten*," *i.e.*, our equipment together again. We were standing in the rain and waited. We did not yet know what was going to happen. Then we were ordered to take off the lock of our rifles and put them in our bread bags. The rifles could not now be used for shooting.

We began to feel what was coming, *viz.*, a night attack with bayonets and hand grenades. So as not to shoot each other in the dark we had to remove the lock from the rifle. We stood there till about 11 o'clock when we were suddenly ordered to camp. We did not know what the whole thing meant, and were especially puzzled by the last order which was, however, welcomed by all of us. We judged from the rolling thunder that the battle had not yet decreased in violence, and the sky was everywhere red from the burning villages and farm houses.

Returning "home" we gathered from the conversation the officers had among themselves that a last attempt was to be made to repel the French; that explained the night assault the order for which had now been cancelled. They had evidently made, or been obliged to make another resolution at the general staff; perhaps they had recognized that no more could be done and had rescinded the order for the attack and decided upon a retreat, which began the next morning at 6 o'clock. We, however, had no idea that it should be our last night at Vitry.

We lodged in a shanty for the night. Being sufficiently tired we were soon in a deep slumber. We had to rise at four o'clock in the morning. Each of us received a loaf of bread; we filled our water bottles, and marched off. Whither we were marching we were not told, but we guessed it. The remaining population of Vitry, too, seemed to be informed; some were lining the streets, and their glances were eloquent. Everywhere a feverish activity was to be observed. We halted outside the town. The captain called us to gather round him and addressed us as follows: "Our troops will evacuate their positions on account of the difficult terrain, and retire to those heights where they will take up new positions."

In saying that he turned round and pointed to a ridge near the horizon. He continued: "There we shall settle down and expect the enemy. New reinforcements will arrive there today, and some days hence you will be able to send a picture postcard home from Paris." I must avow that the majority of us believed that humbug at the time. Other portions of the army were already arriving from all directions. We had been marching for some hours when we heard that Vitry had already been occupied again by the French and that all the material stored at Vitry, together with all the hospitals, doctors and men, and whole companies of the medical service had been taken there.

Towards two o'clock in the afternoon we reached the heights the captain had shown us, but he had evidently forgotten everything, for we marched on and on. Even the most stupid amongst us now began to fear that we had been humbugged. The streets became ever more densely crowded with retreating troops and trains; from all sides they came and wanted to use the main road that was also being used by us, and the consequence was that the road became too congested and that we were continually pushed more to the rear. Munition wagons raced past us, singly, without any organisation. Order was no longer observed. Canteen and baggage wagons went past, and here already a wild confusion arose.

Every moment there was a stop and all got wedged. Many would not wait, and some wagons were driven by the side of the road, through fields turned sodden by the rain, in an attempt to get along. One wagon would be overturned, another one would stick in the mud. No great trouble was taken to recover the vehicles, the horses were taken out and the wagon was left. The drivers took the horses and tried to get along; every one was intent upon finding safety. Thus one incident followed upon another.

An officer came riding up and delivered an order to our captain.

We did not know what it was. But we halted and stepped into the field. Having stacked our rifles we were allowed to lie down. We lay down by the side of the road and gazed at the columns, field kitchens, transports, medical trains, field post wagons, all filing past us in picturesque confusion. Wounded men were lying or sitting on all the vehicles. Their faces showed that riding on those heavy wagons caused them pain. But they, too, wanted to get along at any price for they knew from personal experience what it meant to fall into the hands of an uncompromising enemy. They would perhaps be considered as little as they and we ourselves had formerly considered the wounded Frenchmen left in our hands. Because they knew this, as all of us did, they did not want to be left behind for anything in the world.

We had as yet not the slightest idea what we were to do. Night came upon us, and it poured again in torrents. We lay on the ground and felt very cold. Our tired bodies no longer gave out any heat. Yet we stayed on the ground too tired to move. Sections of artillery now began to arrive, but most of the batteries had no longer their full number (6) of guns. One had lost three, another two; many guns even arriving singly. Quite a number of limbers, some 50 or so, passed without guns. Those batteries had only been able to save the horses and had been obliged to leave the guns in the hands of the French. Others had only two or four horses instead of six.

Presently some fifteen motorcars, fine solid cars, came along. We gazed in astonishment at the strong, elegant vehicles. "Ah!" my neighbours exclaimed, "the General Staff!" Duke Albrecht of Wurttemberg and his faithful retainers! We were getting rebellious again. Every one felt wild, and it rained curses. One man said, "After having sent thousands to their doom they are now making off in motorcars." We were lying in the swamp, and nobody noticed us. The automobiles raced past and soon left all behind them. We were still quite in the dark as to our purpose in that place. We lay there for hours, till ten o'clock at night. The troops were surging back largely in dissolved formations. Machine-gun sections arrived with empty wagons; they had lost all their guns. In the west we heard the thunder of guns coming nearer and nearer. We did not know whether we were going to be sent into battle again or not.

The confusion in the road became worse and worse and degenerated in the darkness into a panic. Refugees, who were wandering about with women and children in that dark night and in the pouring rain, got under the wheels of wagons; wounded men in flight were likewise crushed by the wheels; and cries for help came from everywhere out of the darkness. The streets were badly worn. Abandoned vehicles were lining the sides of the road. We began to move at three o'clock in the morning, and before we were fully aware of what was happening we found ourselves with the rear-guard. Regiments of infantry, shot to pieces, arrived in a pitiful condition. They had cast away their knapsacks and all unnecessary impediments, and were trying to get along as fast as possible. Soon after, the first shrapnel of the enemy began to burst above our heads, which caused us to accelerate our march continually.

The road, which had also been used during the advance, was still marked by deep shell holes that were filled with water to the very edge, for it rained without interruption. It was pitch-dark, and every now and then somebody would fall into one of those shell holes. We were all wet through, but continued to press on. Some would stumble over something in the dark, but nobody paid any attention. The great thing was to get along. Dead horses and men lay in the middle of the road, but nobody took the trouble to remove the "obstacle."

It was almost light when we reached a small village and halted. The whole place was at once occupied and put in a state of defence as well as was possible. We took up positions behind the walls of the cemetery. Other troops arrived incessantly, but all in disorder, in a wild confused jumble. Cavalry and artillery also arrived together with a machine-gun section. These, however, had kept their formations intact; there was some disorder, but no sign of panic. One could see that they had suffered considerable losses though their casualties had not been as heavy as ours. The enemy was bombarding us with his guns in an increasing degree, but his fire had no effect. Some houses had been hit and set alight by shells. Far away from us hostile cavalry patrols showed themselves, but disappeared again. Everything was quiet.

Ten minutes afterwards things in front of us began to get lively; we saw whole columns of the enemy approach. Without firing a shot we turned and retired farther back. Mounted artillery were stationed behind the village and were firing already into the advancing enemy. A cavalry patrol came galloping across the open field, their horses being covered with foam. We heard the leader of the patrol, an officer, call out in passing to a cavalry officer that strong forces of the enemy were coming on by all the roads. We left the village behind us and sought to get along as quickly as possible. We had no idea where we were. The cavalry and artillery sections that had been left behind were keeping the enemy under fire.

Towards noon shrapnel was again exploding above our heads, but the projectiles were bursting too high up in the air to do any damage to us. Yet it was a serious warning to us, for it gave us to understand that the enemy was keeping close on our heels—a sufficient reason to convert our retreat into a flight. We therefore tried to get away as fast as our tired out bones would let us. We knew there was no chance of a rest today. So we hurried on in the drenching rain.

The number of those who dropped by the way from exhaustion became larger and larger. They belonged to various portions of the army. We could not help them, and there were no more wagons; these were more in front. Those unfortunate men, some of whom were unconscious, were left behind just as the exhausted horses. Those that had sufficient strength left crawled to the side of the road; but the unconscious ones remained where they fell, exposed to the hoofs of the horses and the wheels of the following last detachments.

If they were lucky enough not to be crushed to atoms they fell into the hands of the enemy. Perhaps those who found our men were men and acted accordingly, but if they were soldiers brutalized by war, patriots filled with hatred, as could also be found in our own ranks, then the "*boche*" (as the French say) had to die a miserable death by the road, die for his "Fatherland." To our shame, be it said, we knew it from our own experience, and summoned all our energy so as not to be left behind. I was thinking of the soldier of the Foreign Legion lying in the desert sand, left behind by his troop and awaiting the hungry hyenas.

The road was covered with the equipment the soldiers had thrown away. We, too, had long ago cast aside all unnecessary ballast. Thus we were marching, when we passed a wood densely packed with refugees. Those hunted people had stretched blankets between the trees so as to protect themselves from the rain. There they were lying in the greatest conceivable misery, all in a jumble, women and men, children and gray-beards. Their camp reached as far as the road, and one could observe that the terrible hours they had lived through had left deep furrows in their faces. They looked at us with weary, tired eyes. The children begged us to give them some bread, but we had nothing whatsoever left and were ourselves tormented by hunger.

The enemy's shrapnel was still accompanying us, and we had scarcely left the wood when shrapnel began to explode there, which caused the refugees, now exposed to the fire, to crowd into the fields in an attempt to reach safety. Many of them joined us, but before long they were forbidden to use the road because they impeded the retreat of the troops. Thus all of them were driven without pity into the fields soaked by the rain.

When we came to a pillaged village towards the evening we were at last granted a short rest, for in consequence of our quick marching we had disengaged ourselves almost completely from the enemy. We heard the noise of the rear-guard actions at a considerable distance behind us, and we wished that they would last a long time, for then we could rest for a longer period. From that village the head man and two citizens were carried off by the Germans, the three being escorted by cavalry. We were not told why those people were being taken along, but each place had to furnish such "hostages," whole troops of whom were being marched off. The remaining cattle had also been taken along; troopers were driving along the cattle in large droves. We were part of the rear-guard. It is therefore easy to understand why we found no more eatables. Hunger began to plague us more and more. Not a mouthful was to be had in the village we had reached, and without having had any food we moved on again after half an hour's rest.

We had marched two miles or so when we came upon a former camping place. Advancing German troops had camped there about a week ago. The bread that had evidently been plentiful at that time now lay scattered in the field. Though the bread had been lying in the open for about a week and had been exposed to a rain lasting for days, we picked it up and swallowed it ravenously. As long as those pangs of hunger could be silenced, it mattered little what it was that one crammed into one's stomach.

15
At the End of the Flight

Night fell again, and there was still no prospect of sleep and recuperation. We had no idea of how far we had to retire. Altogether we knew very little of how things were going. We saw by the strange surroundings that we were not using the same road on which we had marched before to the Marne as "victors." "Before!" It seemed to us as if there was an eternity between that "before" and the present time, for many a one who was with us then was now no longer among us.

One kept thinking and thinking, one hour chased the other. Involuntarily one was drawn along. We slept whilst walking. Our boots were literally filled with water. Complaining was of no use. We had to keep on marching. Another night passed. Next morning troops belonging to the main army were distributed among the rear-guard. In long columns they were lying by the side of the road to let us pass in order to join up behind. We breathed a sigh of relief, for now we were no longer exposed to the enemy's artillery fire. After a march of some five hours we halted and were lucky enough to find ourselves close to a company of infantry that had happily saved its field kitchen.

After the infantrymen had eaten we were given the rest, about a pint of bean soup each. Some sappers of our company were still among that section of the infantry. They had not been able to find us and had joined the infantry. We thought they were dead or had been taken prisoners, but they had only been scattered and had lost their way. We had hopes to recover still many a one of our missing comrades in a similar manner, but we found only a few more afterwards. In the evening of the same day we saw another fellow of our company sitting on the limber of the artillery. When he saw us he joined us immediately and told us what had happened to him. The section he belonged to had its retreat across the Marne cut off; nearly all had been made prisoners already and the French were about to disarm them when he fled and was lucky enough to reach the other side of the Marne by swimming across the river.

He, too, could not or did not want to find our company, and joined the artillery so as not to be forced to walk, so he explained. Our opinion was that he would have done better by remaining a prisoner, for in that case the murdering business would have ended as far as he was concerned. We told him so, and he agreed with us. "However," he observed, "is it sure that the French would have spared us? I know how we ourselves acted; and if they had cut us down remorselessly we should now be dead. Who could have known it?" I knew him too well not to be aware that he for one had every reason to expect from the enemy what he had often done in his moments of bloodthirst; when he was the "victor" he knew neither humanity nor pity.

It was not yet quite dark when we reached a large village. We were to find quarters there and rest as long as was possible. But we knew well enough that we should be able to rest only for as long as the rear-guard could keep the enemy back. Our quarters were in the public school, and on account of the lack of food we were allowed to consume our iron rations. Of course, we had long ago lost or eaten that can of meat and the little bag of biscuits. We therefore lay down with rumbling stomachs.

Already at 11 o'clock in the night alarm was sounded. In the greatest hurry we had to get ready to march off, and started at once. The night was pitch-dark, and it was still raining steadily. The officers kept on urging us to hurry up, and the firing of rifles told us that the enemy was again close at our heels. At day-break we passed the town of St. Menehould which was completely intact. Here we turned to the east, still stubbornly pursued by the French, and reached Clermont-en-Argonne at noon. Again we got some hours of rest, but in the evening we had to move on again all night long in a veritable forced march. We felt more tired from hour to hour, but there was no stopping.

The rain had stopped when we left the road at ten o'clock in the morning and we were ordered to occupy positions. We breathed again freely, for that exhausting retreat lasting for days had reduced us to a condition that was no longer bearable. So we began to dig ourselves in. We had not half finished digging our trenches when a hail of artillery projectiles was poured on us. Fortunately we lost but few men, but it was impossible to remain any longer, and we were immediately ordered to retreat. We marched on over country roads, and it was dark when we began to dig in again. We were in the neighborhood of Challerange quite near the village of Cerney-en-Dormois. It was very dark and a thick mist surrounded us. We soldiers had no knowledge of the whereabouts of the enemy. As quickly as possible we tried to deepen our trench, avoiding every unnecessary noise. Now and then we heard secret patrols of the enemy approach, only to disappear again immediately.

It was there we got our first reinforcements. They came up in the dark in long rows, all of them fresh troops and mostly men of the *landwehr*, large numbers of whom were still in blue uniforms. By their uniforms and equipment one could see that the men had been equipped and sent off in great haste. They had not yet heard the whistle of a bullet, and were anxiously inquiring whether the place was dangerous. They brought up numerous machine-guns and in a jiffy we had prepared everything for the defence.

We could not get to know where the French were supposed to be. The officers only told us to keep in our places. Our trench was thickly crowded with men, and provided with numerous machine-guns. We instructed the new arrivals in the way they would have to behave if an attack should be made, and told them to keep quite still and cool during the attack and aim accurately.

They were mostly married men that had been dragged from their occupations and had been landed right in our midst without understanding clearly what was happening to them. They had no idea where, in what part of the country they were, and they overwhelmed us with all sorts of questions. They were not acquainted with the handling of the new 98-rifle. They were provided with a remodelled rifle of the 88 pattern for which our ammunition could be used. Though no shots were fired the "new ones" anxiously avoided putting their heads above the edge of the trench. They provided us liberally with eatables and cigars.

It was getting light, and as yet we had not seen much of the enemy. Slowly the mist began to disappear, and now we observed the French occupying positions some hundred yards in front of us. They had made themselves new positions during the night exactly as we had done. Immediately firing became lively on both sides. Our opponent left his trench and attempted an attack, but our great mass of machine-guns literally mowed down his ranks. An infernal firing had set in, and the attack was beaten off after only a few steps had been made by the opposing troops. The French renewed their attack again and again, and when at noon we had beaten back eight assaults of that kind hundreds upon hundreds of dead Frenchmen were covering the ground between our trenches and theirs. The enemy had come to the conclusion that it was impossible to break down our iron wall and stopped his attacks.

At that time we had no idea that this was to be the beginning of a murderous exhausting war of position, the beginning of a slow, systematic, and useless slaughter. For months and months we were to fight on in the same trench, without gaining or losing ground, sent forward again and again to murder like raving beasts and driven back again. Perhaps it was well that we did not know at that time that hundreds of thousands of men were to lose their lives in that senseless slaughter.

The wounded men between the trenches had to perish miserably. Nobody dared help them as the opposing side kept up their fire. They perished slowly, quite slowly. Their cries died away after long hours, one after the other. One man after the other had lain down to sleep, never to awake again. Some we could hear for days; night and day they begged and implored one to assist them, but nobody could help. Their cries became softer and softer until at last they died away—all suffering had ceased. There was no possibility of burying the dead. They remained where they fell for weeks. The bodies began to decompose and spread pestilential stenches, but nobody dared to come and bury the dead.

If a Frenchman showed himself to look for a friend or a brother among the dead he was fired at from all directions. His life was dearer to him and he never tried again. We had exactly the same experience. The French tried the red cross flag. We laughed and shot it to pieces. The impulse to shoot down the "enemy" suppressed every feeling of humanity, and the "red cross" had lost its significance when raised by a Frenchman. Suspicion was nourished artificially, so that we thought the "enemy" was only abusing the flag; and that was why we wanted to shoot him and the flag to bits.

But we ourselves took the French for barbarians because they paid us back in kind and prevented us from removing our own wounded men to safety. The dead remained where they were, and when ten weeks later we were sent to another part of the front they were still there.

We had been fortunate in beating back all attacks and had inflicted enormous losses upon the enemy without having ourselves lost many dead or wounded men. Under those circumstances no further attack was to be expected for the time being. So we employed all our strength to fortify our position as strongly as possible. Half of the men remained in their places, and the other half made the trenches wider and deeper. But both sides maintained a continuous lively fire. The losses we suffered that day were not especially large, but most of the men who were hit were struck in the head, for the rest of the body was protected by the trench.

When darkness began to descend the firing increased in violence. Though we could not see anything we fired away blindly because we thought the enemy would not attempt an attack in that case. We had no target and fired always in the direction of the enemy's trench. Throughout the night ammunition and materials were brought up, and new troops kept arriving. Sand bags were brought in great quantities, filled and utilized as cover, as a protection from the bullets. The sappers were relieved towards morning. We had to assemble at a farm behind the firing line. The farmhouse had been completely preserved, and all the animals were still there; but that splendour was destined to disappear soon. Gradually several hundreds of soldiers collected there, and then began a wild chase after ducks, geese, pigeons, etc. The feathered tribe, numbering more than 500 head, had been captured in a few hours, and everywhere cooking operations were in full swing.

There were more than eighty cows and bullocks in a neighbouring field. All of them were shot by the soldiers and worked into food by the field kitchens. In that place everything was taken. Stores of hay and grain had been dragged away in a few hours. Even the straw sheds and outbuildings were broken up, the wood being used as fuel. In a few hours that splendid farm had become a wreck, and its proprietor had been reduced to beggary. I had seen the owner that morning; but he had suddenly disappeared with his wife and children, and nobody knew whither. The farm was within reach of the artillery fire, and the farmer sought safety somewhere else. Not a soul cared where he had gone.

Rifle bullets, aimed too high, were continually flying about us, but nobody cared in the least though several soldiers had been hit. A man of our company, named Mertens, was sitting on the ground cleaning his rifle when he was shot through the neck; he died a few minutes after. We buried him in the garden of the farm, placed his helmet on his grave, and forgot all about him.

Near the farm a German howitzer battery was in position. The battery was heavily shelled by the enemy. Just then a munition train consisting of three wagons came up to carry ammunition to the battery. We had amongst us a sergeant called Luwie, from Frankfort-on-the-Main. One of his brothers, also a sergeant, was in the column that was passing by. That had aroused our interest, and we watched the column to see whether it should succeed in reaching the battery through the fire the enemy was keeping up. Everything seemed to go along all right when suddenly the sergeant, the brother of the sapper sergeant, was hit by a shell and torn to pieces, together with his horse.

All that his own brother was watching. It was hard to tell what was passing through his mind. He was seen to quiver. That was all; then he stood motionless. Presently he went straight to the place of the catastrophe without heeding the shells that were striking everywhere, fetched the body of his brother and laid it down. Part of the left foot of the dead man was missing and nearly the whole right leg; a piece of shell as big as a fist stuck in his chest. He laid down his brother and hurried back to recover the missing limbs. He brought back the leg, but could not find the foot that had been torn off. When we had buried the mangled corpse the sergeant borrowed a map of the general staff from an officer and marked the exact spot of the grave so as to find it again after the war.

The farmhouse had meanwhile been turned into a bandaging station. Our losses increased very greatly judging from the wounded men who arrived in large numbers. The farmhouse offered a good target to the enemy's artillery. Though it was hidden by a hillock some very high poplars towered above that elevation. We felled those trees. Towards evening we had to go back to the trench, for the French were renewing their attacks, but without any effect. The fresh troops were all very excited, and it was hard for them to get accustomed to the continued rolling rifle fire. Many of them had scarcely taken up their place when they were killed. Their blue uniforms offered a good target when they approached our positions from behind.

At night it was fairly quiet, and we conversed with the new arrivals. Some of them had had the chance of remaining in garrison service, but had volunteered for the front. Though they had had only one day in the firing line they declared quite frankly that they repented of their decision. They had had quite a different idea of what war was like, and believed it an adventure, had believed in the fine French wine, had dreamt of some splendid castle where one was quartered for weeks; they had thought that one would get as much to eat and drink as one wished. It was war, and in war one simply took what one wanted.

Such nonsense and similar stuff they had heard of veterans of the war of 1870-71, and they had believed that they went forward to a life of adventure and ease. Bitterly disappointed they were now sitting in the rain in a dirty trench, with a vast army of corpses before them. And every minute they were in danger of losing their life! That was a war quite different from the one they had pictured to themselves. They knew nothing of our retreat and were therefore not a little surprised when we related to them the events of the last few days.

16

The Beginning of Trench Warfare

On the next morning, at daybreak, we quitted the trench again in order to rest for two days. We went across the fields and took up quarters at Cerney-en-Dormois. We lodged in one of the abandoned houses in the centre of the village. Our field kitchen had not yet arrived, so we were obliged to find our own food. Members of the feathered tribe were no longer to be discovered, but if by any chance a chicken showed its head it was immediately chased by a score of men. No meat being found we resolved to be vegetarians for the time being, and roamed through the gardens in search of potatoes and vegetables. On that expedition we discovered an officer's horse tied to a fence. We knew by experience that the saddle bags of officers' horses always concealed something that could be eaten. We were hungry enough, and quickly resolved to lead the horse away. We searched him thoroughly under "cover," and found in the saddle bags quite a larder of fine foodstuffs, butter and lard among them. Then we turned the horse loose and used the captured treasure to prepare a meal, the like of which we had not tasted for a long time.

It tasted fine in spite of our guilty conscience. One man made the fire, another peeled the potatoes, etc. Pots and a stove we found in one of the kitchens of the houses in the neighborhood.

Towards evening long trains with provisions and endless rows of fresh troops arrived. In long columns they marched to the front and relieved the exhausted men. Soon the whole place was crowded with soldiers. After a two days' rest we had to take up again the regular night duties of the sapper. Every night we had to visit the position to construct wire entanglements. The noise caused by the ramming in of the posts mostly drew the attention of the French upon us, and thus we suffered losses almost every night. But our rest during the daytime was soon to be put an end to, for the enemy's artillery began to shell the place regularly.

Curiously enough, the shelling took place always at definite hours. Thus, at the beginning, every noon from 12 to 2 o'clock from fifty to eighty shells used to fall in the place. At times the missiles were shrapnel from the field artillery. One got accustomed to it, though soldiers of other arms were killed or wounded daily. Once we were lying at noon in our lodgings when a shrapnel shell exploded in our room, happily without doing any damage. The whole room was filled with dust and smoke, but not one troubled to leave his place. That sort of shooting was repeated almost daily with increasing violence. The remaining inhabitants of the village, mostly old people, were all lodged in a barn for fear of espionage. There they were guarded by soldiers.

As the village was being bombarded always at certain hours the officer in command of the place believed that somebody in the village communicated with the enemy with a hidden telephone. They even went so far as to remove the hands of the church clock, because somebody had seen quite distinctly "that the hands of the clock (which was not going) had moved and were pointing to 6 and immediately afterwards to 5." Of course, the spy that had signalled to the enemy by means of the church clock could be discovered as little as the man with the concealed telephone. But in order to be quite sure to catch the "real" culprit all the civilians were interned in the barn. Those civilian prisoners were provided with food and drink like the soldiers, but like the soldiers they were also exposed to the daily bombardment, which gradually devastated the whole village.

Two women and a child had already been killed in consequence and yet the people were not removed. Almost daily a house burned down at some spot or other in the village, and the shells now began falling at 8 o'clock in the evening. The shells were of a large size. We knew exactly that the first shell arrived punctually at 8 o'clock, and we left the place every night. The whole village became empty, and exactly at 8 o'clock the first shell came buzzing heavily over to our side. At short intervals, fourteen or sixteen at the most, but never more, followed it. Those sixteen we nicknamed the "iron portion." Our opinion was that the gun was sent forward by the French when it became dark, that it fired a few shots, and was then taken to the rear again. When we returned from our "walk," as we called that nightly excursion, we had to go to our positions. There we had to perform all imaginable kinds of work

One evening we had to fortify a small farm we had taken from the French the day before. We were to construct machine-gun emplacements. The moon was shining fairly brightly. In an adjoining garden there were some fruit trees, an apple tree among them, with some apples still attached to it. A Frenchman had hanged himself on that tree. Though the body must have hung for some days—for it smelled considerably—some of our sappers were eager to get the apples. The soldiers took the apples without troubling in the least about the dead man.

Near that farm we used mine throwers for the first time. The instruments we used there were of a very primitive kind. They consisted of a pipe made of strong steel plate and resting on an iron stand. An unexploded shell or shrapnel was filled with dynamite, provided with a fuse and cap, and placed in the tube of the mine thrower. Behind it was placed a driving charge of black powder of a size corresponding with the distance of the target and the weight of the projectile. The driving charge, too, was provided with a fuse that was of such a length that the explosion was only produced after the man lighting the fuse had had time to return to a place of safety.

The fuse of the mine was lit at the same time as the former, but was of a length commensurate with the time of flight of the mine, so as to explode the latter when the mine struck the target, or after a calculated period should the mark be missed. The driving charge must be of such strength that it throws the projectile no farther than is intended. The mine thrower is not fired horizontally but at a steep angle. The tube from which the mine is fired is, for instance, placed at an angle of 45 degrees, and receives a charge of fifteen grams of black powder when the distance is 400 yards.

It happens that the driving charge does not explode, and the projectile remains in the tube. The fuse of the mine continues burning, and the mine explodes in the tube and demolishes the stand and everything in its neighborhood. When we used those mine throwers here for the first time an accident of the kind described happened. Two volunteers and a sapper who were in charge of the mine thrower in question thought the explosion took too long a time. They believed it was a miss. When they had approached to the distance of some five paces the mine exploded and all three of them were wounded very severely.

We had too little experience in the management of mine throwers. They had been forgotten, had long ago been thrown on the junk heap, giving way to more modern technical appliances of war. Thus, when they suddenly cropped up again during the war of position, we had to learn their management from the beginning. The officers, who understood those implements still less than we ourselves did, could not give us any hints, so it was no wonder that accidents like the foregoing happened frequently.

Those mine throwers cannot be employed for long distances; at 600 yards they reach the utmost limit of their effectiveness.

Besides handling the mine throwers we had to furnish secret patrols every night. The chief purpose of those excursions was the destruction of the enemy's defences or to harry the enemy's sentries so as to deprive them of sleep.

We carried hand grenades for attack and defence. When starting on such an excursion we were always instructed to find out especially the number of the army section that an opponent we might kill belonged to. The French generally have their regimental number on the collars of their coat or on their cap. So whenever we "spiflicated" one and succeeded in getting near him we would cut that number out of his coat with a knife or take away his coat or cap. In that way the German army command identified the opposing army corps. They thus got to know exactly the force our opponent was employing and whether his best troops were in front of us.

All of us greatly feared those night patrols, for the hundreds of men killed months ago were still lying between the lines. Those corpses were decomposed to a pulp. So when a man went on nocturnal patrol duty and when he had to crawl in the utter darkness on hands and knees over all those bodies he would now and then land in the decomposed faces of the dead. If then a man happened to have a tiny wound in his hands his life was greatly endangered by the septic virus. As a matter of fact three sappers and two infantrymen of the *landwehr* regiment No. 17 died in consequence of poisoning by septic virus. Later on that kind of patrolling was given up or only resorted to in urgent cases, and only such men were employed who were free of wounds. That led to nearly all of us inflicting skin wounds to ourselves to escape patrol duty.

Our camping place, Cerney-en-Dormois, was still being bombarded violently by the enemy every day. The firing became so heavy at last that we could no longer sleep during the day. The large shells penetrated the houses and reached the cellars. The civilian prisoners were sent away after some had been killed by shells. We ourselves, however, remained in the place very much against our inclination in spite of the continuous bombardment. Part of our company lived in a large farmhouse, where recently arrived reserves were also lodged. One day, at noon, the village was suddenly overwhelmed by a hail of shells of a large size. Five of them struck the farmhouse mentioned, almost at the same time. All the men were resting in the spacious rooms. The whole building was demolished, and our loss consisted of 17 dead and 28 wounded men. The field kitchen in the yard was also completely destroyed. Without waiting for orders we all cleared out of the village and collected again outside.

But the captain ordered us to return to the place because, so he said, he had not yet received orders from the divisional commander to evacuate the village. Thereupon we went back to our old quarters and embarked again on a miserable existence. After living in the trenches during the night, in continual danger of life, we arrived in the morning, after those hours of trial, with shattered nerves, at our lodgings. We could not hope to get any rest and sleep, for the shells kept falling everywhere in the village. In time, however, one becomes accustomed to everything. When a shell came shrieking along we knew exactly whereabouts it would strike.

By the sound it made we knew whether it was of large or small size and whether the shell, having come down, would burst or not. Similarly the soldiers formed a reliable judgment in regard to the nationality of an aeroplane. When an aeroplane was seen at a great distance near the horizon the soldiers could mostly say exactly whether it was a German or a French flying machine. It is hard to say by what we recognized the machines. One seems to feel whether it is a friend or a foe that is coming. Of course, a soldier also remembers the characteristic noise of the motor and the construction of the aeroplane.

When a French flier passed over our camp the streets would quickly empty themselves. The reason was not that we were afraid of the flying man; we disappeared because we knew that a bombardment would follow after he had landed and reported. We left the streets so as to convey the impression that the place was denuded of troops. But the trick was not of much use. Every day houses were set alight, and the church, which had been furnished as a hospital, was also struck several times.

Up to that time it had been comparatively quiet at the front. We had protected our position with wide wire entanglements. Quite a maze of trenches, a thing that defies description, had been constructed. One must have seen it in order to comprehend what immense masses of soil had been dug up.

Our principal position consisted of from 6 to 8 trenches, one behind the other and each provided with strong parapets and barbed wire entanglements; each trench had been separately fortified. The distance between the various trenches was sometimes 20 yards, sometimes a hundred and more, all according to the requirements of the terrain. All those positions were joined by lines of approach. Those connecting roads are not wide, are only used by the relieving troops and for transporting purposes, and are constructed in a way that prevents the enemy from enfilading them; they run in a zigzag course. To the rear of the communication trenches are the shelters of the resting troops (reserves). Two companies of infantry, for instance, will have to defend in the first trench a section of the front measuring some two hundred yards.

One company is always on duty, whilst the other is resting in the rear. However, the company at rest must ever be ready for the firing line and is likely to be alarmed at any minute for service at a moment's notice should the enemy attack. The company is in telephonic communication with the one doing trench duty. Wherever the country (as on swampy ground) does not permit the construction of several trenches and the housing of the reserves the latter are stationed far in the rear, often in the nearest village. In such places, relieving operations, though carried out only at night are very difficult and almost always accompanied by casualties. Relief is not brought up at fixed hours, for the enemy must be deceived.

But the enemy will be informed of local conditions by his fliers, patrols or the statements of prisoners, and will keep the country under a continual heavy curtain fire, so that the relieving troops coming up across the open field almost always suffer losses. Food and ammunition are also forwarded at night. The following incident will illustrate the difficulty even one man by himself experiences in approaching such positions.

Myself, a sergeant, and three others had been ordered on secret patrol duty one night. Towards ten o'clock we came upon the line of the curtain fire. We were lying flat on the ground, waiting for a favourable opportunity to cross. However, one shell after the other exploded in front of us, and it would have been madness to attempt to pass at that point. Next to me lay a sapper of my own annual military class; nothing could be seen of the sergeant and the two other privates. On a slight elevation in front of us we saw in the moonlight the shadowy forms of some persons who were lying flat on the ground like ourselves.

We thought it impossible to pass here. My mate, pointing to the shapes before us said, "There's Sergeant Mertens and the others; I think I'll go up to them and tell him that we had better wait a while until it gets more quiet." "Yes; do so," I replied. He crawled to the place on his hands and knees, and I observed him lying near the others. He returned immediately. The shapes turned out to be four dead Frenchmen of the colonial army, who had been there for weeks. He had only seen who they were when he received no answer to his report. The dead thus lay scattered over the whole country. Nothing could be seen of the sergeant and the other men. So we seized a favourable opportunity to slip through, surrounded by exploding shells. We could find out nothing about our companions.

Our search in the trench was likewise unsuccessful; nobody could give us the slightest information though sappers were well known among the infantry, because we had to work at all the points of the front. An hour later the relieving infantry arrived. They had lost five men in breaking through the barrier fire. Our sergeant was among the wounded they brought in. Not a trace was ever found of the two other soldiers. Nobody knew what had become of them.

Under such and similar conditions we spent every night outside. We also suffered losses in our camp almost every day. Though reserves from our garrison town had arrived twice already our company had a fighting strength of only 75 men. But at last we cleared out of the village, and were stationed at the village of Boucoville, about a mile and a half to the northeast of Cerney-en-Dormois. Cerney-en-Dormois was gradually shelled to pieces, and when at night we had to go to the trench we described a wide circle around that formerly flourishing village.

At Boucoville we received the first letters from home by the field post. They had been on their journey for a long, long time, and arrived irregularly and in sheaves. But many were returned, marked, "Addressee killed," "Addressee missing," "Wounded." However, many had to be marked, "Addressee no longer with the army detachment." They could not quite make out the disappearance of many "addressees," but many of us had just suspicions about them, and we wished good luck to those "missing men" in crossing some neutral frontier.

The letters we received were dated the first days of August, had wandered everywhere, bore the stamps of various field post-offices and, in contrast with the ones we received later on, were still full of enthusiasm. Mothers were not yet begging their sons not to risk their lives in order to gain the iron cross; that imploring prayer should arrive later on again and again. It was also at that place that we received the first of those small field post-parcels containing cigars and chocolate.

After staying some ten weeks in that part of the country we were directed to another part of the front. Nobody knew, however, whither we were going to be sent. It was all the same to us. The chance of getting out of the firing line for a few days had such a charm for us that our destination did not concern us in the least. It gave us a wonderful feeling of relief, when we left the firing zone on our march to the railroad station at Challerange. For the first time in a long period we found ourselves in a state of existence where our lives were not immediately endangered; even the most far-reaching guns could no longer harm us. A man must have lived through such moments in order to appreciate justly the importance of such a feeling. However much one has got accustomed to being in constant danger of one's life, that danger never ceases to oppress one, to weigh one down.

At the station we got into a train made up of second and third-class coaches. The train moved slowly through the beautiful autumnal landscape, and for the first time we got an insight into the life behind the front. All the depots, the railroad crossings and bridges were held by the military. There all the men of the *landsturm* were apparently leading quite an easy life, and had made themselves comfortable in the depots and shanties of the road-men. They all looked well nourished and were well clad.

Whenever the train stopped those older men treated us liberally to coffee, bread, and fruit. They could see by our looks that we had not had the same good time that they were having. They asked us whence we came. Behind the front things were very lively everywhere. At all the larger places we could see long railway trains laden with agricultural machinery of every description. The crew of our train were men of the Prusso-Hessian state railroads. They had come through those parts many times before, and told us that the agricultural machines were being removed from the whole of the occupied territory and sent to East Prussia in order to replace what the Russians had destroyed there. The same was being done with all industrial machinery that could be spared. Again and again one could observe the finest machines on their way to Germany.

Towards midnight we passed Sédan. There we were fed by the Red Cross. The Red Cross had erected feeding stations for passing troops in long wooden sheds. Early next morning we found ourselves at Montmédy. There we had to leave the train, and were allowed to visit the town for a few hours.

17
Friendly Relations With the Enemy

There was no lack of food at Montmédy. The canteens were provided with everything; prices were high, however. Montmédy is a third-class French fortress and is situated like Ehrenbreitstein on a height which is very steep on one side; the town is situated at the foot of the hill. The fortress was taken by the Germans without a struggle. The garrison who had prepared for defence before the fortress, had their retreat cut off. A railroad tunnel passes through the hill under the fortress, but that had been blown up by the French. The Germans laid the rails round the hill through the town so as to establish railroad communications with their front. It looked almost comical to watch the transport trains come rolling on through the main street and across the market place.

Everywhere along the Meuse the destroyed bridges had been replaced by wooden ones. Montmédy was the chief base of the Fifth Army (that of the Crown Prince), and contained immense stores of war material. Besides that it harboured the field post-office, the headquarters for army provisions, a railroad management, and a great number of hospitals. The largest of them used to be called the "theatre hospital," on account of its being installed in the municipal theater and the adjoining houses, and always contained from 500 to 600 wounded.

Things were very lively at Montmédy. One chiefly observed convalescent soldiers walking through the streets and a remarkable number of officers, all of whom had been attached to the various departments. They loitered about in their faultless uniforms, or rode along whip in hand. Moreover, they had not yet the slightest idea of what war was like, and when we met them they expected us to salute them in the prescribed manner. Many of them accosted us and asked us rudely why we did not salute. After a few hours we got sick of life twenty miles behind the Verdun front.

At Montmédy we were about twenty miles behind Verdun and some sixty miles away from our former position. When towards one o'clock p. m. we began to move on we guessed that we were to be dragged to the country round Verdun. After a march of nine miles we reached the village of Fametz. There we were lodged in various barns. Nearly all of the inhabitants had stayed on; they seemed to be on quite friendly terms with the soldiers. Time had brought them closer to each other, and we, too, got an entirely different idea of our "hereditary enemy" on closer acquaintance. When walking through the place we were offered all kinds of things by the inhabitants, were treated to coffee, meat, and milk, exactly as is done by German patriots during manoeuvres and we were even treated better than at home. To reward them for these marks of attention we murdered the sons of those people who desired nothing better than living in peace.

Early next morning we moved on, and when we arrived at Damvillers in the evening we heard that we were some three miles behind the firing line. That very night we marched to the small village of Warville. That was our destination, and there we took up our quarters in a house that had been abandoned by its inhabitants. We were attached to the ninth reserve division, and the following day already we had to take up our positions. Fifteen of us were attached to a company of infantry. No rifle firing was to be heard along the line, only the artillery of the two sides maintained a weak fire. We were not accustomed to such quietness in the trenches, but the men who had been here for a long time told us that sometimes not a shot was fired for days and that there was not the slightest activity on either side. It seemed to us that we were going to have a nice quiet time.

The trench in that section crossed the main road leading from Damvillers to Verdun (a distance of some fifteen miles). The enemy's position was about 800 yards in front of us. German and French troops were always patrolling the road from six o'clock at night till the morning. At night time those troops were always standing together. Germans and Frenchmen met, and the German soldiers had a liking for that duty. Neither side thought for a moment to shoot at the other one; everybody had just to be at his post. In time both sides had cast away suspicions; every night the "hereditary enemies" shook hands with each other; and on the following morning the relieved sentries related to us with pleasure how liberally the Frenchmen had shared everything with them. They always exchanged newspapers with them, and so it came about that we got French papers every day, the contents of which were translated to us by a soldier who spoke the French language.

By day we were able to leave the trench, and we would be relieved across the open field without running any danger. The French had no ideas of shooting at us; neither did we think of shooting at the French. When we were relieved we saluted our enemies by waving our helmets, and immediately the others replied by waving their caps. When we wanted water we had to go to a farm situated between the lines. The French too, fetched their water from there. It would have been easy for each side to prevent the other from using that well, but we used to go up to it quite unconcerned, watched by the French. The latter used to wait till we trotted off again with our cooking pots filled, and then they would come up and provide themselves with water.

At night it often happened that we and the Frenchmen arrived at the well at the same time. In such a case one of the parties would wait politely until the other had done. Thus it happened that three of us were at the well without any arms when a score of Frenchmen arrived with cooking pots. Though the Frenchmen were seven times as numerous as ourselves the thought never struck them that they might fall upon us. The twenty men just waited quietly till we had done; we then saluted them and went off.

One night a French sergeant came to our trench. He spoke German very well, said he was a deserter, and begged us to regard him as our prisoner. But the infantrymen became angry and told him to get back to the French as quickly as possible. Meanwhile a second Frenchman had come up and asked excitedly whether a man of theirs had not deserted to us a short while ago. Then our section leader, a young lieutenant, arrived upon the scene, and the Frenchman who had come last begged him to send the deserter back. "For," so he remarked, "if our officers get to know that one of our men has voluntarily given himself up we shall have to say goodbye to the good time we are having, and the shooting will begin again."

We, too, appreciated the argument that such incidents would only make our position worse. The lieutenant vanished; he did not want to have a finger in that pie; very likely he also desired that things remain as they were. We quickly surrendered the deserter; each one of the two Frenchmen was presented with a cigarette, and then they scurried away full steam ahead.

We felt quite happy under those circumstances and did not wish for anything better. On our daily return journeys we observed that an immense force of artillery was being gathered and were placed in position further back. New guns arrived every day, but were not fired. The same lively activity could be observed in regard to the transportation of ammunition and material. At that time we did not yet suspect that these were the first preparations for a strong offensive.

After staying in that part of the country some four weeks we were again ordered to some other part of the front. As usual we had no idea of our new destination. Various rumours were in circulation. Some thought it would be Flanders, others thought it would be Russia; but none guessed right.

We marched off and reached Dun-sur-Meuse in the afternoon. We had scarcely got to the town when the German Crown Prince, accompanied by some officers and a great number of hounds, rode past us. "Good day, sappers!" he called to us, looking at us closely. He spoke to our captain, and an officer of his staff took us to an establishment of the Red Cross where we received good food and wine. The headquarters of the Hohenzollern scion was here at Dun-sur-Meuse. The ladies of the Red Cross treated us very well. We asked them whether all the troops passing through the place were cared for as well as that. "O yes," a young lady replied; "only few pass through here, but the Crown Prince has a special liking for sappers."

We lodged there for the night, and the soldiers told us that Dun-sur-Meuse was the headquarters of the Fifth Army, that life was often very jolly there, and every day there was an open air concert. We heard that the officers often received ladies from Germany, but, of course, the ladies only came to distribute gifts among the soldiers.

Richly provided with food we continued our march the next morning, and kept along the side of the Meuse. In the evening we were lodged at Stenay.

18

Fighting in the Argonnes

Finally, after two days, we landed at Apremont-en-Argonne. For the time being we were quartered in a large farm to the northeast of Apremont. We found ourselves quite close to the Argonnes. All the soldiers whom we met and who had been there for some time told us of uninterrupted daily fighting in those woods.

Our first task was to construct underground shelters that should serve as living rooms. We commenced work at about a mile and three quarters behind the front, but had to move on after some shells had destroyed our work again. We then constructed, about a mile and a quarter behind the front, a camp consisting of thirty-five underground shelters.

A hole is dug, some five yards square and two yards deep. Short tree trunks are laid across it, and about two yards of earth piled upon them. We had no straw, so we had to sleep on the bare ground for a while. Rifle bullets coming from the direction of the front kept flying above our heads and struck the trees. We were attached to the various companies of infantry; I myself was with the tenth company of the infantry regiment No. 67.

The soil had been completely ploughed up by continued use, and the paths and roads had been covered with sticks and tree trunks so that they could be used by men and wagons. After an arduous march we reached the foremost position. It was no easy task to find one's way in that maze of trenches. The water was more than a foot deep in those trenches. At last we arrived at the most advanced position and reported to the captain of the tenth company of the 67th regiment of infantry. Of course, the conditions obtaining there were quite unknown to us, but the men of the infantry soon explained things to us as far as they could. After two or three days we were already quite familiar with our surroundings, and our many-sided duty began.

The French lay only some ten yards away from us. The second day we were engaged in a fight with hand grenades. In that fight Sapper Beschtel from Saarbrucken was killed. He was our first casualty in the Argonnes, but many were to follow him in the time that followed. In the rear trenches we had established an engineering depot. There 25 men made nothing but hand grenades. Thus we soon had made ourselves at home, and were ready for all emergencies.

At the camp we were divided in various sections. That division in various sections gave us an idea of the endless ways and means employed in our new position. There were mining, sapping, hand grenade sections, sections for mine throwing and illuminating pistols. Others again constructed wire entanglements, *chevaux-de-frise*, or projectiles for the primitive mine throwers. At one time one worked in one section then again in another. The forest country was very difficult. The thick, tangled underwood formed by itself an almost insuperable obstacle. All the trees were shot down up to the firing level. Cut off clean by the machine-guns they lay in all directions on the ground, forming a natural barricade.

The infantrymen had told us about the difficulties under which fighting was carried on uninterruptedly. Not a day passed without casualties. Firing went on without a pause. The men had never experienced an interval in the firing. We soon were to get an idea of that mass murder, that systematic slaughter. The largest part of our company was turned into a mine laying section, and we began to mine our most advanced trench. For a distance of some 500 yards, a yard apart, we dug in boxes of dynamite, each weighing 50 pounds. Each of those mines was provided with a fuse and all were connected so that all the mines could be exploded at the same instant. The mines were then covered with soil again and the connecting wires taken some hundred yards to the rear.

At that time the French were making attacks every few days. We were told to abandon the foremost trench should an attack be made. The mines had been laid two days when the expected attack occurred, and without offering any great resistance we retreated to the second trench. The French occupied the captured trench without knowing that several thousands of pounds of explosives lay buried under their feet. So as to cause our opponents to bring as many troops as possible into the occupied trench we pretended to make counter attacks. As a matter of fact the French trench was soon closely manned by French soldiers who tried to retain it.

But that very moment our mines were exploded. There was a mighty bang, and several hundreds of Frenchmen were literally torn to pieces and blown up into the air. It all happened in a moment. Parts of human bodies spread over a large stretch of ground, and the arms, legs, and rags of uniforms hanging in the trees, were the only signs of a well planned mass murder. In view of that catastrophe all we had experienced before seemed to us to be child's play. That "heroic deed" was celebrated by a lusty hurrah.

For some days one had gained a little advantage, only to lose it again soon. In order to make advances the most diverse methods were used, as was said before. The mining section would cut a subterranean passage up to the enemy's position. The passage would branch out to the right and left a yard or so before the position of our opponent, and run parallel with it. The work takes of course weeks to accomplish, for the whole of the loosened soil must be taken to the rear on small mining wagons. Naturally, the soil taken out must not be heaped in one place, for if that were done the enemy would get wind of our intentions and would spoil everything by countermining.

As soon as work is advanced far enough the whole passage running parallel with the enemy's trench is provided with explosives and dammed up. When the mine is exploded the whole of the enemy's trench is covered by the soil that is thrown up, burying many soldiers alive. Usually such an explosion is followed by an assault. The sapping section, on the other hand, have to dig open trenches running towards the enemy's position. These are connected by transversal trenches, the purpose being to get one's own position always closer to the enemy's. As soon as one's position has approached near enough to make it possible to throw hand grenades into the enemy's position the hand grenade sections have to take up their places and bombard the enemy's trenches continually with hand grenades, day and night.

Some few hundred yards to the rear are the heavy modern mine throwers firing a projectile weighing 140 pounds. Those projectiles, which look like sugar loaves, fly cumbrously over to the enemy where they do great damage. The trade of war must not stop at night; so the darkness is made bright by means of illuminating rockets. The illuminating cartridge is fired from a pistol, and for a second all is bright as day. As all that kind of work was done by sappers the French hated the sappers especially, and French prisoners often told us that German prisoners with white buttons and black ribbons on their caps (sappers) would be treated without any mercy. Warned by the statements of those prisoners nearly all provided themselves with infantry uniforms. We knew that we had gradually become some specialty in the trenches.

If the infantry were molested somewhere by the enemy's hand grenades they used to come running up to us and begged us to go and meet the attack. Each of us received a cigar to light the hand grenades, and then we were off. Ten or twenty of us rained hand grenades on the enemy's trench for hours until one's arm got too stiff with throwing.

Thus the slaughter continued, day after day, night after night. We had 48 hours in the trenches and 12 hours' sleep. It was found impossible to divide the time differently, for we were too few. The whole of the forest had been shot and torn to tatters. The artillery was everywhere and kept the villages behind the enemy's position under fire. Once one of the many batteries which we always passed on our way from camp to the front was just firing when we came by. I interrogated one of the sighting gunners what their target might be. "Some village or other," the gunner replied. The representative of the leader of the battery, a lieutenant-colonel, was present. One of my mates inquired whether women and children might not be in the villages. "That's neither here nor there," said the lieutenant-colonel, "the women and children are French, too, so what's the harm done? Even their litter must be annihilated so as to knock out of that nation for a hundred years any idea of war."

If that "gentleman" thought to win applause he was mistaken. We went our way, leaving him to his "enjoyment."

On that day an assault on the enemy's position had been ordered, and we had to be in our places at seven o'clock in the morning. The 67th regiment was to attack punctually at half past eight, the sappers taking the lead. The latter had been provided with hand grenades for that purpose. We were only some twenty yards away from the enemy. Those attacks, which were repeated every week, were prepared by artillery fire half an hour before the assault began. The artillery had to calculate their fire very carefully, because the distance between the trench and that of the enemy was very small. That distance varied from three to a hundred yards, it was nowhere more than that. At our place it was twenty yards.

Punctually at eight o'clock the artillery began to thunder forth. The first three shots struck our own trench, but those following squarely hit the mark, *i.e.*, the French trench. The artillery had got the exact range and then the volleys of whole batteries began to scream above our heads. Every time the enemy's trench or the roads leading to it were hit with wonderful accuracy. One could hear the wounded cry, a sign that many a one had already been crippled. An artillery officer made observations in the first trench and directed the fire by telephone.

The artillery became silent exactly at half past eight, and we passed to the assault. But the 11th company of regiment No. 67, of which I spoke before, found itself in a such a violent machine-gun fire that eighteen men had been killed a few paces from our trench. The dead and wounded had got entangled in the wild jumble of the trees and branches encumbering the ground. Whoever could run tried to reach the enemy's trench as quickly as possible. Some of the enemy defended themselves desperately in their trench, which was filled with mud and water, and violent hand to hand fighting ensued. We stood in the water up to our knees, killing the rest of our opponents.

Seriously wounded men were lying flat in the mud with only their mouths and noses showing above the water. But what did we care! They were stamped deeper in the mud, for we could not see where we were stepping; and so we rolled up the whole trench. Thereupon the conquered position was fortified as well as it could be done in all haste. Again we had won a few yards of the Argonnes at the price of many lives. That trench had changed its owners innumerable times before, a matter of course in the Argonnes, and we awaited the usual counter attack.

Presently the "mules" began to get active. "Mules" are the guns of the French mountain artillery. As those guns are drawn by mules, the soldier in the Argonnes calls them "mules" for short. They are very light guns with a flat trajectory, and are fired from a distance of only 50-100 yards behind the French front. The shells of those guns whistled above our heads. Cutting their way through the branches they fly along with lightning rapidity to explode in or above some trench. In consequence of the rapid flight and the short distance the noise of the firing and the explosion almost unite in a single bang. Those "mules" are much feared by the German soldiers, because those guns are active day and night. Thus day by day we lived through the same misery.

19

Christmas in the Trenches

Winter had arrived and it was icy cold. The trenches, all of which had underground water, had been turned into mere mud holes. The cold at night was intense, and we had to do 48 hours' work with 12 hours' sleep. Every week we had to make an attack the result of which was in no proportion to the immense losses. During the entire four months that I was in the Argonnes we had a gain of terrain some 400 yards deep. The following fact will show the high price that was paid in human life for that little piece of France. All the regiments (some of these were the infantry regiments Nos. 145, 67, 173, and the Hirschberg sharpshooting battalion No. 5) had their own cemetery. When we were relieved in the Argonnes there were more dead in our cemetery than our regiment counted men.

The 67th regiment had buried more than 2000 men in its cemetery, all of whom, with the exception of a few sappers, had belonged to regiment No. 67. Not a day passed without the loss of human lives, and on a "storming day" death had an extraordinarily rich harvest. Each day had its victims, sometimes more, sometimes fewer. It must appear quite natural that under such conditions the soldiers were not in the best of moods. The men were all completely stupefied. Just as they formerly went to work regularly to feed the wife and children they now went to the trenches in just the same regular way. That business of slaughtering and working had become an every day affair. When they conversed it was always the army leaders, the Crown Prince and Lieutenant-General von Mudra, the general in command of the 16th Army Corps, that were most criticized.

The troops in the Argonnes belonged to the 16th Army Corps, to the 33rd and 34th division of infantry. Neither of the two leaders, neither the Crown Prince nor von Mudra, have I ever seen in the trenches. The staff of the crown prince had among its members the old General-Fieldmarshal Count von Haeseler, the former commander of the 16th Army Corps, a man who in times of peace was already known as a relentless slave driver. The "triplets," as we called the trio, the Crown Prince, von Mudra, and Count von Haeseler, were more hated by most of the soldiers than the Frenchman who was out with his gun to take our miserable life.

Many miles behind the front the scion of the Hohenzollerns found no difficulty to spout his "knock them hard!" and, at the price of thousands of human lives, to make himself popular with the patriots at home who were sitting there behind the snug stove or at the beer table complaining that we did not advance fast enough. Von Mudra got the order "*Pour le merite*"; they did not think of his soldiers who had not seen a bed, nor taken off their trousers or boots for months; these were provided with food—and shells, and were almost being eaten up by vermin.

That we were covered with body lice was not to be wondered at, for we had scarcely enough water for drinking purposes, and could not think of having a wash. We had worn our clothes for months without changing them; the hair on our heads and our beards had grown to great length. When we had some hours in which to rest, the lice would not let us sleep.

The air in the shelters was downright pestiferous, and to that foul stench of perspiration and putrefaction was added the plague of lice. At times one was sitting up for hours and could not sleep, though one was dead tired. One could catch lice, and the more one caught the worse they got. We were urgently in want of sleep, but it was impossible to close the eyes on account of the vermin. We led a loathsome, pitiful life, and at times we said to one another that nobody at home even suspected the condition we were in. We often told one another that if later on we should relate to our families the facts as they really were they would not believe them. Many soldiers tried to put our daily experience in verse.

There were many of such jingles illustrating our barbarous handicraft.

It was in the month of December and the weather was extremely cold. At times we often stood in the trenches with the mud running into our trousers' pockets. In those icy cold nights we used to sit in the trenches almost frozen to a lump of ice, and when utter exhaustion sometimes vanquished us and put us to sleep we found our boots frozen to the ground on waking up. Quite a number of soldiers suffered from frost-bitten limbs; it was mostly their toes that were frost-bitten. They had to be taken to the hospital. The soldiers on duty fired incessantly so as to keep their fingers warm.

Not all the soldiers are as a rule kept ready to give battle. If no attack is expected or intended, only sentries occupy the trench. About three yards apart a man is posted behind his protective shield of steel. Nevertheless all the men are in the trench. The sentries keep their section under a continual fire, especially when it is cold and dark. The fingers get warm when one pulls the trigger. Of course, one cannot aim in the darkness, and the shots are fired at random. The sentry sweeps his section so that no hostile patrol can approach, for he is never safe in that thicket. Thus it happens that the firing is generally more violent at night than at day; but there is never an interval. The rifles are fired continually; the bullets keep whistling above our trench and patter against the branches.

The mines, too, come flying over at night, dropping at a high angle. Everybody knows the scarcely audible thud, and knows at once that it is a mine without seeing anything. He warns the others by calling out, "Mine coming!" and everybody looks in the darkness for the "glowworm," *i.e.*, the burning fuse of the mine. The glowing fuse betrays the direction of the mine, and there are always a few short seconds left to get round some corner. The same is the case with the hand grenades. They, too, betray the line of their flight at night by their burning fuse. If they do not happen to arrive in too great numbers one mostly succeeds in getting out of their way. In daylight that is not so hard because one can overlook everything.

It often happens that one cannot save oneself in time from the approaching hand grenade. In that case there is only one alternative—either to remain alive or be torn to atoms. Should a hand grenade suddenly fall before one's feet one picks it up without hesitation as swiftly as possible and throws it away, if possible back into the enemy's trench. Often, however, the fuse is of such a length that the grenade does not even explode after reaching the enemy's trench again, and the Frenchman throws it back again with fabulous celerity. In order to avoid the danger of having a grenade returned the fuse is made as short as possible, and yet a grenade will come back now and again in spite of all.

To return a grenade is of course dangerous work, but a man has no great choice; if he leaves the grenade where it drops he is lost, as he cannot run away; and he knows he will be crushed to atoms, and thus his only chance is to pick up the grenade and throw it away even at the risk of having the bomb explode in his hand. I know of hand grenades thrown by the French that flew hither and thither several times. One was thrown by the French and immediately returned; it came back again in an instant, and again we threw it over to them; it did not reach the enemy's trench that time, but exploded in the air.

Though in general the infantry bullets cannot do much damage while one is in the trench it happens daily that men are killed by ricochet bullets. The thousands of bullets that cut through the air every minute all pass above our heads. But some strike a tree or branch and glance off. If in that case they hit a man in the trench they cause terrible injuries, because they do not strike with their heads but lengthwise. Whenever we heard of dum-dum bullets we thought of those ricochet bullets, though we did not doubt that there were dum-dum bullets in existence. I doubt, however, if dum-dum bullets are manufactured in factories, for the following reasons:—first, because a dum-dum bullet can easily damage the barrel of a rifle and make it useless; secondly, because the average soldier would refuse to carry such ammunition, for if a man is captured and such bullets are found on him, the enemy in whose power he is would punish him by the laws of war as pitilessly as such an inhuman practice deserves to be punished. Generally, of course, a soldier only executes his orders.

However, there exist dum-dum bullets, as I mentioned before. They are manufactured by the soldiers themselves. If the point is filed or cut off a German infantry bullet, so that the nickel case is cut through and the lead core is laid bare, the bullet explodes when striking or penetrating an object. Should a man be hit in the upper arm by such a projectile the latter, by its explosive force, can mangle the arm to such an extent that it only hangs by a piece of skin.

Christmas came along, and we still found ourselves at the same place without any hope of a change. We received all kinds of gifts from our relations at home and other people. We were at last able to change our underwear which we had worn for months.

Christmas in the trenches! It was bitterly cold. We had procured a pine tree, for there were no fir trees to be had. We had decorated the tree with candles and cookies, and had imitated the snow with wadding.

Christmas trees were burning everywhere in the trenches, and at midnight all the trees were lifted on to the parapet with their burning candles, and along the whole line German soldiers began to sing Christmas songs in chorus. "O, thou blissful, O, thou joyous, mercy bringing Christmas time!" Hundreds of men were singing the song in that fearful wood. Not a shot was fired; the French had ceased firing along the whole line. That night I was with a company that was only five paces away from the enemy. The Christmas candles were burning brightly, and were renewed again and again. For the first time we heard no shots. From everywhere, throughout the forest, one could hear powerful carols come floating over—"Peace on earth—"

The French left their trenches and stood on the parapet without any fear. There they stood, quite overpowered by emotion, and all of them with cap in hand. We, too, had issued from our trenches. We exchanged gifts with the French—chocolate, cigarettes, etc. They were all laughing, and so were we; why, we did not know. Then everybody went back to his trench, and incessantly the carol resounded, ever more solemnly, ever more longingly—"O, thou blissful—"

All around silence reigned; even the murdered trees seemed to listen; the charm continued, and one scarcely dared to speak. Why could it not always be as peaceful? We thought and thought, we were as dreamers, and had forgotten everything about us.—Suddenly a shot rang out; then another one was fired somewhere. The spell was broken. All rushed to their rifles. A rolling fire. Our Christmas was over.

We took up again our old existence. A young infantryman stood next to me. He tried to get out of the trench. I told him: "Stay here; the French will shoot you to pieces."

"I left a box of cigars up there, and must have it back." Another one told him to wait till things quieted down somewhat. "They won't hit me; I have been here three months, and they never caught me yet."

"As you wish; go ahead!"

Scarcely had he put his head above the parapet when he tumbled back. Part of his brains was sticking to my belt. His cap flew high up into the air. His skull was shattered. He was dead on the spot. His trials were over. The cigars were later on fetched by another man.

On the following Christmas day an army order was read out. We were forbidden to wear or have in our possession things of French origin; for, every soldier who was found in possession of such things would be put before a court-martial as a marauder by the French if they captured him. We were forbidden to use objects captured from the French, and we were especially forbidden to make use of woollen blankets, because the French were infected with scabies. Scabies is an itching skin disease, which it takes at least a week to cure. But the order had a contrary effect. If one was the owner of such an "itch-blanket" one had a chance of getting into the hospital for some days. The illness was not of a serious nature, and one was at least safe from bullets for a few days. Every day soldiers were sent to the hospital, and we, too, were watching for a chance to grab such a French blanket. What did a man care, if he could only get out of that hell!

20

The "Itch"—A Saviour

On January 5th the Germans attacked along the whole forest front, and took more than 1800 prisoners. We alone had captured 700 men of the French infantry regiment No. 120. The hand to hand fighting lasted till six o'clock at night. On that day I, together with another sapper, got into a trench section that was still being defended by eight Frenchmen. We could not back out, so we had to take up the unequal struggle. Fortunately we were well provided with hand grenades. We cut the fuses so short that they exploded at the earliest moment. I threw one in the midst of the eight Frenchmen. They had scarcely escaped the first one, when the second arrived into which they ran. We utilized their momentary confusion by throwing five more in quick succession. We had reduced our opponents to four. Then we opened a rifle fire, creeping closer and closer up to them. Their bullets kept whistling above our heads.

One of the Frenchmen was shot in the mouth; three more were left. These turned to flee. In such moments one is seized with an indescribable rage and forgets all about the danger that surrounds one. We had come quite near to them, when the last one stumbled and fell forward on his face. In a trice I was on him; he fought desperately with his fists; my mate was following the other two. I kept on wrestling with my opponent. He was bleeding from his mouth; I had knocked out some of his teeth. Then he surrendered and raised his hands. I let go and then had a good look at him. He was some 35 years old, about ten years older than myself. I now felt sorry for him. He pointed to his wedding ring, talking to me all the while. I understood what he wanted—he wanted to be kept alive.

He handed me his bottle, inviting me to drink wine. He cried; maybe he thought of his wife and children. I pressed his hand, and he showed me his bleeding teeth. "You are a silly fellow," I told him; "you have been lucky. The few missing teeth don't matter. For you the slaughtering is finished; come along!" I was glad I had not killed him, and took him along myself so as to protect him from being ill-treated. When I handed him over he pressed my hand thankfully and laughed; he was happy to be safe. However bad the time he might have as prisoner he would be better off at any rate than in the trenches. At least he had a chance of getting home again.

In the evening we took some of the forbidden blankets, hundreds of which we had captured that day. Ten of us were lying in a shelter, all provided with blankets. Everybody wanted to get the "itch," however strange that may sound. We undressed and rolled ourselves in those blankets. Twenty-four hours later little red pimples showed themselves all over the body, and twelve men reported sick. The blankets were used in the whole company, but all of them had not the desired effect. The doctor sent nine of us to the hospital at Montmédy, and that very evening we left the camp in high glee.

The railroad depot at Apremont had been badly shelled; the next station was Chatel. Both places are a little more than three miles behind the front. At Apremont the prisoners were divided into sections. Some of the prisoners had their homes at Apremont. Their families were still occupying their houses, and the prisoners asked to be allowed to pay them a visit. I chanced to observe one of those meetings at Apremont. Two men of the *landstrum* led one of the prisoners to the house which he pointed out to them as his own. The young wife of the prisoner was sitting in the kitchen with her three children. We followed the men into the house. The woman became as white as a sheet when she beheld her husband suddenly. They rushed to meet each other and fell into each other's arms. We went out, for we felt that we were not wanted. The wife had not been able to get the slightest signs from her husband for the last five months, for the German forces had been between her and him.

He, on the other hand, had been in the trench for months knowing that his wife and children must be there, on the other side, very near, yet not to be reached. He did not know whether they were alive or dead. He heard the French shells scream above his head. Would they hit Apremont? He wondered whether it was his own house that had been set alight by a shell and was reddening the sky at night. He did not know. The uncertainty tortured him, and life became hell. Now he was at home, though only for a few hours. He had to leave again a prisoner; but now he could send a letter to his wife by the field post. He had to take leave. She had nothing she could give him—no underwear, no food, absolutely nothing. She had lost all and had to rely on the charity of the soldiers. She handed him her last money, but he returned it.

We could not understand what they told each other. She took the money back; it was German money, five and ten *pfennig* pieces and some coppers—her whole belongings. We could no longer contain ourselves and made a collection among ourselves. We got more than ten *marks* together which we gave to the young woman. At first she refused to take it and looked at her husband. Then she took it and wanted to kiss our hands. We warded her off, and she ran to the nearest canteen and bought things. Returning with cigars, tobacco, matches, and sausage, she handed all over to her husband with a radiant face. She laughed, once again perhaps in a long time, and sent us grateful looks. The children clung round their father and kissed him again and again.

She accompanied her husband, who carried two of the kiddies, one on each arm, while his wife carried the third child. Beaming with happiness the family marched along between the two *landsturm* men who had their bayonets fixed. When they had to take leave, all of them, parents and children began to weep. She knew that her husband was no longer in constant danger, and she was happy, for though she had lost much, she still had her most precious possessions.

Thousands of poor men and women have met such a fate near their homes.

Regular trains left Chatel. We quitted the place at 11 o'clock at night, heartily glad to leave the Argonnes behind us. We had to change trains at Vouzières, and took the train to Diedenhofen. There we saw twelve soldiers with fixed bayonets take along three Frenchmen. They were elderly men in civilian dress. We had no idea what it signified, so we entered into a conversation with one of our fellow travellers. He was a merchant, a Frenchman living at Vouzières, and spoke German fluently. The merchant was on a business trip to Sédan, and told us that the three civilian prisoners were citizens of his town.

He said: "We obtain our means of life from the German military authorities, but mostly we do not receive enough to live, and the people have nothing left of their own; all the cattle and food have been commandeered. Those three men refused to keep on working for the military authorities, because they could not live on the things they were given. They were arrested and are now being transported to Germany. Of course, we don't know what will happen to them."

The man also told us that all the young men had been taken away by the Germans; all of them had been interned in Germany.

At Sédan we had to wait for five hours; for hospital trains were constantly arriving. It was 2 o'clock in the afternoon of the following day when we reached Montmédy, where we went to the hospital. There all our clothes were disinfected in the "unlousing establishment," and we could take a proper bath. We were lodged in the large barracks. There one met people from all parts of the front, and all of them had only known the same misery; there was not one among them who did not curse this war. All of them were glad to be in safety, and all of them tried their best to be "sick" as long as possible. Each day we were twice treated with ointment; otherwise we were at liberty to walk about the place.

One day we paid a visit to the fortress of Montmédy high up on a hill. Several hundreds of prisoners were just being fed there. They were standing about in the yard of the fortress and were eating their soup. One of the prisoners came straight up to me. I had not noticed him particularly, and recognized him only when he stood before me. He was the man I had struggled with on January 5th, and we greeted each other cordially. He had brought along a prisoner who spoke German well and who interpreted for us all we had to say to each other. He had seen me standing about and had recognized me at once. Again and again he told me how glad he was to be a prisoner. Like myself he was a soldier because he had to be, and not from choice. At that time we had fought with each other in blind rage; for a moment we had been deadly enemies. I felt happy at having stayed my fury at that time, and again I became aware of the utter idiocy of that barbarous slaughter. We separated with a firm handshake.

A fortnight I remained at the hospital; then I had to return to the front. We had been treated well at the hospital, so we started on our return journey with mixed feelings. As soon as we arrived at Chatel, the terminus, we heard the incessant gun fire. It was no use kicking, we had to go into the forest again. When we reached our old camp, we found that different troops were occupying it. Our company had left, nobody knew for what destination. Wherever we asked, nobody could give us any information. So we had to go back to the command of our corps, the headquarters of which were at Corney at that time.

We left Chatel again by a hospital train, and reached Corney after half an hour's journey. Corney harboured the General Staff of the 16th Army Corps, and we thought they surely ought to know where our company was. General von Mudra and his officers had taken up their quarters in a large villa. The house was guarded by three double sentries. We showed our pay books and hospital certificates, and an orderly led us to a spacious room. It was the telephone room. There the wires from all the divisional fronts ran together, and the apparatus were in constant use.

A sergeant-major looked into the lists and upon the maps. In two minutes he had found our company. He showed us on the map where it was fighting and where its camp was. "The camp is at the northern end of Verennes," he said, "and the company belongs to the 34th division; formerly it was part of the 33rd. The position it is in is in the villages of Vauquois and Boureuilles." Then he explained to us on the map the direction we were to take, and we could trot off. We returned by rail to Chatel, and went on foot from there to Apremont. We spent the night in the half destroyed depot of Apremont. In order to get to Varennes we had to march to the south.

On our way we saw French prisoners mending the roads. Most of them were black colonial troops in picturesque uniforms. On that road Austrian motor batteries were posted. Three of those 30.5-cm. howitzers were standing behind a rocky slope, but did not fire. When at noon we reached the height of Varennes we saw the whole wide plan in front of us. Varennes itself was immediately in front of us in the valley. A little farther up on the heights was Vauquois. No houses were to be seen; one could only notice a heap of rubbish through the field glasses. Shells kept exploding in that rubbish heap continually, and we felt a cold sweat run down our backs at the thought that the place up there was our destination.

We had scarcely passed the ridge when some shells exploded behind us. At that place the French were shooting with artillery at individuals. As long as Vauquois had been in their power they had been able to survey the whole country, and we comprehended why that heap of rubbish was so bitterly fought for. We ran down the slope and found ourselves in Varennes. The southern portion of the village had been shelled to pieces and gutted. Only most of the chimneys which were built apart from the bottom upward, had remained standing, thin blackened forms rising out of the ruins into the air.

Everywhere we saw groups of soldiers collecting the remaining more expensive metals which were sent to Germany. Among other things church-bells melted into shapeless lumps were also loaded on wagons and taken away. All the copper, brass, tin, and lead that could be got was collected.

21

In the Hell of Vauquois

We soon found our company, and our comrades told us what hell they had gotten into. The next morning our turn came, too. We had to reach the position before daybreak, for as soon as it got light the French kept all approaches under constant fire. There was no trace of trenches at Vauquois. All that could be seen were pieces of stones. Not a stone had literally remained on the other at Vauquois. That heap of ruins, once a village, had changed hands no less than fifteen times. When we arrived half of the place was in the possession of the Germans. But the French dominated the highest point, whence they could survey the whole country for many miles around. In the absence of a trench we sought cover behind stones, for it was absolutely impossible to construct trenches; the artillery was shooting everything to pieces.

Thus the soldiers squatted behind piles of stones and fired as fast as their rifles would allow. Guns of all sizes were bombarding the village incessantly. There was an army of corpses, Frenchmen and Germans, all lying about pell-mell. At first we thought that that terrible state of things was only temporary, but after a few days we recognized that a slaughter worse than madness was a continuous state of things at that place. Day and night, ever the same. With Verdun[1] as a base of operations the French continually brought up fresh masses of troops. They had carried along a field railroad the heavy pieces of the neighbouring forts of Verdun, and in the spring of 1915 an offensive of a local, but murderous kind was begun.

The artillery of both sides bombarded the place to such an extent that not a foot of ground could be found that was not torn up by shells. Thousands upon thousands of shells of all sizes were employed.

---

1. *'Neath Verdun* by Maurice Genevoix, The Experiences of a French Soldier During the Early Months of the First World War, is also published by Leonaur.

The bombardment from both sides lasted three days and three nights, until at last not a soldier, neither French nor German, was left in the village. Both sides had been obliged to retreat before the infernal fire of the opponent, for not a man would have escaped alive out of that inferno. The whole slope and height were veiled in an impenetrable smoke. In the evening of the third day the enemy's bombardment died down a little, and we were ordered to go forward again into the shell torn ruins. It was not yet quite dark when the French advanced in close order.

We were in possession of almost the whole of the village, and had placed one machine-gun next to the other. We could see the projectiles of the artillery burst in great numbers among the reserves of the attackers. Our machine-guns literally mowed down the first ranks. Five times the French renewed their attack during that night, their artillery meanwhile making great gaps in our ranks. We soldiers calculated that the two sides had together some three or four thousand men killed in that one night. Next morning the French eased their attacks, and their guns treated us again to the accustomed drum fire. We stood it until 10 o'clock in the morning; then we retreated again without awaiting orders, leaving innumerable dead men behind.

Again the French advanced in the face of a violent German artillery fire, and effected a lodgment at the northern edge of the village of Vauquois that used to be. A few piles of stones was all that still belonged to us. We managed to put a few stones before us as a protection. The guns of neither side could hurt us or them, for they, the enemy, were but ten paces away. But the country behind us was plowed by projectiles. In face of the machine gun fire it was found impossible to bring up ammunition.

The sappers undid the coils of rope worn round their bodies, and three men or more crept back with them. One of them was killed; the others arrived safely and attached the packets of cartridges to the rope. Thus we brought up the ammunition by means of a rope running in a circle, until we had enough or till the rope was shot through. At three o'clock in the afternoon we attacked again, but found it impossible to rise from the ground on account of the hail of bullets. Everybody was shouting, "Sappers to the front with hand grenades!" Not a sapper stirred. We are only human, after all.

A sergeant-major of the infantry came creeping up. He looked as if demented, his eyes were bloodshot. "You're a sapper?"

"Yes,"

"Advance!"

"Alone?"

"We're coming along!"

We had to roar at each other in order to make ourselves understood in the deafening, confounded row. Another sapper lay beside me. When the sergeant-major saw that he could do nothing with me he turned to the other fellow. That man motioned to him to desist, but the sergeant-major got ever more insistent, until the sapper showed him his dagger, and then our superior slung his hook. Some twenty hand grenades were lying in front of us. Ten of them I had attached to my belt for all emergencies. I said to myself that if all of them exploded there would not be much left of me. I had a lighted cigar in my mouth. I lit one bomb after the other and threw them over to some Frenchmen who were working a machine-gun in front of me, behind a heap of stones. All around me the bullets of the machine-guns were splitting the stones.

I had already thrown four grenades, but all of them had overshot the mark. I took some stones and threw them to find out how far I would have to throw in order to hit the fire spitting machine in front. My aim got more accurate each time until I hit the barrel of the gun. "If it had only been a hand grenade," I thought. An infantryman close to me was shot through the shell of one ear, half of which was cut in pieces; the blood was streaming down his neck. I had no more material for bandaging except some wadding, which I attached to his wound. In my pocket I had a roll of insulating ribbon, rubber used to insulate wires; with that I bandaged him. He pointed to the machine-gun. Thereupon I gave him my cigar, telling him to keep it well alight so as to make the fuse which I desired to light by it burn well. In quick succession I threw six hand grenades. I don't know how many of them took effect, but the rags of uniforms flying about and a demolished machine-gun said enough. When we advanced later on I observed three dead men lying round the machine-gun.

That was only one example of the usual, daily occurrences that happen day and night, again and again and everywhere, and the immense number of such actions of individual soldiers makes the enormous loss of human life comprehensible.

We were still lying there without proceeding to the attack. Again ammunition was brought up by ropes from the rear. A hand grenade duel ensued; hundreds of hand grenades were thrown by both sides. Things could not go on long like that; we felt that something was bound to happen. Without receiving an order and yet as if by command we all jumped up and advanced with the dagger in our hands right through the murderous fire, and engaged in the maddest hand to hand fighting. The daggers, sharp as razors, were plunged into head after head, chest after chest. One stood on corpses in order to make other men corpses. New enemies came running up. One had scarcely finished with one when three more appeared on the scene.

We, too, got reinforcements. One continued to murder and expected to be struck down oneself the next moment. One did not care a cent for one's life, but fought like an animal. I stumbled and fell on the stones. At that very moment I caught sight of a gigantic Frenchman before me who was on the point of bringing his sapper's spade down on me. I moved aside with lightning speed, and the blow fell upon the stone. In a moment my dagger was in his stomach more than up to the hilt. He went down with a horrible cry, rolling in his blood in maddening pain. I put the bloody dagger back in my boot and took hold of the spade. All around me I beheld new enemies.

The spade I found to be a handy weapon. I hit one opponent between head and shoulder. The sharp spade half went through the body; I heard the cracking of the bones that were struck. Another enemy was close to me. I dropped the spade and took hold of my dagger again. All happened as in a flash. My opponent struck me in the face, and the blood came pouring out of my mouth and nose. We began to wrestle with each other. I had the dagger in my right hand. We had taken hold of each other round the chest. He was no stronger than myself, but he held me as firmly as I held him. We tried to fight each other with our teeth. I had the dagger in my hand, but could not strike. Who was it to be? He or I? One of us two was sure to go down. I got the dagger in such a position that its point rested on his back. Then I pressed his trembling body still more firmly to myself. He fastened his teeth in my shaggy beard, and I felt a terrible pain. I pressed him still more firmly so that his ribs almost began to crack and, summoning all my strength, I pushed the dagger into the right side of his back, just below the shoulder-blade. In frightful pain he turned himself round several times, fell on his face, and lay groaning on the ground. I withdrew my dagger; he bled to death like many thousands.

We had pushed back the French for some yards when we received strong assistance. After a short fight the enemy turned and fled, and we followed him as far as the southern edge of the village. There the French made a counterattack with fresh bodies of men and threw us back again for some 50 yards. Then the attack was halted, and we found ourselves again where we had been at the beginning of that four days' slaughter. Thousands of corpses were covering the ruins of Vauquois, all sacrificed in vain.

22

Sent on Furlough

For four days and nights, without food and sleep, we had been raging like barbarians, and had spent all our strength. We were soon relieved. To our astonishment we were relieved by cavalry. They were Saxon chasseurs on horseback who were to do duty as infantrymen. It had been found impossible to make good the enormous losses of the preceding days by sending up men of the depot. So they had called upon the cavalry who, by the way, were frequently employed during that time. The soldiers who had been in a life and death struggle for four days were demoralized to such an extent that they had no longer any fighting value. We were relieved very quietly, and could then return to our camp. We did not hear before the next day that during the period described our company had suffered a total loss of 49 men. The fate of most of them was unknown; one did not know whether they were dead or prisoners or whether they lay wounded in some ambulance station.

The village of Varennes was continually bombarded by French guns of large size. Several French families were still living in a part of the village that had not been so badly damaged. Every day several of the enemy's 28-cm. shells came down in that quarter. Though many inhabitants had been wounded by the shells the people could not be induced to leave their houses.

Our quarters were situated near a very steep slope and were thus protected against artillery fire. They consisted of wooden shanties built by ourselves. We had brought up furniture from everywhere and had made ourselves at home; for Varennes was, after all, nearly two miles behind the front. But all the shanties were not occupied, for the number of our men diminished from day to day. At last the longed-for men from the depot arrived. Many new sapper formations had to be got together for all parts of the front, and it was therefore impossible to supply the existing sapper detachments with their regular reserves. Joyfully we greeted the new arrivals. They were, as was always the case, men of very different ages; a young boyish volunteer of 17 years would march next to an old man of the *landsturm* who had likewise volunteered. All of them, without any exception, have bitterly repented of their "free choice" and made no secret of it. "It's a shame," a comrade told me, "that those seventeen-year-old children should be led to the slaughter, and that their young life is being poisoned, as it needs must be in these surroundings; scarcely out of boyhood, they are being shot down like mad dogs."

It took but a few days for the volunteers—all of them without an exception—to repent bitterly of their resolve, and every soldier who had been in the war for any length of time would reproach them when they gave expression to their great disappointment. "But you have come voluntarily," they were told; "we had to go, else we should have been off long ago." Yet we knew that all those young people had been under some influence and had been given a wrong picture of the war.

Those soldiers who had been in the war from the start who had not been wounded, but had gone through all the fighting, were gradually all sent home on furlough for ten days. Though our company contained but 14 unwounded soldiers it was very hard to obtain the furlough. We had lost several times the number of men on our muster-roll, but all our officers were still in good physical condition.

It was not until September that I managed to obtain furlough at the request of my relations, and I left for home with a resolve that at times seemed to me impossible to execute. All went well until I got to Diedenhofen.

As far as that station the railroads are operated by the army authorities. At Diedenhofen they are taken over by the Imperial Railroads of Alsace-Lorraine and the Prusso-Hessian State Railroads. So I had to change, and got on a train that went to Saarbrucken. I had scarcely taken a seat in a compartment in my dirty and ragged uniform when a conductor came along to inspect the tickets. Of course, I had no ticket; I had only a furlough certificate and a pass which had been handed to me at the field railroad depot of Chatel. The conductor looked at the papers and asked me again for my ticket. I drew his attention to my pass. "That is only good for the territory of the war operations," he said; "you are now travelling on a state railroad and have to buy a ticket."

I told him that I should not buy a ticket, and asked him to inform the station manager. "You," I told him, "only act according to instructions. I am not angry with you for asking of me what I shall do under no circumstances."

He went off and came back with the manager. The latter also inspected my papers and told me I had to pay for the journey. "I have no means for that purpose," I told him. "For these last three years I have been in these clothes" (I pointed to my uniform), "and for three years I have therefore been without any income. Whence am I to get the money to pay for this journey?"

"If you have no money for travelling you can't take furlough."

I thought to myself that if they took me deep into France they were in conscience bound to take me back to where they had fetched me. Was I to be a soldier for three years and fight for the Fatherland for more than a year only to find that now they refused the free use of their railroads to a ragged soldier? I explained that I was not going to pay, that I could not save the fare from the few *pfennigs'* pay. I refused explicitly to pay a soldier's journey with my private money, even if—as was the case here—that soldier was myself. Finally I told him, "I must request you to inform the military railroad commander; the depot command attends to soldiers, not you." He sent me a furious look through his horn spectacles and disappeared. Two civilians were sitting in the same compartment with me; they thought it an unheard-of thing that a soldier coming from the front should be asked for his fare. Presently the depot commander came up with a sergeant. He demanded to see my furlough certificate, pay books, and all my other papers.

"Have you any money?"

"No."

"Where do you come from?"

"From Chatel in the Argonnes."

"How long were you at the front?"

"In the fourteenth month."

"Been wounded?"

"No."

"Have you no money at all?"

"No; you don't want money at the front."

"The fare must be paid. If you can't, the company must pay. Please sign this paper."

I signed it without looking at it. It was all one to me what I signed, as long as they left me alone. Then the sergeant came back.

"You can not travel in that compartment; you must also not converse with travellers. You have to take the first carriage marked 'Only for the military.' Get into that."

"I see," I observed; "in the dogs' compartment."

He turned round again and said, "Cut out those remarks."

The train started, and I arrived safely home. After the first hours of meeting all at home again had passed I found myself provided with faultless underwear and had taken the urgently needed bath. Once more I could put on the civilian dress I had missed for so long a time. All of it appeared strange to me. I began to think. Under no conditions was I going to return to the front. But I did not know how I should succeed in getting across the frontier. I could choose between two countries only—Switzerland and Holland. It was no use going to Switzerland, for that country was surrounded by belligerent states, and it needed only a little spark to bring Switzerland into the war, and then there would be no loophole for me. There was only the nearest country left for me to choose—Holland. But how was I to get there? There was the rub. I concocted a thousand plans and discarded them again. Nobody, not even my relatives, must know about it.

23

The Flight to Holland

My furlough soon neared its end; there were only four days left. I remembered a good old friend in a Rhenish town. My plan was made. Without my family noticing it I packed a suit, boots, and all necessities, and told them at home that I was going to visit my friend. To him I revealed my intentions, and he was ready to help me in every possible manner.

My furlough was over. I put on my uniform, and my relations were left in the belief that I was returning to the front. I went, however, to my friend and changed into civilian clothes. I destroyed my uniform and arms, throwing the lot into the river near by. Thus having destroyed all traces, I left and arrived at Cologne after some criss-cross travelling. Thence I journeyed to Dusseldorf and stayed at night at an hotel. I had already overstayed my leave several days. Thousands of thoughts went through my brain. I was fully aware that I would lose my life if everything did not come to pass according to the program. I intended to cross the frontier near Venlo (Holland). I knew, however, that the frontier was closely guarded.

The country round Venlo, the course of the frontier in those parts were unknown to me; in fact, I was a complete stranger. I made another plan. I returned to my friend and told him that it was absolutely necessary for me to get to know the frontier district and to procure a map showing the terrain. I also informed him that I had to get hold of a false identification paper. He gave me a *landsturm* certificate which was to identify me in case of need. In my note-book I drew the exact course of the frontier from a railway map, and then I departed again.

Dead tired, I reached Crefeld that night by the last train. I could not go on. So I went into the first hotel and hired a room. I wrote the name that was on the false paper into the register and went to sleep. At six o'clock in the morning there was a knock at my door.

"Who is there?"

"The police."

"The police?"

"Yes; the political police."

I opened the door.

"Here lives ——? (he mentioned the name in which I had registered).

"Yes."

"Have you any identification papers?"

"If you please," I said, handing him the *landsturm* certificate.

"Everything in order; pardon me for having disturbed you."

"You're welcome; you're welcome," I hastened to reply, and thought how polite the police was.

That well-known leaden weight fell from my chest, but I had no mind to go to sleep again. Whilst I was dressing I heard him visit all the guests of the hotel. I had not thought of the customary inspection of strangers in frontier towns. It was a good thing I had been armed for that event.

Without taking breakfast (my appetite had vanished) I went to the depot and risked travelling to Kempten in spite of the great number of policemen that were about. I calculated by the map that the frontier was still some fifteen miles away. I had not much baggage with me, only a small bag, a raincoat and an umbrella. I marched along the country road and in five hours I reached the village of Herongen. To the left of that place was the village of Niederhofen. Everywhere I saw farmers working in the fields. They would have to inform me of how the line of the frontier ran and how it was being watched. In order to procure that information I selected only those people who, to judge by their appearance, were no "great lights of the church."

Without arousing suspicion I got to know that the names of the two places were "Herongen" and "Niederhofen," and that a troop of *cuirassiers* were quartered at Herongen. The man told me that the soldiers were lodged in the dancing hall of the Schwarz Inn. Presently I met a man who was cutting a hedge. He was a Hollander who went home across the frontier every night; he had a passport. "You are the man for me," I thought to myself, and said aloud that I had met several Hollanders in that part of the country (he was the first one), and gave him a cigar. I mentioned to him that I had visited an acquaintance in the Schwarz Inn at Herongen.

"Yes," he said; "they are there."

"But my friend had to go on duty, so I am having a look round."

"They have got plenty to do near the frontier."

"Indeed?"

"Every thirty minutes and oftener a cavalry patrol, and every quarter of an hour an infantry patrol go scouting along the frontier."

"And how does the frontier run?" I queried, offering him a light for his cigar.

He showed me with his hand.

"Here in front of you, then right through the woods, then up there; those high steeples towering over the woods belong to the factories of Venlo."

I knew enough. After a few remarks I left him. All goes according to my program, I thought. But there was a new undertaking before me. I had to venture close enough to the frontier to be able to watch the patrols without being seen by them. That I succeeded in doing during the following night.

I hid in the thick underwood; open country was in front of me. I remained at that spot for three days and nights. It rained and at night it was very chilly. On the evening of the third day I resolved to execute my plan that night.

Regularly every fifteen minutes a patrol of from three to six soldiers arrived. When it had got dark I changed my place for one more to the right, some five hundred yards from the frontier. I said to myself that I would have to venture out as soon as it got a little lighter. In the darkness I could not see anything. It would have to be done in twilight. I had rolled my overcoat into a bundle to avoid making a noise against the trees. I advanced just after a patrol had passed. I went forward slowly and stepped out cautiously without making a noise. Then I walked with ever increasing rapidity.

Suddenly a patrol appeared on my right. The frontier was about three hundred yards away from me. The patrol had about two hundred yards to the point of the frontier nearest to me. Victory would fall to the best and swiftest runner. The patrol consisted of five men; they fired several times. That did not bother me. I threw everything away and, summoning all my strength, I made in huge leaps for the frontier which I passed like a whirlwind. I ran past the pointed frontier stone and stopped fifty yards away from it. I was quite out of breath, and an indescribable happy feeling took hold of me. I felt like crying into the world that at last I was free.

I seated myself on the stump of a tree and lit a cigar, quite steadily and slowly; for now I had time. Scarcely fifty yards away, near the frontier stone, was the disappointed patrol. I read on the side of the frontier stone facing me, "*Koningrjk der Nederlanden*" (Kingdom of the Netherlands). I had to laugh with joy.

"Who are you?" one of the German patrol called to me.

"The Hollanders have now the right to ask that question; you've got that right no longer, old fellow," I replied.

They called me all manner of names, but that did not excite me. I asked them: "Why don't you throw me over my bag which I threw away in the hurry? It contains some washing I took along with me so as to get into a decent country like a decent man."

Attracted by that conversation, a Dutch patrol, a sergeant and three men, came up. The sergeant questioned me, and I told him all. He put his hand on my shoulder and said, "Be glad that you are here—*wij Hollanders weuschen de vrede* (we Hollanders wish for peace), and you are welcome here in hospitable Holland."

I had to go with the soldiers to their guard-room and take breakfast with them. Thereupon they showed me the nearest road to Venlo, where I arrived at seven o'clock in the morning. From Venlo I travelled to Rotterdam. I soon obtained a well-paid position and became a man again, a man who could live and not merely exist. Thousands upon thousands of Belgian refugees are living in Holland, (as at 1917), and are treated as the guests of the people. There are also great numbers of German deserters in Holland, where their number is estimated to be between fifteen and twenty thousand. Those deserters enjoy the full protection of the Dutch authorities.

I would have never thought of leaving that hospitable country with its fairly liberal constitution if the political sky had not been so over-clouded in the month of March, 1916.

24

America and Safety

What I have still to relate does not concern actual war experiences. But the reader might want to know how I came to America. That must be done in a few short sentences.

In Holland war was believed to be unavoidable. Again I had to choose another domicile. After much reflection and making of plans I decided to go to America.

After having left my place I executed that plan. Some days after I was informed that the steamer *Zyldyk* of the Holland-American line was leaving for New York in the night from the 17th to the 18th of March. According to my plan I packed my things in a sailor's bundle and began the risky game.

I had never been on a sea-going steamer before. The boat was a small trader. I had found out that the crew had to be on board by midnight. I had an idea that the men would not turn up earlier than was necessary. With my sailor's bundle I stood ready on the pier as early as ten o'clock. All I had packed together in the excitement consisted of about seven pounds of bread and a tin containing some ten quarts of water. At midnight the sailors and stokers of the boat arrived. Most of them were drunk and came tumbling along with their bundles on their backs. I mixed with the crowd and tumbled along with them. I reached the deck without being discovered. I observed next to me a deep black hole with an iron ladder leading downwards.

I threw my bundle down that hole and climbed after it. All was dark. I groped my way to the coal bunker. I would have struck a match, but I dared not make a light. So I crawled onto the coal which filled the space right up to the ceiling. Pushing my bundle in front of me I made my way through the coal, filling again the opening behind me with coal. Having in that manner traversed some thirty yards I came upon a wall. There I pushed the coal aside so as to have room to lie down. I turned my back against the outer wall of the boat.

Nobody suspected in the slightest degree that I was on board. Now the journey can start, I thought to myself. At last the engines began to work; we were off. After many long hours the engines stopped. Now we are in England I guessed. Perhaps we were off Dover or somewhere else; I did not know. Everything was darkness down there. While the boat was stopping I heard the thunder of guns close to us. I had no idea what that might mean. I said to myself, "If the English find me my voyage is ended." But they did not turn up.

At last we proceeded; I did not know how long we had stopped. All went well; I scarcely felt the boat move. However, it was bitterly cold, and I noticed that the cold increased steadily. Then the weather became rougher and rougher. Days must have passed. I never knew whether it was day or night. Down in my place it was always night. I ate bread and drank water. But I had scarcely eaten when all came up again. Thus my stomach was always empty.

Through the rolling of the boat I was nearly buried by the coal. It got worse and worse, and I had to use all my strength to keep the coal away from me. The big lumps wounded me all about the head; I felt the blood run over my face. My store of bread was nearly finished, and the water tasted stale. I lit a match and saw that the bread was quite black.

I wondered whether we were nearly there. No more bread. I felt my strength leave me more and more. The boat went up and down, and I was thrown hither and thither for hours, for days. I felt I could not stand it much longer. I wondered how long we had been on the water. I had no idea. I was awfully hungry. Days passed again. I noticed that I had become quite thin.

At last the engines stopped again. But soon we were off once more. After long, long hours the boat stopped. I listened. All was quiet. Then I heard them unloading with cranes.

New York!—After a while I crept forth. I found that half of the coal had been taken away. Not a soul was there. Then I climbed down a ladder into the stokehole; nobody was there either. I noticed a pail and filled it with warm water. With it I hastened into a dark corner and washed myself. I was terribly tired and had to hold on to something so as not to collapse. When I had washed I took my pocket mirror and gazed at my face. My own face frightened me; for I looked pale as a sheet and like a bundle of skin and bones. I wondered how long the voyage had lasted. I had to laugh in spite of my misery—I had crossed the ocean and had never seen it!

The problem was now to get on land. What should I say if they caught me? I thought that if I were caught now I should simply say I wanted to get to Holland as a stowaway in order to reach Germany. In that case, I thought, they would quickly enough put me back on land. With firm resolve I climbed on deck which was full of workmen.

I noticed a stairway leading to the warehouse. Gathering all my strength I loitered up to it in a careless way and—two minutes later I had landed. I found myself in the street outside the warehouse.

Up to that time I had kept on my legs. But now my strength left me, and I dropped on the nearest steps.

It was only then that I became aware of the fact that I was not in New York, but in Philadelphia. It was 5 o'clock in the afternoon of April 5th, 1916. I had reckoned on twelve days and the voyage had taken eighteen.

Physically a wreck, I became acquainted with native Americans in the evening. They afforded me every assistance that one human being can give to another. One of those most noble-minded humanitarians took me to New York. I could not leave my room for a week on account of the hardships I had undergone; I recovered only slowly.

But today I have recovered sufficiently to take up again in the ranks of the American Socialists the fight against capitalism the extirpation of which must be the aim of every class-conscious worker. A relentless struggle to the bitter end is necessary to show the ruling war provoking capitalist caste who is the stronger, so that it no longer may be in the power of that class to provoke such a murderous war as that in which the working-class of Europe is now bleeding to death.

The Diary of a German Soldier

Contents

Preface	155
The Diary of a German Soldier	157
Mobilisation	159
The Departure	163
Luxemburg	165
Arlon	168
Lenglier	173
Bertrix	176
Matton	178
Autrecourt	181
Raucourt	183
The Battle of the Marne	188
Rheims	194
The March on Roye	196
Ercheu—Solente—Champieu	200
Roye	202
The Germans at Roye	205
The Formation of the 56th Division	211
Givry	214

In Champagne	217
Across Germany and Austria	223
In Galicia	226
First Battles in Galicia	230
Radawa	234
Last Battles in Galicia and Our Return to France	239
Hérin	244
Headquarters at Valenciennes	246
The Battle of Champagne	252
Douai—in Champagne	258
Verdun—Frankfort—Mayence	263
At the Danish Border	267

Preface

A very few pages of these war memoirs will convince the reader that their author held an important position in the German army. Although Sergeant C—— only bore the chevrons of a non-commissioned officer, he was, nevertheless, virtually an officer in everything but name. His duties, as sometimes also happens in the French army, were akin to those of an officer. He played an important part on the so-called staff of his battalion. In turn, he was secretary, interpreter, and liaison officer. He frequently performed missions of trust and often carried confidential dispatches. Besides, he enjoyed all the prestige which the German Army attaches to the rank of *"Einjährig-Freiwillige."*[1] He dined with his superior officers and, when not on duty, mingled with them on an equal footing.

The special and relatively independent position which this rather well-informed and observant young man occupied, from August 1st, 1914, to October, 1916, enabled him to see much and to give us a vivid picture, always interesting, though presented with extreme simplicity, of the events of which he was an eye-witness. As a matter of fact, C—— is no writer and kept a diary much more for his personal satisfaction than because of any literary aspirations. It is precisely because of this complete lack of pretension and because of the author's undeniable freedom of thought that it seemed to us that these memoirs would find favour in the eyes of the French public.

We shall see some of those barbaric scenes and acts of vandalism which have dishonoured the German Army, presented in broad daylight. C——, with great accuracy, gives the places, the date, and almost always the name, the rank and the unit of the German officers who so often delighted in overwhelming innocent civilians with all

---

1. A young man of the upper classes, who, at his own expense, serves in the army for one year. There is no corresponding term in English.—Translator.

possible abuses, committed with barbaric brutality and lewd passion. In this respect, the testimony of C—— constitutes a valuable document to support the indictment which the Allies have been drawing up against Germany for the past three years: those atrocious crimes, as for instance the secret massacre of twenty French civilians, both male and female, with bayonets, ordered at Braucourt on August 29th, 1914, by Colonel Puder, have been verified in every detail and with all necessary care.

This little book possesses still another interest of a purely historic nature; for these simple daily jottings in reality constitute the complete history, for the first two years of the war, of a German battalion which was closely connected with its regiment, its brigade, its division and often even its army corps. Even though the author is far from being an artist, or perhaps just because of that, this book faithfully portrays the aspect and the local colour of the different phases of the war on various fronts: Luxemburg, Artois, Picardy, Champagne, Galicia and the Vosges. For instance we learn under what conditions a German division went back and forth between the French and Russian fronts and how long it took them to do it in those distant days when they still did.

In 1916, the author, thoroughly disgusted with Prussian militarism, decided to escape to Denmark, and it is from that country that this work has reached us. After fighting bravely for nineteen months both in France and Galicia, Feldwebel C—— was seriously wounded at the beginning of the attack on Verdun (February 23rd, 1916) and spent four months in a hospital at Frankfort. He had scarcely recovered when he was returned to the front. However, the surgeons again sent him back to Germany, where the authorities finally recognized him to be unfit for active service. He was transferred to the auxiliary service and was sent to join a non-combatant battalion which was working on the fortifications of the Danish border in Schleswig. Thus Feldwebel C—— left the German Army after having discharged his full duty and at a moment when he was not under fire. His desertion has nothing dishonourable about it and this is important as regards the extent of confidence which we should place in his opinions and criticisms.

We believe that this rather sternly written but complete book forms a unique document: the war experiences of a German witness, a brave soldier, but still very liberal minded and above all perfectly straightforward and sincere.

Louis-Paul Alaux.

Paris, January 15, 1918.

The Diary of a German Soldier

On October 1st, 1913, I joined the 2nd Battalion, 6th Company, of the 88th Regiment as a "*Freiwilliger.*"[1] My regiment formed part of the 42nd Infantry Brigade (21st Division, 18th Army Corps) . As all the "*Freiwillige*" do, I entered the reserve officers' training corps.

As soon as war was declared, I was assigned, because of my knowledge of French, as interpreter and attached to the so-called staff of my battalion. I held this position for the first two years of the war and shared the fortunes of the second battalion up to the moment when I was transferred to the auxiliary service because of a serious wound which I received during the attack on Verdun on February 23rd, 1916.

Perhaps the reader of these simple campaign notes will sometimes be tempted to believe that I have exaggerated a little. Nevertheless, in the following pages, I have only told of those happenings at which I was actually present, of those sights which I beheld with my own eyes. Besides I am sure that later on the tales of the inhabitants of the invaded territories will fully confirm these memoirs.

---

1 See footnote, of Preface.

1
Mobilisation

Immediately after the assassination of the heir to the Austrian throne at Sarajevo an almost undefinable restlessness was noticeable all over Germany. Many people said that this event could bring on grave complications in which Germany might be entangled and that it might even result in a European war. Alas, our anxiety was justified. As a matter of fact, on the 23rd of July, 1914, on the very day on which the Austrian ultimatum was dispatched to Serbia, an order of the general commanding the 18th Army Corps informed us that the manoeuvres for which we were preparing had been called off and that we were to hold ourselves in readiness for a general mobilization order. From the 23rd to the 30th of July all the men from our corps who were on leave were recalled and ordered to join their regiments with all possible speed.

At 3 p.m. on July 30th, 1914, the 2nd Battalion was ordered to guard the bridges over the Main, the railroads, and the approaches to the powder works at Hanau-on-the-Main. I, personally, received an order to take a detachment of twenty-four men to guard the great railroad bridge which crosses the Main between Hanau and Klein-Steinheim. Lieutenant Merbach accompanied us as far as the bridge, to give me the necessary instructions. I asked him to do me the favour of calling at the station for my mother whom I expected that day. Then, after placing my sentinels, I had nothing to do but watch the many trains crowded with soldiers which were continually crossing the bridge. My mother told Merbach that the 47th Artillery Regiment (11th Corps) had already left in field-grey.

Every person passing over the bridge had to be brought to me and my instructions were to question them all carefully, keeping on the look-out for spies. Several officer patrols passed by, all cautioning me to watch diligently and to look out for everything.

At 4 a.m. on the thirty-first the soldiers who brought us our coffee told us that the men of the 5th Company were already in field-grey. A guardsman, named Wagner, from Flesheim, then called out:

"Well, that's something more than a hoax; it begins to look serious. This means that the crown prince has gained his point and the emperor will not delay the declaration of war. Why should he care? His six boys are not going to be under fire; but we'll have to burn our fingers pulling their chestnuts out of the fire. We are going to sell our skins, but will you just tell me why and for whom?"

I told him to keep quiet or I would have to punish him, but he kept on:

"Oh, come on! Sir, there are many soldiers and non-commissioned officers too who do not want war. As for me, I am a socialist...."

Again I told him to keep quiet, or I would have him taken to prison on the spot.

When I spoke to Merbach about this on the following day, he told me not to punish Wagner in any way.

At four o'clock in the afternoon we were relieved.

In many places, in order to get back to the barracks we had to break through an enthusiastic and excited crowd composed mainly of women. The people were shouting: "Hurrah for the 88th!" "Long live the emperor!" and were singing patriotic songs at the top of their voices. In some streets it was impossible to make headway. The entire population of Hanau had turned out. Especially in front of the barracks there was an enormous crowd. Every time that a courier appeared the civilians fell upon him, shouting: "What have you got? Has war been declared? Not yet? What a pity!" It was a delirious joy. Where is that joy now?

We had hardly returned to the barracks when our company commander. Captain Otto Gaup, assembled us all in order to address us. During the ten months I had been in his company, I had more often seen him drunk than sober. Sometimes we were forced to put him on his horse, for he would have been quite incapable of mounting unaided. This is about what he said to us:

Dear soldiers:

Great historic events are under way. Threatening clouds are beginning to obscure the political horizon. What will be the consequences of the Sarajevo assassination? Our enemies boldly dare to challenge us and are making use of assassins in order to have an excuse for war. They wish it. Very well, they shall have it. Come what may, we are prepared and we shall know how to receive them. Dear friends, I do not believe that I personally will have the good fortune to lead you on to victory, but I am sure that you will not only preserve the ancient glory of Germany unsullied, but that you will also bring back new laurels. Let us place trust in our emperor and our government, in our people and above all in ourselves. With this hope I ask you to shout with me: 'Long live our Emperor and King!'

Thereupon he shook hands with us and left. I overheard Lieutenant Dehes say to Lieutenant Popp: "He must surely have had a little too much to make him talk such nonsense."

On August 1st about half-past five a dispatch arrived at headquarters. As soon as the commanding officer, Kuhl, opened it he ran down into the courtyard of the barracks, terribly excited, shouting:

"Soldiers, men and women, old and young, listen, all of you. His Majesty the Emperor has ordered mobilization to commence on August 2nd. We are ready and since they dare to disturb our peace we shall show those brigands from across the Rhine and those assassins from St. Petersburg of what metal we are made. Dear comrades, long live our emperor, for whom we joyfully go to war and for whom we are ready to die." Thereupon Captain Raabe, commanding the 5th Company, with tears in his eyes, began to sing: "*Heil Dir im Siegerkranz.*"[1]

A beelike activity immediately reigned all over the barracks. Everyone ran from one place to another without knowing why. Bayonets were taken to the armoury to be sharpened. Soldiers' relatives were coming into the barracks and soldiers were going out to the city. Every one was singing in the streets and civilians invited soldiers to have a drink, telling them: "See that you give the French a good licking!" Bells were ringing at full peal. Why? Because one nation was jealous of the other and because there were too many people in Germany and too little room for them. O bells, your former sweet sound was wild on that evening; you were no longer calling to Christians, but to bloodthirsty wild beasts.

On August 3rd a nun was arrested near the powder works on the suspicion of being a spy entrusted with blowing them up. Today she is a Red Cross nurse in the hospital of Saint Vincent at Hanau, caring

---

1. "Hail to Thee, Crowned Victor"—(The German National Anthem).

for the wounded.

On the afternoon of August 5th, when all were ready to depart, a thorough inspection of equipment took place. Major Kuhl handed over the command of the 2nd Battalion to Major Schmidt. Both addressed us, and we all shouted: "Long live his Majesty, the Emperor and the King." After that every one sang in chorus "*Deutschland Uber Alles*" and "*Die Wacht Am Rhein.*"

Then we were told that we would leave at 2 a. m. Now that the hour of departure was close at hand, the courage of many a braggart began to fail and give place to a gloomy resignation. The food was quite tolerable that evening; some jokers called it a funeral feast. I went to the city to do a little shopping and to say goodbye to some friends. Later we assembled for the last time at the home of Lieutenant Popp of the 5th Company and then returned to the barracks.

2

The Departure

In the barracks soldiers, instead of resting, were playing cards or writing home. They paid no attention to the officers and non-commissioned officers, who came in and advised them to sleep. At midnight the reveille sounded and coffee was served.

Moreover a fine racket had been going on everywhere in the city all evening long. The cafes and restaurants were filled with civilians and soldiers who had not reported at evening roll-call.

A crowd of people surrounded the barracks. There were many relatives of soldiers among them. An order had been issued preventing civilians from entering the barracks. In order to avoid affecting scenes and the farewells of sobbing mothers and wives, Major Schmidt decided to advance the hour of departure, so that the battalion left for the station at ten minutes past one.

The band of the 3rd Engineers marched first. The people running alongside sang and yelled so that you might think you were surrounded by a crowd of lunatics. All windows were opened wide and filled with men and women in their night clothes, who shouted their good wishes and threw us dainties and cigarettes.

When we arrived at the station we were immediately ordered into the train so that we would be promptly and completely cut off from the crowd and farewell scenes would be necessarily brief. Only some officers' wives had obtained permission to stay on the platform. Lieutenant Eger's wife fainted after kissing her husband. While some ladies carried her into the waiting room, Eger, without showing any emotion whatsoever, calmly sought his compartment.

I found myself in a compartment with Lieutenants Merbach and Popp. All of a sudden the latter began to cry. Finally the train started and passed out into the black night.

At Frankfort refreshments were waiting for us on the platform. The ladies of the Red Cross served the soldiers, who were almost all downcast. The ladies tried to revive their spirits and said to them: "Courage, friends; show that you are men, happy and proud to be permitted to shed your blood for the emperor and the German fatherland."

Probably these ladies had nothing to do, and, being bored at home, they came to the station to pass the time. Otherwise they would not have talked such nonsense. It is certainly an honour to die for your country if it is attacked. But had we been attacked?

We had been ordered to remove our shoulder straps so that no one could tell to what unit we belonged. In the stations, when civilians asked us where we came from, we answered: "From hell," or "From the moon."

Various inscriptions were painted on the coaches, such as: "Paris Express," "Down with France!" or again "Further declarations of war received here."

In the morning, Popp, Merbach, Loffelhardt and I left our compartment for a car filled with baggage from which we could calmly survey the landscape.

Towards six in the evening we finally arrived at Zerf where we passed the night. We were coldly received by the inhabitants. These people had once been French and they remembered it. Captain Ziekenrath, Merbach, Loffelhardt and I were quartered in the home of a citizen who told us that all his beds were occupied by his wife and daughters. We had to be content with some straw which Merbach's orderly brought us. He had stolen it somewhere or other. We were so tired that we slept soundly on that straw, so soundly, in fact, that next morning we were late for roll-call.

On August 7th, 1914, we left Zerf. Our train passed through Irsh, Saarburg, Littdorf, Frissel, Nittel and Wellen, where we crossed the Moselle and the Luxemburg frontier. All the soldiers, tired out, were now sad and discouraged.

3
Luxemburg

It was about half-past eleven when we arrived at Alingen. Almost immediately Major Schmidt assembled the staff of the battalion in order to give us his instructions as to the treatment to be accorded to the inhabitants of the country. These people were really thoroughly familiar with the German language, but they pretended not to understand a word of it and insisted on talking French. The men composing the staff of the 2nd Battalion of the 88th Infantry were Major Schmidt; Lieutenant Wunderlich, *aide-decamp*; Dr. Schafer, the head of the medical staff; Dr. Wolkewiz; Lieutenant Merbach; Sergeant-Major Hauser; Loffelhardt; and myself.

As interpreter, I was ordered to inform the inhabitants that it would be greatly to their advantage to welcome the soldiers and to do their utmost to avoid quarrels.

Merbach, Loffelhardt and I were quartered on a woman whose brother had left Paris on August 4th, 1914. He told us that every one in Paris blamed the Crown Prince for starting the war. Merbach answered that he was only one of the many guilty ones. This woman gave us an excellent dinner. In the afternoon, the doctor inspected the men's feet because several of them had been complaining of soreness.

At five o'clock, the whole battalion was assembled on the road leading from Alingen to Mensdorf. Colonel Puder, commanding the 88th, greeted and addressed us. Then, led by a band, we left for the city of Luxemburg, arriving there at noon on the eighth. The natives who watched us pass showed without exception only hostility. Merbach, Loffelhardt and I went on ahead to order the people to place pails of water in front of their houses so that the soldiers, whose throats were parched by the heat, might have a chance to drink.

The battalion halted at Esch, five kilometres from the capital of

Luxemburg. The men were put up in barns and the officers were billeted on the inhabitants.

Merbach and I were assigned to a priest who received us very badly, telling us that he could only give us one single bed. Merbach gravely replied that two young men could not possibly sleep in one bed, especially in the home of a Catholic priest.

"What is your religion?" asked the priest.

"I am a Catholic," Merbach answered, although he was really a Protestant.

Merbach and I were ordered to go to Luxemburg immediately to buy cigarettes and various things for the battalion. In the tobacco shop two ladies were behind the counter as we entered. Merbach told them in German that we wanted some cigarettes and that we would pay for them. The ladies pretended not to understand, and one of them said in French:

"Gentlemen, if you were French, I would give you everything you wish for nothing. But we cannot bear the sight of '*sauerkrauts.*'"

"Madam," I answered in French, "be careful of what you say and whom you address in this manner. Some day your words may come back to you in an unpleasant fashion." Thereupon she became thoroughly frightened and embarrassed, for she had not thought that we could understand French.

I reassured her, saying that I would not give her away. Then she decided to speak German, greatly to the satisfaction of Sergeant-Major Vetter who could now make the purchases on which he hoped to gain a fine profit. This swindler really resold these goods to the men for much more than he paid for them. His thefts assumed such large proportions that Major Schmidt was forced to remove him. Later on he was killed in the first engagement of the battalion.

Immediately upon his return to the cantonment, Major Schmidt invited us to have coffee, and then our time was our own.

Our priest received us a little more cordially this time. We dined with him. The dinner was so good that I did not pay the slightest attention to Merbach's puns.

On the following day, Merbach, Loffelhardt and I were ordered to make a careful inspection of the wagons of the battalion. While we were thus occupied, the other officers spent their time in the cafes, drinking and playing cards.

At seven o'clock we received the following order:

The 2nd Battalion of the 88th Infantry will advance from Luxemburg to Arlon, and will find out whether or not the city is still occupied by the enemy. Half a section of the 6th Uhlans will supplement the 2nd Battalion. Patrols commanded by officers and non-commissioned officers will reconnoitre.

By chance, we three, Merbach, Loffelhardt and myself, were again chosen by the commander to be sent to reconnoitre. Our hearts beat a little faster, but we could not object, since, as they say, orders are sacred. Soon we arrived in the city. Those inhabitants whom I questioned told us that the Belgian soldiers had just left Arlon, scarcely two hours ago. The city seemed quiet, so we returned to the battalion where Major Schmidt ordered us to report to Baron Von Schenk, infantry general and commander of the army corps. He was then at Luxemburg. The general had a copy of our report made by his chief *aide-de-camp*, Major Martens,

Towards ten o'clock, the battalion, led by a band, entered Arlon. All precautions were taken to guard against an attack. Arlon was occupied by our battalion, a company of machine gunners, who set up their loaded pieces right in the heart of the city, the 6th Uhlans and a battery of the 63rd Artillery. The 5th Company took possession of the barracks of the city; the three other companies were billeted in various places. Brigadier-General Von der Esch and the chief of staff of the 42nd Brigade lived at the Hotel Continental. All the officers and non-commissioned officers had to live with the men in the cantonments.

But Major Schmidt gave Merbach, Loffelhardt and myself permission to live in the city at the house of the deputy-major. We stayed there up to the very moment of our departure.

4

Arlon

When we entered Arlon, all the inhabitants, probably out of curiosity, were at their windows or doors. Bands were playing and the soldiers singing. The mayor of Arlon, a lawyer, was taken as a hostage and placed in the town hall under armed guard. The following proclamation was issued:

To the citizens of Arlon!

I am having the following proclamation made public and I hope that every one will heed its commands.

The city of Arlon is occupied by German troops. Every one must submit to the will of the conqueror. Any infraction of the following orders will be severely punished.

1. The inhabitants must welcome the soldiers and treat them politely;

2. All arms and munitions must be brought to the town hall as soon as possible;

3. The gathering of more than three persons on the streets is forbidden;

4. The inhabitants must stay in their homes from 7 p. m. to 7 a. m.;

5. From 8 p. m. on, there may be no light in the houses. Fires must be put out at the same time and no smoke allowed to be seen;

6. Every person having any knowledge of the movements of the enemy, is asked to report all information immediately under pain of severe punishment;

7. I have taken the mayor of Arlon as a hostage. He will be set

free as soon as the population has conformed to my orders and as soon as other guarantees shall have been given.

Arlon, August 10, 1914.
von der Esch,
Brigadier-General."

A special detachment was ordered to announce this proclamation. It was composed of Lieutenant Popp, accompanied by two non-commissioned officers, two drummers, two trumpeters and eight men with fixed bayonets.

I was selected to read the proclamation. At every street corner the drums were beaten and the civilians gathered to hear the reading of General von der Esch's orders. I had to read it at least thirty times before I was able to return to the house where I lived with Merbach and Loffelhardt.

We had hardly returned when Major Schmidt sent for us to order us to go to the city and requisition some bread and meat at the bakers and butchers. In the streets we saw lots of soldiers talking with the inhabitants by means of signs, which was rather amusing.

In several shops they told us that soldiers had taken things by force without paying for them and had insulted the proprietors. Merbach quieted these people by giving them vouchers. In one tobacco shop, a soldier had in this manner taken eighty *francs*' worth of cigarettes for his captain and had never come back to pay for them. Private Bessler, of the 6th Company, had gone into a jeweller's—supposedly to buy some jewellery. He stuffed everything the woman showed him into his pockets, and was just about to go off with his booty when we came on the scene. Merbach boxed his ears and made him return the stolen jewels.

Towards half-past eight as Merbach, returning to Major Schmidt, was passing police headquarters a revolver was fired at him. He was not wounded. A policeman was just then standing in front of the door. He was immediately arrested and a council of war was hastily organised. It was composed of the following members:

Major Schmidt, chairman.

First Lieutenant Bertram, prosecuting attorney.

Lieutenant Eger, counsel for the defence.

Brigadier-General von der Esch, A captain of the 63rd Artillery, and Lieutenant Kaufmann of the 6th Uhlans, judges

I was the interpreter.

The accused was one Louis Empereur, a policeman of the city of Arlon, married and the father of four children. He had had so far an absolutely clear record with the German military authorities. Before the opening of the session, I was able to say a few words to him: I told him that he had a good chairman and I advised him to remember his wife and children and to be careful of what he said. He answered me that he knew what he had to do and that I need not worry about him. The session commenced and Lieutenant Bertram delivered his address. Empereur was accused of:

1. Having fired at the Prussian Lieutenant Merbach, without wounding him;

2. Having disobeyed the commands of the Brigadier-General's proclamation which ordered the inhabitants to give up their arms and to carry them to the town hall.

Since the accused did not seem to regret his action, the prosecuting attorney asked the war-council to make an example of him by imposing the death sentence.

Lieutenant Eger, counsel for the defence, pleaded on behalf of Empereur, basing his arguments on the fact that no arms were found in his possession. But the accused cried out: "Yes, it was I who fired, and I have only one regret: that I did not succeed in killing a German!"

After this avowal he could only be sentenced. He was executed at 2 p. m.

At four o'clock someone fired on a patrol of the 6th Uhlans, but again without wounding any one. The shot came from a window of a disorderly house in front of which the patrol was passing. Immediately the Uhlans dismounted and, assisted by some foot-soldiers of the 8th Company of our battalion, went into the house where they commenced to maltreat the women and to plunder everything. After they had stolen all they could carry off they arrested two men and two women who were in the house and led them before the General. At the conclusion of a summary examination the men were set free, after the girls had declared them to be innocent, saying that they themselves had fired on the Uhlans. They were immediately executed without a council of war. Then the house was given over to pillage. Everything that the soldiers could not carry off was broken or thrown out of the windows. The officers were greatly amused at soldiers who had put on women's chemises over their uniforms and were running around the streets in that costume.

On August 12th I left, by automobile, with Merbach, Loffelhardt and two men to reconnoitre in the *château* at B——. We had orders to take photographs and to satisfy ourselves as to the side from which a future attack might come. We had requisitioned six automobiles in Arlon. Loffelhardt, who was a good chauffeur, drove. German pickets outside of Arlon had taken such careful precautions and had dug so many ditches across the roads leading into the town that we were more than an hour getting across it.

The *château* of B—— was situated in the midst of a large and beautiful park. As soon as we arrived, the caretaker came out to meet us. He took us into his own house where his sixteen or seventeen-year-old daughter begged us to spare him. We told her to have no fear, for we were not waging war on civilians. Her mother was sick in bed.

After visiting the *château*, and appropriating some arms, we went down to the cellars, which were stocked with wine and all sorts of provisions. Merbach, who did not wish to carry off anything without orders from the major, sealed all the doors and gave the caretaker a paper forbidding any one to take away anything from the *château*.

As soon as we returned we reported to General von der Esch, telling him that we had not seen the enemy. Then we hurried to our major in order to tell him of our discovery. He gave us permission to return to the *château* immediately, and to bring back all the wines and provisions we wished. The drum-major accompanied us to lend a hand in case of need.

As we had taken all the keys, it was easy for us to re-enter the *château*. I immediately went in search of the caretaker, but was greatly surprised to find his house empty and in a frightful disorder. A labourer, passing by, told us of what had happened during our absence. Four German soldiers of the 42nd Brigade had entered the caretaker's house and after maltreating the inmates who fled in terror, had ransacked the place, amusing themselves by breaking whatever they could not carry off with them. I asked this man if he knew what these blackguards had done to the young girl, but he could give me no information on that score.

We then went into the *château* and had the contents of the cellars loaded onto carts and wagons, belonging to the place, which we found in the coach house. We also took away all the horses in the stables. While this was going on, Merbach on the first floor was cramming a large trunk full of linen. The non-commissioned officers. Lurch and

Loser, as their share, were breaking open the drawers and taking all the jewels and valuables they could find. They gave away many of them to their friends. September, 1916, found Paymaster Herbert of the 2nd Battalion still wearing a bracelet which he got at this time. We also took all the saddles and harnesses from the stables. Then the expedition started for Arlon. Major Schmidt congratulated us, saying that we had surpassed his expectations.

Up to August 17th, we led a fairly agreeable existence at Arlon and Luxemburg. Almost every day Merbach, Loffelhardt and I rode out in an automobile to reconnoitre. But Merbach always took us to Luxemburg where we spent our time. On our return we presented some sketch or other of a spot on which we had never set foot, saying that we had seen no trace of the enemy. And General von der Esch was delighted to have such fine soldiers.

On August 17th, 1914, we were ordered to leave Arlon which did not especially please the soldiers, for they would rather have stayed on there, eating, drinking, and smoking stuff stolen from the inhabitants of the country.

5

Lenglier

We advanced for two days, reconnoitring right and left for fear of a surprise attack.

Finally on August 20th, 1914, war began in earnest for us. It was our first serious engagement and it showed me how a most gentle fellow, like my friend Merbach, could suddenly become savage in the excitement of battle.

It was about 6 a. m. and we had just left Tintage, where we had been quartered. We were marching along the road which leads from Martelange to Neufchâteau, taking all precautions necessary to our safety. Our battalion was leading. Behind us came the 1st and 5th Battalions of the 87th Infantry. The 80th Fusiliers and the 81st Infantry were on our left.

About 1 p. m. a patrol coming from Lenglier notified us that we could advance without danger since that locality was not occupied by the enemy. After having some soup, prepared by the field kitchens, we resumed our march. All of a sudden, on our right, we heard an unwonted noise, altogether new to us. We knew right away what it was: a shell. Several dropped quite close to us. Major Schmidt immediately gave the following order:

"The 5th, 6th and 7th Companies will advance in skirmish line, taking shelter behind the hill which lies before them. The 8th Company will stay behind in reserve."

All the officers, sword in hand, marched in front of their men, as in a review.

The French and Belgians aimed very well and, sad to say, were aided by our own 27th Artillery who fired at us. After being reinforced by the 87th Infantry, Colonel Puder ordered the attack.

We could see now with our own eyes what war, which we only

knew from books, really is. Men hit by a bullet flung up their arms, turned about and fell, dead or wounded. Everywhere one heard cries of pain and groans mingling with the whizzing of bullets and shells, the hurrahs of the soldiers and the commands of the officers.

Captain Dunker was wounded twice and died that very evening. Lieutenant Eger, wounded in the hand, soon fell down in a faint. The 8th Company, which had until now been held in reserve, advanced in its turn to the left of the 5th Company.

All of a sudden the village of Lenglier began to burn and the two last named companies were ordered to take possession of it. The staff of the 2nd Battalion, to which I belonged, was now on the right wing of the 2nd Company. Lieutenant Brunn, an officer much loved by all his soldiers, fell just as he was giving an order, pierced through the heart. Non-Commissioned Officer Steinbach fell at the same time.

At last we actually entered Lenglier, which presented a sad spectacle. Houses were burning everywhere; the streets were strewn with the bodies of soldiers and horses. A Belgian officer was lying across a beam that was still burning. His body was half burnt and his distorted face expressed horrible pain. This unfortunate man had fallen there, wounded, and must have been slowly burned alive.

Merbach and I, with our orderlies, were just then at a telephone post in the depot. All of a sudden we heard the screams of women and children. Going out into the street we saw a group of civilians, composed of four men, two women and five children, in the midst of a troop of officers and soldiers. Soldiers were kicking these unfortunate people and striking them with their rifle butts. The soldiers accused them of having fired at Colonel von Kriestein, commanding the 87th Infantry, who had just been wounded. He died in Germany shortly after. Their guilt could not be proven, for French, Belgian and German bullets were whizzing in every direction. Merbach took these unhappy people under his protection. In another house nearby a woman, holding a young child in her arms, was killed by a musket blow in the presence of her husband. He was later stabbed with a bayonet by a soldier of the 87th. I do not know what became of the child.

In front of the station a young lieutenant of the 87th was ordering a non-commissioned officer and two men to set fire to the hotel, under the pretext that it was from there that von Kriestein might have been fired at. These three men first entered the hotel cellars in the hope of finding some wine. They found it, to be sure, but they immediately began to quarrel because the non-commissioned officer wanted to keep all the champagne for himself. So a man of the 88th was chosen to set fire to the hotel, which he did, floor by floor. Many houses were destroyed in this way.

About six o'clock Merbach and I were sent to look for the paymaster, in order that rations might be distributed. We followed a little path between two hills to the right of the station. Soon we met a group of German soldiers, a seriously wounded French lieutenant in their midst. When he saw us, this officer said in German: "Gentlemen, I beg of you to deliver me from these wild beasts." The poor man had a bullet in his abdomen and seemed to be suffering intensely.

Merbach suddenly became very much excited and answered brutally: "Take care of what you say and don't talk that way about brave soldiers who are fighting to deliver the world from the filthy French. As sure as I am standing here, I will not leave you until you have died before my eyes."

"Lieutenant Merbach," said Paymaster Herbert who had just joined us, "remember that he is an officer like yourself and that he is wounded."

But Merbach did not wish to listen to anything and sent us away. He remained alone with the dying man.

I told Major Schmidt of this affair and he ordered Merbach to take command of the 8th Company, whose captain, Zieckenrath, had been wounded. Two days afterwards, in the Battle of Bertrix, Merbach was killed by a French soldier who dealt him a musket blow on the head. He was one of my best friends.

In the Battle of Lenglier the 2nd Battalion lost five officers and sixty men.

Night fell and we lay down in the midst of the dead and wounded, whose cries we heard all around us. Our camp was in a place about two kilometres east of Lenglier, which continued to burn all through the night.

It was impossible for most of us to rest because we were all unnerved. Many soldiers thanked God for having protected them. Others boasted of having killed many Belgians and French. Whenever, utterly tired out, we began to doze a little, nightmares or shells would rudely awaken us.

At dawn we went on. For eight hours we marched around Neufchâteau, where a battle seemed to have taken place, and then we were ordered to bivouac at Bercheux. We had the 87th French Infantry aided by a company of Belgian cyclists opposite us.

6

Bertrix

On August 22nd the reveille sounded at five o'clock in the morning. We marched off at seven, following the road to the left of Lenglier. After passing through Tournay-en-Ardennes, we entered the forest of Huquant where we snatched a moment's rest. Almost all the inhabitants of the village had fled precipitately, leaving their houses intact in the hands of the Germans, who were pillaging, breaking, and plundering everything. The soldiers, for their own amusement, were throwing furniture and dishes out of the windows. Schmidt, it is true, from time to time said that he would kill anyone who went into the houses; but the soldiers did as they pleased and did not obey Schmidt or anyone else.

At eleven o'clock near the Luchy forest, on the way from Bertrix to Recogne, we received for the last time two days' rations. About two o'clock an order from the Army Corps was received. We were to attack immediately because the enemy, in great numbers, was getting ready to block our path, and perhaps to attempt to drive us back. Two of our companies advanced on the left side of the road and two on the right. We were assisted on the right by the 1st Battalion, and on the left by the 80th Fusiliers.

The 7th Company was ordered to form in skirmish line, occupying the outskirts of the forest, and to open the attack. The first one to be killed was First Lieutenant Bertram. He fell, struck by the bullet of a German soldier named Schleisinger, whom the Lieutenant had punished before the war by three days' imprisonment, and who wished to avenge himself, and had moreover so expressed himself to his comrades. His bullet made a little hole in the nape of Bertram's neck. This Schleisinger not only went unpunished, but a little while later received the Iron Cross for bravery. He died in the hospital at

Nesle of wounds received in battle.

The Battle of Bertrix was one of the most important in which our battalion took part. The French occupied a favourable position and tried their utmost to prevent our advance. In order to avoid being driven back we had to sacrifice all our reserves. The fighting was desperate and both sides displayed equal valour. The French artillery and machine gunners aimed very well and caused us great losses.

A great many soldiers fell, dead or wounded, and it was impossible to bring aid to any one because each one of us had enough to do to shelter himself from bullets and shells. At one time we thought that everything was lost and that we would have to retreat, when, fortunately, the 3rd Artillery Regiment of the Mayence fortress broke through the forest and arrived on the field. Hardly had the horses come out from the sheltering trees when they fell, overwhelmed by the French fire. Officers and soldiers set to work dragging the guns and pushing the wheels in order to be able to open fire as soon as possible. Many were killed.

At last the 3rd Artillery was ready to fire and our cause took a turn for the better. Some soldiers of the 5th and 8th companies succeeded in gaining possession of guns belonging to the 18th French Artillery. The Frenchmen defended their guns, revolver in hand, and died bravely for their country. Then the Prussians cheered. The French, seeing a part of their artillery lost and one of their aviators fall, began to retreat slowly and to offer less resistance.

The battle was over for that day and the last rays of the sun gloomily lit up the field, covered with the wounded and dying.

The next morning, August 23rd, the conflict began again, but less violently than on the previous day. Still keeping in skirmish line, we advanced, leaving Bertrix on our left. The soldiers were hungry and many of them opened the knapsacks of dead French and Germans in order to find something to eat. Bertrix was burning and we advanced through a field of unmowed grain. We spent the night between Fontenoille and Chassepierre on the French border.

The next day, at eight o'clock, we engaged in our first battle on French soil, in the neighbourhood of Matton, and in Matton itself.

7

Matton

On the morning of August 24th our battalion again happened to march at the head of the line. This did not please Major Schmidt or the soldiers at all because we had already lost more men than all the other battalions. But Schmidt was the youngest commander and he had to obey.

The French who were beating a slow retreat had assumed the defensive in the woods near Matton. We attacked them and a short while afterwards occupied their positions. Since we had no orders we stayed right there in the trenches until the 80th came to relieve us. The field kitchens, which were two kilometres behind us, were waiting to give us a hot meal. The men were satisfied and had already forgotten the hardships of the previous days. But their happiness was of short duration. Indeed the French had just made a counter attack and had pushed aside the 80th, who lost the positions which we had gained. As soon as he was told of this, the Commander of the Army Corps, Baron von Schenk, ordered Schmidt to attack immediately. Schmidt replied:

"Your Excellency, my battalion has lost more men than all the others put together. My men have fought like lions. They have had almost nothing to eat for three days and they can stand it no longer."

"What's that? Are you not ashamed of yourself?" said Schenk. "You will attack immediately and the knapsacks will remain here."

Schmidt, with tears in his eyes, grasped the battalion standard and placed himself at the head of his men. He was seeking death. Because of this incident, Schmidt became popular with all the soldiers. On the other hand, he was unfavourably regarded by his superiors and ended by handing in his resignation in April, 1915.

Our artillery, which had done pretty good work that day, helped us take Matton, which was already completely demolished, only a few houses remaining intact. When the 80th came to relieve us the soldiers exchanged musket blows and kicks. Our men called them cowards and full dress soldiers. Our officers said nothing but spat on the ground to express their disgust before their comrades of the 80th.

We had to go about twelve kilometres to get our knapsacks and at about 8 p. m. we took up our quarters in more or less ruined houses.

The soldiers broke everything that was still whole. They made fires of furniture and planks torn from the floors. They found a good deal of linen, especially women's underwear. Many men threw aside their shirts and put on women's chemises, which they said were much more comfortable in the heat. No one could forbid them anything, for most of them were drunk and would not obey. They quarrelled in front of the cellar entrances and had only one fear: that they might leave some wine for others. Often in their haste they forgot to turn off the taps so that the cellars were flooded with wine. Besides, many officers, especially reserve officers, were the first to set a bad example.

I lived with Major Schmidt and his entire staff in the house of a retired French captain, that was still intact. He told Schmidt that he could not understand how, in an army like ours, which had such a reputation for discipline, the soldiers could be permitted to plunder and steal as they had just done at Matton. Schmidt asked me to answer him by saying that unfortunately he could not punish the soldiers because too many officers themselves had given such a bad example.

"How does it happen?" the old French captain went on, "that you mobilised so quickly? In France there was so little thought of war that we did not even have the time necessary to prepare for our defence."

Lieutenant Wunderlich made him understand that Germany had been preparing for a new war for forty-four years, while in France the people had only begun to think of such a thing about a year or two ago, (as at 1919).

On the next morning, August 25th, at half-past nine Paymaster Herbert arrived with supply wagons in order to distribute provisions among the kitchens. Then we saw who the true thieves, the greatest plunderers, were. What had they not stolen? Full trunks, clothing, materials, clocks, phonographs and even umbrellas, canes and other things of no earthly use to a soldier. Beside the regulation wagons there were a lot of others loaded with loot. Some were entirely filled with wine. When he saw this Schmidt asked since when had he become a robber captain. The paymaster answered, without moving a muscle, that there had been no way of preventing the soldiers from entering abandoned houses.

"Fine excuses," answered Schmidt. "I believe you are war profiteers. While the soldiers at the front are sacrificing their skins, you gentlemen to the rear steal at leisure."

This band of thieves brought with them a quantity of provisions stolen from the houses and stores, and all sorts of poultry, geese actually hanging out of the wagons.

At 2 p. m. the regiment left Matton to march on Carignan. Along the road we could see ambulances and shattered wagons and the bodies of soldiers and horses which, because of the heat, were beginning to pollute the air. We also saw dead cows and pigs which the soldiers had left to rot after they had cut from them such meat as they wanted at the moment. It was the work of marauders who wage war for their own personal gain and only appear in their units to get their pay.

At Carignan, for lack of space, we had to camp out. On the twenty-sixth, we acted as reserves for the troops fighting around Mouzon. During the night it rained so hard that we had to go into the houses for shelter. Naturally the soldiers had to stay indoors and that caused some grumbling. I overheard Klein, a first class private, express himself as follows:

"Whenever there is anything good to be had, it's for the officers. As for us, they leave us wherever we are and don't even look at us. But let the battle come, then they are scared; they compliment us and flatter us because they are afraid. Then they are just like little children, but when the danger is over, they resume their authoritative tone and treat us like dogs."

On August 27th, we crossed the Meuse, near Carignan, without any difficulty.

We encamped at Villemontry which had not suffered much. But the inhabitants complained of the raids and pillages of the soldiers who, through their threats, got money and other valuables.

In the evening every soldier received a bottle of wine. The men, already fed by the kitchens, nevertheless prepared another meal for themselves, composed of chickens and other provisions, stolen from the village. Indeed nothing was left of the chickens and geese except the feathers which flew around in the streets.

On August 28th, reveille sounded at five o'clock, the last reveille, alas, for the many of us who were to fall on that day.

8

Autrecourt

We formed part of the left wing of the 21st Division and participated in the battle waged in and around Sedan. We were stationed between Haraucourt and Autrecourt. The 25th Division was on our left. The French artillery aimed very well, but with small results, because most of their projectiles did not explode. The shrapnel shells were the most dangerous, because when they burst it was at a certain height and a shower of bullets rained down upon us. They caused us great losses. We were lying on the crest of a small hill to the east of Autrecourt and we could not possibly advance because of the murderous fire of the French, who shot at all those who were foolish enough to raise their heads.

Major Schmidt, Reserve-Lieutenant Beck, Loffelhardt and I marched with the battalion, while Lieutenant Wunderlich, a drum-major and a non-commissioned officer stayed about fifty paces behind us with the telephone in order to keep up communication with the rest of the regiment. A shell, which exploded right where they stood, struck a telephone operator, so that he was literally cut to pieces, and wounded Lieutenant Wunderlich in the back and in the arm.

After we had surged forward and backward several times we ended by succeeding in getting into the village which was completely destroyed. As at Lenglier I saw half-burned corpses lying among the ruins. The wounded groaned and the frightened animals bellowed loudly in the stables.

It was about two o'clock when we entered Autrecourt. In order to try to see Wunderlich, I, together with the major, sought the field hospital which had been installed in the church.

A frightful spectacle met our eyes and our nerves were subjected to a severe test. At first, it was impossible to find Wunderlich, so filled was the church with the wounded. We would have had to step over their bodies. Among others I remember the son of a merchant from Hanau-on-the-Main, who had lost both eyes. He screamed fit to break one's heart and kept calling for his mother. In his agony he tore off the dressing, and we could see how horrible his wound was. Others had one or two limbs shot away, or had their stomachs torn open by shells. Some bore their suffering resignedly; others on the contrary uttered loud shrieks.

In a garden, to the right of the church, were the French wounded. I must say that most of them did not scream, either because they were afraid to or because of national pride and for the sake of setting the Germans a good example of courage.

We asked the nurses why they did not carry these wounded Frenchmen into the houses instead of letting them lie out in the open. "We have no room," they answered. "Besides it is not cold during the night and they are well covered." Let it be said in passing that the nurses are the greatest thieves on earth.

We camped north of Autrecourt. The companies assembled to report their losses in dead, wounded and prisoners. Only then I realised how hot the fighting had been. All the companies had lost more than half of their fighting force in dead or wounded.

Many of the soldiers walked over the battlefield to find their friends, but most of them were not ashamed to explore the pockets of the dead. To any questions they answered that they were looking for identification tags. To put these ghouls to flight it was necessary for Schmidt to issue a formal order, threatening to shoot immediately any man who should touch a corpse.

The Meuse flowed calmly at our feet, indifferent to all this wretchedness of which, nevertheless, it was the primary cause.

In order that the convoys might cross the river, the 21st Pioneers had built a bridge at Villers, just ahead of Mouzon. Because one could not see very well there and as the crossing was making slow progress the Pioneers set fire to the houses nearest to the river. But the fires spread over the village and soon it was all aflame, so that one could see as though in full daylight. The general commanding the army-corps congratulated the 21st Pioneers.

9

Raucourt

On August 29th, 1914, after having received a fresh supply of rations, we set out for Raucourt. During the march our new *aide-de-camp*, Lieutenant Kédor, especially distinguished himself. He was a booby who maltreated the soldiers who were already suffering greatly from the heat and from thirst. As they were not marching quickly enough, he threatened them with his crop, insulted them and called them dogs, pigs, band of peasants, herd of cows, etc. Nevertheless, during the battle, no one ever saw this hero, who preferred to stay near the kitchens where shells and bullets did not fall. This, however, did not prevent him from being one of the first in the regiment to receive the Iron Cross.

About 3 p. m. we arrived at Raucourt. Here something happened which ought not to have occurred, but, honestly speaking, who in the German army still had any respect for the Red Cross, non-combatants, women, etc.? Not many.

The 87th Infantry which was in the lead had not neglected to take all precautions and had sent patrols in various directions. Some of these patrols preferred to remain quietly at an inn at Raucourt, rather than fulfil their mission. They stripped the entire house and after taking whatever pleased them, went into the cellar. There they seized a lot of wine, especially champagne, as was afterwards proved by the number of empty bottles lying about on the ground. It was not long before they were completely drunk. Then, whether it was the result of a quarrel, or whether it was by accident, one of the soldiers was killed by the sideboard in the dining room. He had been hit by the butt-end of a rifle which had opened his skull like a melon. His brain oozed out. His eyes, as big as fists, hung from their sockets. He was completely disfigured. So that no one could identify him the murderers had hidden his papers and taken his military certificate out of his knapsack, which was still lying in front of him, with the contents all thrown about. What indicated that the murderers were not civilians was the fact that he still held his own gun and that the murderer's gun, the butt all covered with blood, was still there.

Lieutenant Kédor, the non-commissioned officers Dorr of the regimental staff, Hallenbach, Loffelhardt and I were the first to enter the house, for a crowd of civilians and soldiers had assembled outside the door without daring to go in. We immediately understood what had happened, and saw that only a German soldier could have committed the murder. Kédor said: "Who will denounce the criminals so that they will be punished for their crime? They will never be found. Nevertheless we cannot allow the honour of the German army to be sullied in this way." With these words he went out of the house and accused the inhabitants of Raucourt of having murdered a Prussian soldier.

Immediately under Colonel Puder's orders, First Lieutenant Schaffitzel, the adjutant of the regiment, arrested all the inhabitants of the houses near the inn, about twenty in number. These miserable people swore that the soldiers were fighting among themselves and that they were innocent. Whereupon Puder shouted: "Kill this whole crowd immediately even though the innocent will suffer with the guilty, and set fire to the hotel and the neighbouring houses." Perhaps he thought that one of these wretches might denounce some one eke, but in this he was mistaken. However, before he could countermand the order the soldiers, like wild beasts, threw themselves on the fifteen or twenty men and women, condemned without a trial by Colonel Puder, and killed them wildly with bayonet thrusts. During this time others hastily set fire to the houses and to the hotel, which were in flames within a few moments.

Then the soldiers scattered over the whole village, maltreating and terrorising all the inhabitants. They were allowed full liberty to do as they pleased.

The battalion camped outside of the village in a field, where the bodies of French colonial soldiers were still lying about. We suffered much for want of tobacco. Major Schmidt and we ourselves smoked tea. The soldiers smoked dry leaves. Many stripped the dead in order to find some tobacco, which they resold for gold. Soldiers gave watches, rings and French or Belgian gold pieces in exchange for a few cigarettes. Where did all this money and these valuables come from since the German soldier is paid only five and three-tenths *marks* every ten days?

On the next day, a Sunday and a day of rest, a religious service was held at which the chaplain of the 21st Division preached, taking as his text: "*Love thy neighbour as thyself.*" At half-past eleven a mass for the Catholic soldiers was held in the church of Raucourt.

Because we of the general staff were in want of wine, Major Schmidt told me to try and sneak out with Loffelhardt and find some. So I started a little investigation among the inhabitants of the village who advised me to apply at a villa, situated at the northern limit of Raucourt. This villa was occupied by an old lady who lived there alone with her son and who was likely to have a lot of wine in her cellar.

When Non-Commissioned Officer Kumpfe, Loffelhardt and I presented ourselves at the villa we were thrown out by a young lieutenant who had already taken up his quarters there.

So we returned to Major Schmidt to tell him of the failure of our mission. Kédor, who was never afraid in such a case, said that we must return there with him. When we arrived the young lieutenant had gone away and we were able to see the lady at once. We explained the purpose of our visit, but she told us:

"Gentlemen, everything in this house has already been taken by the general who lives here."

"And where is this gentleman?" I asked.

"He has gone out," she said.

"Very well. When he returns you will show him our certificate of requisition."

Whereupon we went down into the cellar and immediately began to pack up some bottles of champagne and other wines.

As we were making ready to leave, with about thirty bottles, the young officer received us at the door of the cellar with these words:

"I'll teach you to drink my champagne! You drink water, you rascals!"

But Kédor, who was not afraid, shouted in his face:

"What are you saying? Who are you? What are you doing in this house?"

"I am the general's adjutant and I order you to leave this wine alone and to quit this place as quickly as possible."

"Shut up; keep your mouth closed! I am older than you. I believe you are only an impostor. You'll hear from me," answered the bold

Kédor.

Finally we arrived at Schmidt's quarters with our stolen wine, but we could not drink much of it since our departure was fixed for half-past four. We had hardly time to have a bite before setting out.

Barely six kilometres from Raucourt we had to halt in order to let other troops go by, because we were the reserves. This delay gave Schmidt an opportunity to send us back to get some more wine because we would probably be going through places which had already been stripped of everything by the troops preceding us. So I set out with Lieutenant Abraham of the 8th Company and Loffelhardt. All of us rode bicycles. We were delighted to be able to annoy the young lieutenant again. In the village Lieutenant Abraham stopped a moment to speak to some soldier acquaintances, so Loffelhardt and I went on ahead and presented ourselves alone at the door of the old lady's villa.

We knocked several times but no one answered. Then we jumped over the garden wall and removed the iron bar in order to open the door and put our bicycles inside. We were very much surprised to hear threatening words in German. The door of the house was also closed so we climbed in at a window, and were soon in the room from which the noise came. There we saw a strange sight. In the room were Non-Commissioned Officer Kumpfe, who was one of our party the first time we had come for the wine, Janecke, a first class private, and the old lady. The latter was completely undressed and appeared about to faint. When she saw us she started to cry, probably thinking that we also had come to hurt her. I told her to dress herself and to tell us what had happened.

"About half an hour ago," she said, "these two gentlemen broke into my room through the window and asked for money. I told them I had none because my son had gone away and taken it with him. Not understanding French, they thought I was refusing to give it to them. I took them into the dining-room to give them something to eat, but they pointed their revolvers at me and dragged me into this room. I tried to make them understand that they would find nothing which would be of the slightest value to them. Then the taller one" (this was Kumpfe) "sat down on my bed and made me understand by signs that I was to get undressed. In like manner, I tried to convey to him that I am an old woman, sixty-three years old, and begged him to remember his mother and to spare me such dishonour. Then this gentleman took a candle and set fire to my bed. I beg you to look at the sheets and blankets. Half mad with fear I tore off my clothes, ready to submit to the inevitable, when luckily you gentlemen came."

Then I explained to the lady why we had come back to see her, that she must not be afraid of us and that we would pay her in requisition certificates, which had the same value as current money. Kumpfe, now thoroughly scared, begged me to say nothing of what we had seen. Both he and Janecke asked the old lady's pardon. She also asked us not to say anything; because she did not want these men to be punished, and because she was embarrassed by the whole business. Loffelhardt and I promised her to keep it secret.

She asked us all to have something to eat, and you may be sure we did not refuse. Lieutenant Abraham, who had just arrived, also accepted her invitation and seemed very much pleased with the good woman. We did not tell him all that she had endured. After supper she herself took us to the cellar to get some wine. Since we could not carry it all with us, we told her to bury the rest, because I had marked on the requisition bill that we had taken everything; but I doubt if she did that. Later on, when Kumpfe wanted to order Janecke to do something, the latter said in a clear voice: "Raucourt." Kumpfe immediately turned pale and gave his orders to another soldier.

In the evening we rejoined the battalion, laden like mules, to Schmidt's great satisfaction.

The villages through which we passed were for the most part completely ruined, and in many of them even the churches were no longer standing.

Now the Battle of the Marne awaited us, the Marne where the French showed the stuff they were made of and where General Joffre closed the door on our hopes and illusions.

Here I wish to tell of some of the foolish ideas of our soldiers in order to show to what extent these illusions were spread about. We were to enter Paris immediately; that went without saying and no one doubted it for a moment. But all the soldiers were convinced that we would be in England very soon as well.

"How are we going to get to England?" asked one.

"Don't worry," replied another. "Wilhelm has already prepared everything. One fine day Dover will be bombarded from Calais and we will quietly set off for London where we can eat our fill of pudding."

10

The Battle of the Marne

We had the good fortune to remain in the rear-guard for five days until September 5th, 1914, when we were led under the deadly French artillery fire, to the north of Heiltz-leMerupt, in order to take part in the great Battle of the Marne. The French artillery aimed so well that on the march toward our position, we lost almost half of our fighting force, in dead or wounded.

We finally arrived at Heiltz-le-Merupt where we had to stop because the village was under fire. Always on the jump on account of the violent fire of the enemy artillery, we reached our positions between Sermaize-les-Bains and Pagny-sur-Saul, on the railroad, where we were sheltered. At this moment our communications with the rear were interrupted because of the close and violent fire of the French artillery which was becoming more and more deadly. We were in relative shelter, but only if we lay in the water. A torrential rain fell unceasingly and we had eaten nothing since 4 a. m. We had to await nightfall before we could leave our disagreeable position where, if we were not shot to death, we would probably be drowned like rats.

At 10 p. m. two field kitchens approached. Without bothering to see to what regiment they might belong the men threw themselves upon them and stripped them of everything in the twinkling of an eye.

Soon Loffelhardt and I were appointed to take the reinforcements which had just arrived from Mayence out to the battalion and to scatter them among the various companies. Some old Hanau acquaintances of ours were with them. The important thing was that they had tobacco and cigarettes, which we had been deprived of for a long time.

We showed the newcomers to their companies. Many had only

joined the colours six weeks before. They were beside themselves at the idea of taking part in a great battle and screamed so that we were obliged to shut them up, for the French were hardly thirty or forty metres away from us. I had hardly spoken when the fusillade began again, very violently, and then it was hard to restrain these valiant warriors who began to run in all directions, especially to the rear. Soon Loffelhardt and I had to lie down flat in a pool of water.

The company orderlies were starting off with new recruits when the order arrived for an immediate attack on the French who were opposite us. That was a real butchery. For the first time, I took part in a hand-to-hand combat. Every conceivable weapon was used: the bayonet, the rifle butt and even the trench knife. The two artilleries thundered on and caused terrible losses on both sides. Neither French nor Germans gave any quarter and no one wished to surrender. Our attack failed, resulting only in enormous losses.

In the morning we saw Kédor approaching with the four company adjutants whom he had gone to look for, back where the field kitchens were. He wished to enrol the new arrivals, but this was impossible because we had no lists and anyway most of them had been initiated by being killed, wounded or made prisoners. For a long while, in Germany, the many requests for information made by soldiers' relatives all received this simple answer: "Missing since the battle of the Marne." Many of these young soldiers did not even have identification tags.

On September 6th, the firing subsided somewhat, but it continued to rain in torrents. I was squatting at the bottom of a hole with Loffelhardt quite close to the major. All of a sudden a French shell fell right into our trench and tore six men to pieces.

About 5 p. M. Loffelhardt and I went to the rear carrying orders from the major to the paymaster. He was stationed with the baggage near Sagny-sur-l'Angle together with all the provisions of the 21st in charge of Rittmeister, a captain of the Hussars. Just as we came up the latter was questioning the mayor of Sagny-sur-l'Angle who had been brought before him and accused of communicating with the French, and of warning them of all our movements by means of an underground telephone. This suspicion was all the more well founded because a German battery, which had only just taken up its position, was immediately wiped out by the French fire. A non-commissioned officer of the 6th Uhlans arrived in the town hall courtyard and ordered the soldiers to arrest all civilians. Three women, among them the daughter of the mayor, a young girl of eighteen, were found in a cellar which had been their hiding place, and were treated just like the men, that is to say with the utmost brutality.

We spent the night with the paymaster and were able to see what an easy and agreeable life these gentlemen of the Quartermaster's Department were leading. While we were doing without everything in the trenches a frightful waste was going on here. They did not deny themselves anything. Wagons filled with plundered goods were standing in line. Because it was raining, comfortable tents had been put up. The paymaster invited us to have dinner with him and treated us just as though we were in a first-class hotel. Many excellent courses and all kinds of wine were served. Since Loffelhardt and I had had virtually nothing to eat for forty-eight hours, our appetites were enormous. Both of us were possessed by the one idea of profiting by this occasion, by eating enough for several days. Everything that we ate at that dinner had been stolen.

A few steps from us some soldiers who were guarding the civilians of Sagny did not hesitate to show their utter lack of respect for the women in a shocking manner. These poor creatures could do nothing and they began to cry, but that did not prevent those brutes from keeping right on. The officers ought to have put an end to such conduct. Are not two officers always detailed to stay with the baggage? Where were they? Probably about to celebrate with stolen wine. They were waging war in their own way.

After we were quite refreshed we responded to the call of duty and rejoined our battalion at about 4 a. m. We had to creep over bodies of dead men and horses and the ruins of wagons, guns and automobiles which littered the battlefield. It was impossible to walk upright without exposing oneself to the enemy fire. So we had to crawl. I shuddered as I touched the dead and reflected that perhaps a moment later I too would be one of these innumerable and unknown corpses. About half-past six we reached the crest of a hill. We offered a fine target to the enemy and their bullets began to whiz over us. So we hid behind a dead horse. Soon we saw some troops in front of us retreating in our direction. How great was our surprise to find that we were in the midst of the first, instead of the second, battalion.

In answer to our questions we were told that the second battalion was now further to the left. We went there and I asked Major Schmidt why we had abandoned the railroad line. He said: "You have heard that the Germans with Von Kluck were twenty kilometres from Paris, but, you see, the matter fell through and we have to beat a retreat. If this goes on, we shall soon have no more men left, for our losses are terrific." We remained there without orders, waiting to be taken prisoners.

"Charlot," Schmidt went on, "if fate wishes us to fall into the hands of the French while we are still alive, let us always stay together. Why didn't I learn more French at school? Well, that's understood, we'll keep together."

We remained there all day long; the French artillery fired to our rear and prevented us from retreating. They were also firing at us and killing many of our men, so that our position became intolerable. The stretcher bearers did not know where to turn next for the wounded were all crying out at the same time, calling them from every direction. Some men began to stick their handkerchiefs on their guns to show that they wished to surrender, but the French did not pay the slightest attention to us, only answering by bullets which very often hit their mark. Every one was demoralised. In order to calm the men, higher officers told them that we were retreating as a precautionary measure, but no one believed that. The soldiers had no compunction about shouting right at the officers: "Yes, yes, you were too hasty with your Paris story. Now the French have given us a beating which we shall never forget."

Finally, on September 8th, about 7 p. m., we escaped out of the death-clutch of the French. We were ordered to begin the retreat, which was wretchedly accomplished because of contradictory orders and counter orders. First they would send us in one direction and then in another. If we had just halted in a spot where we could get a little rest, another order would immediately come telling us to leave it. This uncertainty among their chiefs exasperated the soldiers, who sometimes even began to insult the officers. Many men, dead beat, refused to go on, but stayed where they were, surrendering to their fate.

On September 9th, about 4 a. m. our regiment was ordered to act as rear-guard of the division and to send out patrols composed of trustworthy men. Until further orders, the bulk of the rear-guard was to occupy the southern part of the Sommeilles forest.

It had stopped raining and the sun was shining brightly. Our little staff made themselves as comfortable as possible on the edge of a sand pit. They brought us coffee from the kitchens. We took it with pleasure and were discussing recent deaths when a French shell, bursting quite near by recalled to us the fact that the war was not yet over. Lieutenant Kédor, who was dangling his legs over the edge of the pit, all of a sudden rolled down, upsetting our coffee and shouting: "Help! Quick! I'm wounded!" Dr. Wolkewiz and two nurses came running but he got up alone and feeling himself all over said: "I thought that a shell had torn me to pieces. But, thank God, I see that there is nothing the matter with me and that I am safe and sound." We all laughed at the courage of this hero, who went on: "Major, I had a narrow escape; that shell whizzed by my ears, so that I thought surely the end had come. It's good that those simpletons aimed badly."

The major answered him: "Kédor, I haven't laughed so much since we mobilised. And just look! the whole battalion is doubling up with laughter. It remains to be seen whether it's on account of your heroism or your acrobatic stunts."

Kédor, who was ill-natured, got angry at these remarks and began to pick a quarrel with the soldiers. But he had hardly opened his mouth when they called out, shaking with laughter: "Help! Quick! I'm wounded!"

In order to end this scene, Schmidt sent Kédor to the kitchens to get us some more coffee.

Soon we continued our retreat. Von Kluck's artillery galloped madly by, with infantry men who could no longer keep up and who did not wish to fall into the hands of the French, hanging onto the gun carriages.

In the villages through which we passed there was no longer any question of maltreating the inhabitants. Some of them asked us if we were looking for the road to Paris. Schmidt, for whom I translated these sarcastic questions, did not get angry and only shrugged his shoulders.

At six o'clock we arrived at Hans where we were to encamp with all of the 88th, the 87th, the 6th Uhlans and the 63rd Artillery. The streets were so crowded with guns and wagons that it was impossible to get through. Officers swore and yelled and soldiers did what they chose. Many of the non-commissioned officers were soundly thrashed by privates. While I was going for orders for the brigade I saw Lieutenant Anspach of the 3rd Battalion swearing at an Uhlan who had touched him with his lance in passing. The Uhlan answered him in a rage: "Shut up, you great big thief; now you're getting back your courage because we're far away from the French. Be off with you, you poor coward, otherwise you'll get something more." Anspach paled and went off. I myself had removed the collar of my cape in order to pass unrecognised, for I realised that the troops were not respecting their superiors just then.

The night passed quietly for the men, but we were kept busy with orders and counter orders.

We left Hans on September 11th about 3 a. m., in skirmish line, and retreated eastward, crossing the trenches between Hans and Somme-Tourbe.

About six o'clock we were relieved by regiments who had not yet been tried out, and we in our turn relieved the Guard which had been beaten at Rheims.

Such was the part which our battalion played in the battle of the Marne.

11

Rheims

We were marching northward in the direction of Vouziers when we were suddenly ordered to change our course. Upon consulting maps, we found that we were being sent to Rheims. Our march on that city was a veritable forced march, for we made about fifty kilometres in one day. Colonel Puder shouted to us: "Well, we'll have to pull other people's chestnuts out of the fire again. It seems that the Guard has been licked and no doubt we're being sent to replace it."

It was at Bourgogne that we met the first soldiers of the Guard. Our men received them with sorry jokes. "Well," they said, "here you are, you brawlers from Berlin. Did the French give you a good licking? You just look at us to see what real soldiers are. You're nothing but full-dress soldiers. You know how to shoot off your mouths; but when the battle comes, you throw away your guns and beat it " The officers said nothing and laughed in their sleeves. Those remarks assured them that we would do our duty and would efface the failure of the Guards who had lost the fort of Brimont. We were being sent to recapture it.

At first no one cared to attack because of the accuracy of the French artillery fire. But Brigadier-General von der Esch ran all along the line, striking the backs of the soldiers with his sword. Thus it was that the brigade retook the fort of Brimont. Afterwards von der Esch told the officers that this was the best way to make the soldiers advance, and to recall them to their duty.

While we were taking the fort we were continuously subjected to the terrible fire of the French artillery, which continued to pick off our men. Our paymaster Herbert, who now had to come a little closer with his supply wagons in order to distribute the goods, was horribly afraid but that did not prevent him from getting the Iron Cross.

During the afternoon of September 17th Major Schleguer of the

1st Battalion and our Major Schmidt ordered Loffelhardt and myself to go to Rheims in search of some champagne to celebrate our victory over the Imperial Guard. We left on bicycles by way of Auménancourt-le-Petit, Bourgogne and Fresnes. As we were coming out of Fresnes, shells began to fall around us. We thought that they came from our artillery whose range might be too short. We were positive that Rheims was not yet occupied by the French. On coming out of the woods, a regular rain of shells greeted us. We did not know what to do, and thought that the best thing would be to get into the city as quickly as possible. There we would be safe.

As we were passing by a farm where a company of infantry was hiding the soldiers asked us: "Where are you going? Good luck to you!" All of a sudden we found ourselves in the midst of an infernal bombardment. Shells came from all directions and burst all around us. As we were going along that beautiful white road the French artillery, who were really occupying Rheims, fired at us as though they were shooting at targets. Realizing our mistake, and seeing that we had long ago passed the German lines, we went back at a dizzy pace. We surely beat all speed records, for we had the whole French artillery firing at our backs to hurry us away and to give us courage.

The road went uphill a bit, but just the same we rode on like world champions in order to get out of this hell. Schmidt, deeply moved, received us with open arms: "My poor fellows," he said, "what an unfortunate order! To risk your lives for a bottle of champagne! You had scarcely left when we were informed that our men no longer held Rheims and that the road was being subjected to a terrific bombardment. Luckily Heaven protected you! Was that you rushing along the road like madmen?"

This story shows what German soldiers are sometimes forced to do. Surely Schmidt alone would never have given such an order, but Schleguer, a Prussian in the true sense of the word, would have insisted upon immediate obedience.

Several soldiers who had eaten their reserve rations were tied to a stake with their hands behind their backs. On this occasion Private Render of the 5th Company, who had served in the Foreign Legion in Africa for five years, said that there he had never seen soldiers subjected to such treatment and that all the stories told about the Foreign Legion in Germany were entirely false.

On September 19th, we were relieved and proceeded to Pignécourt where we took up our quarters on a large estate.

12

The March on Roye

On September 20th we began our march towards Roye. About three o'clock we passed through Neufchâtel. We met detached groups of soldiers, belonging to other regiments, leading numbers of pigs, horses, cows, etc., which they had taken from the inhabitants. They said they were taking them to their regiments. Upon Schmidt's reminding them that pillaging was forbidden they answered that their superiors had ordered them to requisition these animals, but that they had not had time to rejoin their units, which had retreated too soon. In reality they were marauders. Neufchâtel had not been shelled, but all the shops had been plundered and the goods thrown helter-skelter into the middle of the streets. A strong box lay in the garden of a villa the windows and doors of which were broken.

On September 20th, Major Schmidt, Dr. Schafer, Dr. Wolkewiz, Lieutenant Kédor, Loffelhardt and I stopped at a farm on the road to Laon, not far from Neufchâtel, to rest and to quench our thirsts. A very sad-looking woman received us and asked us if we also had come to bring dishonour upon her daughters.

Schmidt told me to question this woman, so I asked her to tell us what had happened. Then she took us into a bedroom where she showed us the traces of the great crime which had just been committed in her house.

"Three or four hours ago at the most," she said, "three soldiers came here and asked me for wine and money. I told them that I had neither one nor the other and that I was alone with my two daughters. They told me to call my daughters. I tried to make them change their minds, but they would not listen to anything, and so, because I was afraid of their threats, I had to obey. Hardly had they appeared when the soldiers, like wild beasts, threw themselves upon my poor children and pushed them into this room, where, despite my cries, they ruined them. One of them put his hand over my mouth and held me back, striking me the while. Here, gentlemen, you see the traces of this wild struggle. I think, from his insignia," she said, "that one of you gentlemen" (she looked at Schafer) "is a doctor. I beg him to give my daughters a careful examination so that he may testify that I speak the truth." Schafer was left alone with the young girls and came back a few moments later, reporting to Major Schmidt that they had been raped by those blackguards. These two poor young ladies, aged respectively eighteen and twenty years, no longer dared to look even at their mother, and stood ashamed before us.

We told the ladies that we would put in a complaint, but that it would probably have no result, for there were so many cads who made war in this fashion on innocent people. Schmidt told me to ask them if there was anything more we could do for them. They begged us to leave them alone.

Schmidt complained to Colonel Puder. The latter answered that he could do nothing because it would be impossible to find those blackguards and punish them, just as it was impossible to punish marauders and thieves. "In that case," he said, "Germany might as well make peace immediately, for I see everyone stealing and everyone has rings on his fingers and jewels in his pockets. We would have to jail almost everyone."

Schmidt said to me, regarding this affair, "Charlot, we speak badly enough of the Russians in Germany, but I think we are no better than they Perhaps we are worse !"

On September 21st, we proceeded slowly along the road from Laon. The soldiers were singing. Lieutenant Kédor, who had a mania for tormenting his men, wished to stop them. But they all began to yell, imitating Kédor's voice: "Help! Quick! I'm wounded!" thus recalling to him his stunt in the sand pit, and making him furious. In his anger he went so far as to strike several men with his crop. During one of our halts, he saw some soldiers lying on the ground and struck one of them on the nape of the neck. This man calmly got up, took his gun, loaded it and aimed at Kédor, who immediately began to run in a zigzag line, calling for his horse. We were at a little distance from this scene and were greatly amused by it. Colonel Puder held his sides with laughter.

Schmidt had the soldier brought to him and told him that he had done right, and that he ought to defend himself against every individual who might attack him, whether friend or enemy. Colonel Puder and General von der Esch himself also congratulated the soldier. Kédor had disappeared. But since he was *aide-de-camp*, he would soon have to come back for orders. Schmidt took advantage of the occasion to say to him: "Kédor, you have already given us proof of your heroism by showing us that even in the face of great danger you keep your wits about you, and know how to get out of it. But the soldier, who surely would have killed you if it had not been for our cries and bursts of laughter, is still braver. In any case, you entertained us very well." Kédor was very much downcast for a short time, and left the soldiers alone.

On the twenty-third, we left for Fressancourt, La Fère, Chauny and Beaugies, where we halted.

Each company had sent ahead a non-commissioned officer to secure quarters for the battalion. The peasants of Beaugies, simple and childlike people, surprised at our strange uniforms which were not French and which they hadn't seen before, asked the quartermasters; "Are you Englishmen?"

"Yes, yes,"[1] the latter answered in order to get good quarters, and warned us, when we arrived, not to let on that we were enemies. These good people fought for the privilege of having soldiers live with them, and showed us all sorts of courtesies. Finally I could not refrain from telling them that we were Germans. They immediately ran away, as though a bomb had fallen in their midst, crying, "The Prussians! The Prussians!" It was very funny.

Thanks to my having made inquiries of the major, Major Schmidt and his whole staff were quartered in a comfortable farm where we found food and some excellent wine which I had advised the major to send us. Several other officers of the battalion came to dine with us and, thanks to the wine, many were soon completely drunk, including our good Major Schmidt. About 1 a. m. I had to go to Maucourt for orders, and I learned that we were to leave at two o'clock. It was about one forty-five when I left Maucourt. I went to the police post to warn the trumpeter to sound the alarm and then returned to the major. I found them all drunk and incapable of understanding me.

Thanks to Dr. Schafer, who seemed a little less intoxicated than the others, we finally made Schmidt understand what he had to do. He immediately ordered the officers to assemble their troops at the village gate within ten minutes. We were supposed to leave at two o'clock,

---

1. In English in the original.

but at two thirty the battalion had not yet been assembled, for while the officers were drinking the soldiers had been doing the same. Also a great many lazy fellows failed to answer the roll-call.

Before arriving at Guiscard we had to halt in order to let other troops go by. Most of the officers and soldiers threw themselves in the ditches along the road, to continue their interrupted slumber and to sleep themselves sober. Only a snapshot was lacking.

At eight o'clock we passed through Guiscard and Libermont.

13
Ercheu—Solente—Champieu

Thanks to our artillery, it was comparatively easy for us to enter the village of Ercheu, which, like the rest, was the scene of the usual pillage. On our right was the 25th Division under the Grand Duke of Hesse-Darmstadt. The French were in possession of Solente, a very favourable position. The Hessians on our right were better located than we were and could advance a little. As for us, no sooner did one of our patrols venture out, than it was immediately shot down. Volunteers were asked for in vain; no one responded.

At nine o'clock we received the formal order to attack at midnight. Loffelhardt, who brought us the order, told us that things were not going well with us in Northern France and Belgium and that the cavalry had been ordered to leave immediately by rail, because the English Army was offering an unexpected resistance.

So the Battle of Solente took place the night of September 24th-25th, 1914. It was terrible. French and Germans fought with blind fury and neither side gave any quarter. The heroic defence of the French again caused us terrible losses, and we entered Solente at 5 a. m. only by literally walking over the dead and wounded.

The eldest son of Major Schmidt, who had joined the battalion only a short time ago, met his death in this slaughter house. The father's grief was heartrending. To those who tried to console him, by saying that his son had died for his country, he answered: "What do I care about your country? Why do we need a war?"

On entering Solente I witnessed a horrible scene. A German soldier had gone into a house to make some coffee. Near the stove was an old woman, sitting up in bed. On her right, an old man in a chair. About two feet from this group, a young woman was sitting nursing her baby. A shell which had exploded in the room had mortally wounded the old woman in the head, the old man was cut in two, the soldier was lying on the ground, dead, while the young woman was sitting in her chair with her head cut off, but the baby in her arms was entirely unharmed. No one who saw this terrible sight could help crying.

During the whole day of the twenty-fifth the fierce struggle continued for the possession of the town of Champieu, which we had to take house by house. Our artillery aimed very well.

Near the City Hall were lying the bodies of more than sixty Frenchmen and dying horses, who must have been kicking about among the wounded. One dead Frenchman still held a German helmet in his hand. Opposite this scene the field kitchens were installed, and drunken soldiers were singing cabaret songs at the top of their voices. A phonograph was going and Private Schreiner of the 6th Company was playing a waltz on his accordion.

In one corner a Munich painter was calmly sketching the scene. In front of every house the bodies of French and Germans were lying all jumbled in a heap. One young Frenchwoman, who had just come out of a cellar where she had been hiding, started to shout in the middle of the street, "Down with the Huns!" She was immediately bayoneted to death.

Many Frenchmen who had suffered only slight bullet wounds were, nevertheless, found dead, their breasts pierced by bayonets or their skulls shattered by musket blows. The order, given by the brigade, to give no quarter, had apparently been carried out by killing the wounded.

On the twenty-seventh we buried the dead. The identification tags of the German soldiers were carefully collected, but no one bothered about the French, who were thrown pell-mell into the trenches, which were then covered with earth. An affecting ceremony was held when Reserve Lieutenant Beck and Major Schmidt's son were buried.

A woman of the village went mad and was sent to a lunatic asylum.

"Why all this massacre? this slaughter? What do those people who started this war really want?" said Colonel Puder himself, much affected by the death of Schmidt's son, for whom he had cared a good deal.

14

Roye

On September 30th, 1914, we began the assault on Roye, the following troops taking part: 80th Fusiliers, 81st, 87th and 88th Infantry regiments of the 18th Army Corps; 82nd, 83rd, 84th and 85th Infantry regiments of the 21st Army Corps. There were thus eight infantry regiments, not to speak of the artillery, who had previously destroyed the town, especially the northern part. This bombardment did the French much harm. The orphanage, which had been turned into a hospital, was set on fire and many of the wounded were burned alive.

We left the town in pursuit of the French. But, almost immediately, we had to seek shelter in a sand pit on the road from Roye to Amiens.

As we were coming out of Roye, six French soldiers who had not been able to rejoin their comrades, surrendered. Major Schlegler of the 3rd Battalion immediately ordered those soldiers who were standing nearby to shoot these unfortunate men. But not one of them would execute this barbaric command and all tried to get away. Then Schlegler with his revolver killed one of the French soldiers, telling his men: "If you don't obey me I'll kill you like him." So the remaining five prisoners were shot down by the soldiers.

Schlegler however couldn't boast for long of his cruelty for hardly had the last prisoner fallen, when he himself was shot from the left. He in his turn fell dead. Lieutenant Abraham delivered the funeral oration: "Such a death was too fine for this murderer."

At almost the same time, Kédor was quite seriously wounded, his right forearm being shattered by a bullet. The soldiers did not hesitate to say that the man who had shot at him had unfortunately not aimed quite accurately enough. Everyone was happy about it, and men came up to him, laughing in their sleeves, while asking him hypocritically:

"Is the lieutenant suffering much?"

"No," answered Kédor, making a wry face.

"Come, come, buck up, and show that you are a Prussian officer," said Schmidt.

The latter showing his right hand, which had just then been slightly scratched by a passing shell, added:

"Now I've had enough of this rotten business—I'm going home. Let those who want to fight, fight! I don't!"

With these words Schmidt bade us goodbye and went to the field hospital. Right after this he left for Germany.

On the next day we heard that Colonel Puder had feigned illness, and that he also had left for Germany.

On our right the 25th Division had just taken possession of Soyécourt and Fresnay-les-Roye; the 87th took Parvillers.

On October 3rd, Lieutenant-Colonel Brentano was made commander of the 88th. Our new battalion chief was Captain Bartsch, a former orderly of the commander of the 21st Division.

On that day we took Quesnoy-en-Santerre, which was in ruins. We found nothing there but some poultry.

On October 7th, 1914, we were joined by reinforcements from Mayence. Among them were many soldiers who had already been wounded and had recovered. They did not show any enthusiasm.

October 5th, 1914, the new trench warfare commenced for us. Each battalion spent two days resting behind the lines and then four days in the trenches. We took up our quarters at Carrépuits, near Roye.

From October 13th to 26th we stayed before Quesnoy-en-Santerre.

During this time the troops had the big job of digging and arranging the trenches.

On October 27th, the French attacked us simultaneously from three sides and we lost our first line trenches. When we reported this bit of news to Lieutenant Anspach, regimental adjutant, he said: "You are a band of cowards, and you ought to be ashamed of being Germans." This Anspach, a fellow of Kédor's type, was himself the greatest coward in the regiment, and during engagements spent most of his time with the kitchens. Now he was almost always in a dugout.

On October 28th, the army corps ordered us to attack in order to regain our first line trenches. But the French gave us a fine reception. We were completely beaten, leaving four hundred prisoners, two guns and four machine guns in the hands of the enemy. We also lost all our telephone apparatus, and had to retreat still further to a place about two hundred metres north of Damery. We had had nothing to eat for two days and in front of us lay more than two hundred German corpses.

Finally, on November 2nd, we were relieved and sent to rest up at Soyécourt until November 6th. Now we had to turn the trenches into veritable forts. They had to be very deep, with communicating passageways. Comfortable and safe shelters were dug, both for officers and soldiers. There were doors, beds, chairs, mattresses. In our battalion we even had a piano. In December, electricity was installed. We were bombarded three times a day, but the shells did not do much damage. Every evening at nine o'clock the kitchens served us a hot meal, with tea, rum and other alcoholic drinks. At four in the morning they brought us hot coffee. Some men thought the life was quite bearable in comparison with our past sufferings.

15

The Germans at Roye

We now spent all our rest periods in Roye itself, in spite of the bombardments, and we remained there four days at a time.

A captain of the 80th was appointed governor of the city. He chose as mayor, a baker named Lefèvre, making him responsible for anything that might come up.

He had to draw up a list of all the inhabitants. All men from sixteen to forty-four were sent to Germany. Everyone else had to work for the Germans.

From December on all the women had to wash for the German soldiers. They earned one *franc* a day, paid by the city with vouchers, while all contributions had to be paid in silver or gold. Others had to make sand bags for the trenches. The men cleaned the streets and pulled down houses which were too badly damaged. Three, named by the mayor, acted as policemen.

As a matter of fact, the soldiers scarcely benefited at all from these rest periods, because every day they had one hour of company drill and at least two hours of battalion drill. At noon there was a medical inspection and a review; at one o'clock, patriotic singing. These prescribed duties had to be completed whether there was a bombardment or not.

Pretending that its steeple served as a target for the French artillery, the chief of staff ordered the church of Roye to be pulled down. It gave our engineers great pleasure to execute this order and soon only the foundations of the building were left. The chairs, stalls, the pulpit, confessionals and the pews were used for firewood by the soldiers.

These men preferred staying in the trenches to resting behind the lines; there they were really better sheltered from shells and furthermore did not have to drill.

The headquarters of the battalions and companies were permanently established in Roye. Every evening the sergeant majors came to the trenches to make their reports. Some men who were in with the non-commissioned officers were permanently attached to the office and walked about town, running after women or getting drunk. The kitchens and all the offices were also at Roye.

Many non-commissioned as well as commissioned officers obtained mistresses, almost always by threat and violence.

On December 22nd, our battalion celebrated Christmas two days ahead of time because on the twenty-fourth, we were to go back to the trenches and it was easier to have a celebration in the city. The captain who commanded the battalion in the absence of Schmidt (who, since his recovery, was commanding a detachment at Ham) addressed us as follows:

Dear Comrades:
We cannot celebrate this German holiday in the midst of our families. A world of enemies is marshalled against us in order to crush us and to seize our property, our wives, our children. Cowards that they are, they attacked us, but we've shown them that we're still the same old Germans who know how, sword in hand, to defend themselves and to protect their country. We are fighting, and we are ready to die for this holy cause. I ask you to shout with me:
    Long live his Majesty, Emperor William II.
    Hoch! Hoch! Hoch!"

Lieutenant Nolte of the 6th Uhlans thanked the captain and then some soldiers, grouped about a piano, started the song: "*Stille Nacht, Heilige Nacht.*"[1]

Just as they finished the last verse, a shell burst behind the wall, in the cemetery. Some soldiers who went out, came back and told us that several graves had been torn open and that the limbs and remains of the dead were scattered all over. This incident rather dampened our enjoyment of this "*Stille Nacht.*" When the celebration was over the soldiers went back to their companies, where they got beer and alcoholic drinks in such quantities that soon all of them were disgustingly drunk. They scattered through the streets, knocking at doors of houses where they knew that ladies were living. It is true, patrols had been ordered, as is usually done on such occasions, but the patrols themselves

---

1. Silent Night, Holy Night.

and their commanders were as drunk as the others and instead of punishing them, they helped them make a racket, and cause disorder.

In our battalion we had a "Beer Evening," at which all the officers were present. One knows what that is. As long as it lasts no other drinks ought to be taken. But there were so many other drinks that soon the officers were as badly off as the soldiers.

On December 24th, 1914, our new chief, Major Rogge, arrived. He was a former captain of the 65th Infantry from Cologne, whence he had been removed because he was too cruel to his men. Then he had been sent to the General Staff at Berlin, where he was made a battalion chief.

After this he became commander of the fort at Stuttgart. Rogge, who was a great coward and was coming to the front for the first time, was very much afraid of shells. When he heard one come, he writhed like a snake. The soldiers hardly ever laughed when shells were falling into the trenches, but no one who saw Rogge could help laughing at him. As soon as he arrived in our dugout his first question was: "Can one live here without being shot?" We tried to calm him by telling him that the enemy was not aiming at us, but at Roye. "You've done your work well," he told us, "everywhere I've been there's not a single house standing. What are all those graves which I saw along the road, marked with caps or helmets? Tell me something about a battle? What really happens?"

Then Lieutenant Nolte gave him a terrifying description in which nothing was lacking—the shattered limbs, cries of the wounded, frenzied horses, etc. "Just imagine, major, I saw one man walking in Tours, with his entrails coming out of his open belly."

Rogge did not wish to hear any more; he turned pale and drops of perspiration beaded his forehead. He did not eat anything during the entire meal. Nolte's talk had taken away his appetite. But he made up for it by drinking like a fish. Nolte signed to us to hide the wine bottles, because it seemed as though Rogge were going to leave nothing for the rest of us. It was astonishing to see how much that man could drink,—a professional would have been afraid to compete with him.

If it had occurred to the French to attack us that evening there would not have been much resistance, although we had taken the precaution of doubling sentries.

On December 31st, we celebrated New Year's Eve at Gruny, near Soyécourt, where we were resting. We heard the muffled roar of cannon and the sky was ablaze with red and white rockets. This did not hinder the soldiers from joyously firing their guns into the air in honour of the New Year which was to bring us peace.

In the evening every one was royally drunk. In our battalion we were all gathered about Rogge, who presided. A drunken soldier tried to force his way in with his gun. After he had been thrown out, he came back with a sabre, and if it had not been for Dr. Wolkewiz, who grabbed my arm, I should have been stabbed to the heart. Rogge wished to have him shot but his comrades had already hidden him. This little incident, however, did not prevent us from going on drinking beer, wine and liquors. Soon several officers rolled under the table. Rogge was happy.

The soldiers were doing the same thing. They fought and made a deafening racket all night long. If there had been an alarm we could not have assembled even a single company.

On January 2nd, a French aviator hovered over our lines for a long while. Our artillery aimed at him in vain. Shrapnel burst about him, but he was not hit. After he had found out what he wished to know, he rose and returned to the French lines, to report. Our officers called the artillery "pigs"—"trash," etc., because of their awkwardness, but they only laughed. They had no doubt done their best because, for every aeroplane brought down, the battery received a barrel of beer.

A few days afterwards we received regimental orders to sound unexpected night alarms, whenever the battalion was not on the march. Under Schmidt these alarms had always taken place at nine o'clock, so that the men could have a night's rest. No one ever failed to report and Schmidt was always pleased. But with Rogge, everything was different.

On January 2nd, 1915, we celebrated the first six months of the war. Sergeant Major Hauser, secretary of the battalion, went to Rogge in the name of all the non-commissioned officers to ask him not to have the alarm sounded that night, because the non-commissioned officers were going to have a little party. Rogge promised. This is how he kept his promise.

It seems that the non-commissioned officers drank a great deal. But with us, as soon as one emptied his glass it would have to be filled again, for Rogge's great pleasure was to make all his guests drunk. Some young lieutenants asked permission to go to bed, but Rogge would let no one leave. About 3 a. m. Lieutenant von Stein was so drunk that he had to be carried to bed. He looked like a dead man, for he no longer moved a muscle. This amused Rogge very much. At four o'clock Rogge ordered us to sound the alarm. We reminded him of his promise, but he answered, "This band of peasants has had enough sleep; they must not forget that they are soldiers." The orderlies left immediately to warn the companies. We tried our best to awake von Stein, but in vain. He did not stir. Rogge then told us to pour a pail of water over his head. This measure met with no success; von Stein continued to snore. So Rogge said to us, "Leave that pig there, the drunkard alone, since there is no way of waking him."

We repaired to the meeting place, where the companies were already assembled. But the soldiers were grumbling and many were missing. Private Merkel, of the 8th Company, whom Lieutenant Nolte reminded that he had forgotten his saucepan, answered;

"Yes, Lieutenant, but I'm not drunk as some others are." The officer commanding the 5th Company was missing, but when Sergeant Major Saltenberger reported this to the chief, the latter answered: "Go to the devil."

Rogge collected the commissioned and non-commissioned officers and said to them: "Gentlemen, this is disgraceful. If you and I can report, I am sure these peasants can do as much."

Sergeant Major Saltenberger assembled the non-commissioned officers of the 5th Company and imitating Rogge addressed them in the following manner:

> Gentlemen, I'm very much pleased with your answer to the alarm. I promised you there would be none, but nevertheless, I had to disturb your sleep. I regret that the commander of the 5th Company should have been absent, for that's a black mark for us. I advise you, gentlemen, not to imitate him, for we superior officers, whatever our rank, ought always to set a good example. Good night, gentlemen. Break ranks.

Rogge, who had heard everything, was furious but could do nothing. A few days later, Sergeant Major Saltenberger was declared unfit for service, by the doctor, because of his nerves, and was sent back to Germany.

Our new position (between Parvillers and Dumery) was more dangerous. All day and all night shells rained down on the trenches. Every day we had fifteen or twenty killed and wounded.

On February 12th, we were sent to Nesles for a two weeks' rest. The city had not suffered much but the inhabitants complained bitterly of the troops, who were plundering everything.

On February 24th, Lieutenant-Colonel Brentano reported sick and left for Germany. Rogge was made commander of the 88th. He "cleaned out the regiment," as he said. Anspach, the regimental adjutant, was made commander of the 7th Company, and von Stein took his place with Rogge. Nolte, although only a reserve officer, was made Rogge's *aide-de-camp*—an unheard of thing, but Rogge could not do without him. Schiellein, a wine merchant from Mayence, who up to now had been in the quartermaster's department, lost his place and was sent with Anspach to the 7th Company. Rogge did this to avenge himself on Schiellein because he owed the latter a large sum and thought to get rid of his creditor by sending him under fire.

A short time before he had asked Schiellein for several cases of champagne, and the latter had refused them to him, because he knew that he would never be able to collect for them. Reserve Lieutenant Rickert, a theological student, was made adjutant of the 2nd Battalion. That same day, Rickert, Loffelhardt and I went to see Major Schmidt, commanding a detachment of young recruits at Ham, to talk over all these changes with him. He told us that there would be a great review in two days, and that he would then ask to be returned to his battalion.

The review did, in fact, take place before Grand Duke Louis of Hesse who said that he was very well satisfied with Schmidt's recruits and awarded the latter a medal for bravery. The training of the recruits was over, so Schmidt asked and obtained permission to resume command of his former battalion. All the soldiers were pleased, for they cared a lot for him and called him "Papa Schmidt."

Of course, relations between Schmidt and Rogge became very much strained. They hated each other and Rogge made use of every opportunity to criticize Schmidt.

16

The Formation of the 56th Division

On March 5th, we were ordered to throw away our guns and ammunition, because we were going to get Russian guns instead. We were also told to move our camp farther on, because the three battalions were to take up quarters on the next day in three villages between Ham and St. Quentin. The 2nd Battalion was to go to Fluquières. The convoys that were bringing ammunition to the batteries of the 210th, stationed at Soyéncourt were there too.

Loffelhardt and I called on the governor of Ham who was also the lieutenant of artillery in charge of the distribution of ammunition. He was living in the *château* at Ham. He greeted us pleasantly, and told us that Major Schmidt and his staff were welcome to live with him in the *château*. That night, for the first time since August 20th, 1914, we did not hear the guns.

In the town, where we went to find quarters for our men, we were badly received by the inhabitants who complained that they had had to entertain soldiers continuously for the last five months. One man said to me: "We no longer know how to protect our wives and daughters. All the Germans try to get mistresses, in any manner possible. The *commandant* always supports the soldiers, and besides he himself keeps a young girl whom he has made his mistress in his *château* by force."

When we saw the *commandant* again we mentioned this matter. Laughing, he asked us if our officers also hunted women and were in love with some little French girls. Loffelhardt told him that we were a fighting unit, and not in the quartermaster's department—also that we waged war on soldiers, not on civilians and above all not on women.

"My friend, you're amusing," replied the lieutenant. "In any case, I'm prudently going to hide my angel so that no harm will come to her!"

With that, he left us, to do as he had said. Who was "his angel"? Probably some unhappy girl whom he was holding in the *château*.

We told Schmidt about this, but he only shrugged his shoulders and said that everyone makes war in his own way. As the officer made our stay at Ham as pleasant as possible, Schmidt said nothing to him about it.

On March 8th we were quartered at Bohain where we remained for some time.

On March 11th we handled our Russian guns for the first time. Instruction in their use began immediately. We could not understand why they gave us such poor ones.

On March 15th, we received the following order:

"The 35th, 88th, and 118th Infantry, the latter two regiments forming part of the 18th Corps, will make up the 112th Brigade of Infantry which will be part of the 56th Division. Each battalion is to furnish twenty men who will form a company of cyclists and accompany the staff of the division. The 55th Division will also comprise a squadron of the 13th Hussars and the 111th and 112th Artillery regiments, to each of which shall be attached three heavy batteries besides their regular ones."

The commander of the new division was a General Eberhard, who had been the instructor of Prince Joachim of Prussia. The commander of the brigade was Colonel Munter, who had commanded the 41st Brigade since December, 1914.

On March 19th, we were ordered to be ready to leave in the morning.

Our battalion, which thus far had behaved pretty decently, spoiled its reputation, on leaving Bohain by stealing a large quantity of wine. Some men of the 7th Company broke open the door of a cellar, which had been sealed by the commandant, and took possession of all the wine they found there. Almost the whole company was drunk. The sergeant major, named Dombach, had two hundred bottles of wine loaded on a wagon, expecting to drink them later on with his friends. But he did not touch one of them, for we told Major Schmidt about it and he ordered it all to be taken for the battalion staff. So after all we were the ones to drink the stolen wine.

At 2 p. m. we took the train for Cateau, Charleville, Sedan and Attigny, where we were to stop.

The journey was gloomy, and the train no longer bore inscriptions, like there were on that which took us to Luxemburg in August,

1914,—"Express for Paris," or "Declarations of War received here."

Nature alone seemed oblivious to the war, for the meadows and grain fields were just beginning to turn green.

17

Givry

About 10 p.m. we were ordered to make ready to leave Attigny for Givry, where we were to stay until further orders. Loffelhardt and I set out to seek quarters for our staff and to find stable room for one hundred and twenty horses.

The governor, a cavalry captain, thought fit to stick Schmidt in a dirty room, which was already occupied by a sick woman, while the rest of us, the doctor included, had to sleep with the men in the barn.

Schmidt's rage may be imagined. He was all the more angry because right opposite to him a young cavalry lieutenant was strutting about a hotel, all by himself. The next day he told the governor that he wished to have the hotel vacated immediately, in order to make room for himself and his staff. The magnificent lieutenant was ordered to pack himself off before noon. The latter then started to strip the hotel and to have all the furniture carried outside, not forgetting the "German stove." Knowing that it would be impossible to find even a single chair in the village, I warned Schmidt of the lieutenant's action, and he stationed a sentinel with loaded rifle in front of the hotel with orders to shoot any one who attempted to carry off anything whatsoever. He told me to inform the lieutenant of this order. No sooner had I delivered my message than this fellow yelled at me insolently:

"And who are you, my good fellow? Get out of my way immediately or I'll strike you in the face with my crop."

It was in vain that I told him that I was only giving him Schmidt's message. He wouldn't listen to anything I said.

Schmidt, told of this, sent me back with Rickert whom he ordered to bring the lieutenant to him, by force if necessary.

When he saw Rickert, the cavalry lieutenant saluted him politely and followed him without any protest.

We had never seen Schmidt in such a rage. He shouted so that all the soldiers, who happened to be in the street ran to hide themselves; they expected that he would strike the lieutenant with his crop, and they did not want to have to testify against him.

As soon as the lieutenant appeared, Schmidt yelled at him: "How dare you, you miserable lazy fellow, insult and threaten anyone who comes in my name? Stand still, not one step or I'll accuse you of insubordination. Give me your name! What's your business here? How can you have the cheek to strip that house?" In exasperation Schmidt brandished his crop.

The lieutenant answered: "I have the honour to report to the major that I was having the beds, the piano and all the furniture removed as well as the stove and all the wines of the place, because I consider them to be my property."

"Aren't you ashamed," answered Schmidt, "to lie that way—But no, you're right—we're just beginning to find out that all of you in the quartermaster's department and in the rear are nothing but a band of shameless robbers, who spoil the reputation of the German Army, while we are having our jaws broken in the trenches. See that the hotel is in order in one hour's time and that not a pin is missing, or I'll have you reported for stealing and that'll teach you to cut up and defy brave soldiers like us who have just come from the front."

Once we were settled in this fellow's quarters Schmidt asked me to try my utmost to find some eggs for breakfast, so I went to the house of a villager who had some chickens.

"I'll tell you, sir," he said, "I've got some chickens, but I'm not allowed to sell them, give them away or eat them myself, and the same with the eggs. Everything is at the disposal of the governor, who sends an orderly every week to see if I still have my quota. If a single one is missing, I've got to pay one hundred *marks*," Schmidt, who was in the humour for putting an end to abuses, started a row at the governor's house and made him rescind his command. The grateful villager sent Schmidt a basket of eggs.

At Givry, I for the first time witnessed a case of insubordination. A soldier threw his gun down in front of Lieutenant Schaller, commanding the 2nd Company, saying:

"Here's your old gun—Stick me in prison; I'm tired of being treated like a kid."

Schaller had the man arrested and taken before the major after drill.

"Well, my good fellow," said Schmidt, "what's got into you? I'm going to give you a taste of the punishment you deserve, but because of your wife and children. Lieutenant Schaller 's complaint shall go no further."

The man was tied to a tree with his hands behind his back and a sentinel with a loaded gun was stationed near him. The sentinel sat in a chair smoking a cigar, which showed the soldier that he had acted like a fool and that it was better to obey orders.

On the twenty-second, we were ordered to Savigny because our division was soon going to return to the trenches. About two o'clock Loffelhardt and I wanted to go into Vouziers, but a policeman stopped us. No one was allowed to enter the city just then because the emperor was reviewing the Guard. Extraordinary precautions were taken to insure the *Kaiser's* safety. A squadron of German aeroplanes flew above Vouziers during the whole of his stay, and he was protected by a regular iron wall. On the following day, the *Ardennes Journal*, a German paper edited in French, announced that His Majesty had gone to the firing line (Vouziers was then hardly twenty kilometres from the front) and had distributed Iron Crosses among his brave soldiers of the Guard (the same who had run away at Rheims and who had lost the fort at Brimont which we had been obliged to retake) .

Vouziers was often bombarded by French aviators. The General Headquarters of General von Einem, Commandant of the Third Army, were located there.

After the review we entered Vouziers. The soldiers of the Guard were walking about the streets, most of them drunk, because beer had been generously distributed after the review.

At Savigny, Kédor, who had had enough of the trenches, pretended that his wounded arm hindered him from riding horseback, and was sent to Mayence.

18

In Champagne

On March 25th, 1915, we took possession of our new sector between Le Mesnil-les-Hurlus and Ville-sur-Tourbe, popularly called "The Devil's Hole." It was a nasty position, a place specially made for breaking one's neck. One was hardly sheltered there and had almost no communication with the rear. During the four days that we stayed in the first line trenches, we could get nothing from the kitchens. Each man, before he set out, got a threepound loaf of bread, a bit of fat (butter or cheese), his canteen and two bottles filled with coffee. This had to do him for four days. The men were prepared to attack, their cloaks roiled up and their bags filled with hand grenades. Behind this position there was a second one called "support." Finally in the third line trenches were the reserves.

We were immediately sent to the first line. Never since the beginning of the war had we been in such a horrible place. We were surrounded on all sides by the bodies of dead Germans and Frenchmen, and since some trenches had a depth of hardly sixty centimetres, we frequently had to use the dead as bulwarks. All those bodies which had not been buried were a terrible sight. I do not know what prevented us from going mad. The French lines were hardly twenty to thirty metres from us. Because the two lines, far from being straight, made all sorts of turns, death approached us from all sides without our ever being able to tell whether the bullets were French or German. The trenches were so shallow that it was impossible to walk upright, and we had to crawl or double up.

We had no shelter, indeed it would have been useless for the French artillery, which never stopped firing, would have destroyed it and besides how could the materials have been brought to us? Every single man who wished to reach the trenches had to slip in between the dead.

In various places arms and legs sticking up from the ground helped to point the way. For instance, we said, "A few metres to the left you will see a hand sticking up from the ground wearing a wedding ring: the left wing of the battalion is about twenty metres in a straight line from there." In order to shoot we had to push aside bodies right and left, and since no one ever knew where they were shooting, because of the irregular line, many soldiers killed their own comrades.

Most of all, we were afraid of aeroplane bombs. We heard them start off, then all of a sudden we saw faintly a sort of a bottle way up in the sky—which, slowly describing a parabola, landed in the trenches and exploded. If we could have sought a shelter as soon as we saw them coming we might have had a chance, but where were we to go? When the bomb had burst all the men, who had lain down flat on the ground, raised themselves in order to see the damage. It was a terrible sight. One time, I remember I saw two men cut in tiny pieces and a third was so terribly riddled that his body was like a skimmer. The head of one of the dead men could not be found. Since no one could be buried, the bodies were simply thrown in front or in back of the trenches. It is impossible to describe our sufferings and our anguish during those four days.

At last the moment of our escape from this hell arrived. But it took us more than three hours to get out of the trenches because we had to take great precautions. The battle field was really continuously lit up by French and German rockets and in order to get away we had to creep in between the bodies in single file so that we looked like a procession of ghosts. If one of our men was wounded we had to let him die there, for it would have been impossible to carry him to the second line, without risking our own lives. All of us had only one idea, to get something to eat as soon as possible for we were literally dying of hunger, since almost all of our provisions had been eaten during the first two days. At last we came to a place where a machine gun was set up and where the ground allowed us to walk upright and to advance more rapidly. Unfortunately the French shells rained on, and killed many more of our men.

Finally this bad half hour was over and we reached the auxiliary position. This really formed a part of the first line, for we were still only sixty or eighty metres from the French, but here there were shelters and we were in relative safety. The aerial bombs could no longer reach us, but the shells and, above all, the shrapnel poured down on us unceasingly; the stretcher bearers and nurses had so much to do that they could not even take time to eat. The wounded were transported to the rear, and the dead were buried in the regimental cemetery, prepared behind the shelter of Schmidt's staff. A helmet or a fragment of the shell that killed him was placed on each man's grave.

One day I was present at the funeral of a non-commissioned officer of the 2nd Company, who had just been killed. Shells rained on us from all sides, while several German aviators who had just arrived on the scene attempted to attack the French. While the soldiers were singing a sort of a funeral hymn and were lowering the body into the grave, a bomb fell in our midst killing six men and wounding just about as many. We left the body without continuing the ceremonies, and every one hurried into the shelter, while a regular storm of French shells beat down on the cemetery.

At the end of eight days, if you count the time we spent in the first line trenches, we were sent to Ripont for four days' rest. It would have been better to have been left where we were, for there was no shelter at Ripont and the French artillery fire was just as bad. Nevertheless, we were able to get a shave for the first time in twelve days. When the artillery was not firing, the soldiers played cards or cleaned their new Russian guns. These often went off by themselves, and caused several accidents. On account of the steady fire we did not have to drill.

When our rest period was over, we had to return to our "Devil's Hole," where during our first four days we had lost fifty-eight dead and as many wounded. All the soldiers were downcast and discouraged. We had hardly arrived when Rogge instructed us to be prepared for a night attack. The men got a mixture of tea and about ninety *per cent,* alcohol. Our attack, which met with no success, was led by Captain Baron von der Recke, who was seriously wounded. On the following day there came an order from the 8th Reserve Army Corps, in which we had been incorporated. The general complained of the cowardice of the battalion, which had failed in the attack, and impressed on us the fact that we had to make still greater effort to drive back the French who had succeeded in penetrating our part of the lines. The soldiers were broken hearted and many wrote home, thinking that it was perhaps for the last time.

That evening the tea contained even more alcohol. Besides, a little while before the attack each group of eight men received a bottle of cognac, so that they all became veritable beasts. At eleven o'clock we crawled out of our holes like ghosts, slipping in between the corpses. We lay on our stomachs, our knives held in our teeth, and our bags full of hand grenades, clutching our rifles, until the moment when the order was given to spring forward. Our men acted like wild beasts. Orders had been given to spare no one, and even the wounded were killed. But the French defended themselves like lions and we had to give way. The only result was, that about half of the battalion were killed or wounded or taken prisoners. We had to go back to our lines creeping in between the dead. French and Germans shot bright rockets into the air, so that the night was turned into day. The 35th and 80th regiments on our left and the 18th on our right never stopped firing all night long and the artillery and French machine guns made a great disturbance on their side. Schmidt said: "Isn't there a bullet for us too? When will this slaughter end?"

This time we were sent to rest between Gratreuil and Ripont in a place where the engineers had dug huge subterranean shelters, each one holding two hundred and fifty men. These shelters were covered with earth and tree trunks, and were out of the way of the shells.

We had hardly arrived there when an order of the 56th Division commanded Schmidt to report sick and to leave immediately for Vouziers. Rogge had complained, accusing Schmidt of having through his incompetence caused our night attacks to fail. Schmidt was sent back, but he was looking for nothing better, and had several times refused to execute Rogge's orders. Once he had even said in my presence, that he had had enough of it all and that he only wished to be sent back to his family in Wiesbaden.

Eger, who, at the beginning of the war, had only been a lieutenant, was appointed to fill Schmidt's place, as battalion chief. He immediately acted like a brute. On the first day of his command he ordered out the band, and forced the battalion to goose step, while the shells poured down on them. As each shell whizzed by, the men trembled but Eger pretended not to notice it. He shouted at them, saying that what they were doing was not a goose step, but a regular funeral march. It was only too true, for all of a sudden a shell burst to the left, killing three men of the 8th Company. Those standing near by were covered with blood and some of them were wounded, and fled.

Nevertheless, Eger continued the parade as though nothing had happened, and ordered the names of the fifteen or twenty men who had disappeared to be noted, so that they might be severely punished. As to the three dead, Eger pronounced their funeral oration by saying to the other soldiers: "Take away those three pigs who didn't know enough to fall in battle and hurry up about it because our drill isn't over yet—Will you hurry? If you don't I'll run over you with my horse, and knock you all in a heap, you band of peasants."

In this way Eger celebrated his promotion as commander of the 2nd Battalion. Six months later, while still in Champagne, he did not himself know enough to have himself killed by a French soldier, for a *German bullet* found his heart.

When he went into the trenches, he always had something to criticize. He had the soldiers build a little hut above his shelter "to breathe a little fresh air," he said. He only stayed there when the French were not firing. They destroyed his hut before two days were over. The following day a note was found nailed to one of the beams which was still standing: "If you wish to take an airing, go into the trenches instead of sitting down in front of the dead and laughing at them. We are patriots, who are fighting for our country, not cowards."

Eger, half mad with anger, said all these pigs had eaten and drunk too much and that he would find a way to kill every one of them. "This evening," he said, "I'm going to treat them all as they deserve."

This was his vengeance, a regular drunkard's vengeance. Every day the companies got some rum. That evening he had only six bottles distributed to each company. The rest was drunk in our shelter. Eger had invited all the officers. Soon he and Lieutenant Boettger, eighteen years old, became so intoxicated that they got into an argument and wanted to come to blows. Boettger was thrown out, and left in the trench, as dead, so that the fresh air might revive him. Eger was pushed into a corner. Lieutenant Tietz of the 6th Company and Lieutenant Schaeffer of the 7th even wished to tie him, in order to keep him quiet.

The German papers are full of tales of such rows, which are always attributed to the Russians. But, nevertheless, they sometimes also occurred in our army, the effect moreover of rum, stolen from the soldiers.

For several days, a rumour had been current that we were going to be replaced and that we would be sent to the Vosges or to Arras. No one knew just exactly what was going to happen. Finally, on May 2nd, 1915, we were relieved by the 65th Reserve Regiment. We were ordered to entrain on May 3rd, for Somme-Py. We did not know where we were going but we were all happy in the thought of leaving this hell, where so many of us had been killed. About six o'clock it was announced that Lodz had just been captured by the Germans. All the assembled soldiers yelled "Hurrah!" But a storm of French shells fell on us and the hurrahs were replaced by the screams and groans of the wounded. There were two non-commissioned officers, Muller and Wolff, both of the 6th Company; one had his right arm shot off, the other both legs shattered. Both of them were expecting their commission as second lieutenants.

In the evening of May 2nd, we left for Somme-Py.

19

Across Germany and Austria

On May 2nd, 1915, about seven o'clock we reached the ruins of Somme-Py. We had some soup, and then got into the train which was waiting for us and was to leave about two o'clock. But first we attended to the loading of the baggage and the horses. It feels queer to travel without knowing where you're going. Some said we were going to Arras, because the men from Wurtemburg could not hold out any longer. Others professed to know from a reliable source that we were bound for Alsace. Those who said nothing were the most sensible, for even the station officials only knew the name of the next station, where we were to stop for something to eat. Our train was run as far as Sedan by soldiers of the 3rd Engineers. After that, we were in the hands of state officials.

At Sedan there was a two hours' stop. The station was guarded by soldiers and no one was allowed to go into the city. We were ordered to remove our chevrons and insignia because no one was supposed to know who we were or where we came from. That was an excellent way to confound spies.

At ten o'clock we left Sedan and the following morning, at four o'clock, we passed through Sarrelouis, where coffee was served. The day before everything around us had spelled ruin and desolation. Today we were back in civilization, far from the war and the thunder of the guns. We could hardly believe our eyes. The ladies of the Red Cross were very sympathetic when we told them that we came from Champagne. The coffee was excellent and the soldiers drank as much as they liked of it. At six o'clock we rode on toward Kaiserslautern. Now we were sure that we were bound for Russia, either to the Carpathians or on into Serbia. The soldiers were delighted, for they knew very well that the fighting was not nearly so severe on the Eastern front, as it had been in France. They sang and seemed suddenly to have forgotten all the horrors of the war. What seemed strangest to us was that we no longer heard the whizzing of shells above our heads.

At eleven o'clock we arrived at Kaiserslautern, where Paymaster Herbert, Rickert and I were ordered to distribute provisions among the various companies. It all went very well and quickly, because everything had been prepared in advance. A meal had been prepared in the station restaurant for us, and you may be sure we did not leave a single crumb on our plates.

After dinner we took a little walk on the station platform to limber up. Many wounded were coming in from Argonne and the Vosges where they had suffered a great deal. A crowd had formed around one of the stretcher bearers. I went there and a Red Cross nurse told me: "It's a wounded Frenchman, who doesn't know any German." I drew nearer and spoke French to this soldier, whom I told that he had nothing to fear, because really it was only the English who were hated in Germany. The man told me that in France every one was sure of winning the war, and of getting back Alsace and Lorraine.

All the way from Klein-Steinheim to Hanau the soldiers were joyfully anticipating passing through our own depot. They hoped to have the chance to see and kiss their parents and their wives. All along the tracks a crowd of civilians had rushed up to see the 2nd Battalion go by. I don't know how they learned of our coming. The train proceeded very slowly in the midst of the hurrahs of soldiers and civilians.

At the station, wounded officers of our battalion were waiting for us. Relatives and friends had been admitted to the platform. One may imagine what heartrending scenes took place. The meal served to the men was excellent—by far the best of the whole trip. Civilians overwhelmed us with dainties and presents.

We left Hanau at eight o'clock, on May 5th. We passed through Chemnitz and Goerlitz. In the latter place the stop was rather long, the station being filled with the militia so that no one could go out. Two of our men succeeded in sneaking through the guard. They were stopped by the militia and taken to the station by six men with fixed bayonets. Eger asked them:

"Why did you go out?"

"We wanted to do some shopping," they answered.

"And you had yourselves arrested by these civilians." (This was Eger's term for all non-combatant troops.) "Aren't you ashamed to be in my battalion and to get yourself locked up by those donkeys who haven't been to war at all?"

Eger sent away the two soldiers without punishing them, because he hated all stay-at-home troops.

The food prepared for the soldiers was not fit to eat. The men complained and said that they would raid the station kitchen if they weren't allowed to eat in the city. The officers tasted the soup and told the station-master that it was scandalous and wicked to treat soldiers just back from the front in this way.

In spite of that no one was allowed to go out, because we were to leave at ten o'clock.

At Koenigshutte we had our last meal on German soil, and entered Austria. We passed through Lansashutte, Kallowitz and Magsolwitz. We were in Galicia.

At Wadowicz we were served by the Austrian Red Cross ladies who were even more amiable than the Germans. They told us to lick the Russians good and plenty, so that the war would soon be over.

We met a train stuffed full with Russian prisoners. In some coaches the sick and wounded were lying all in a heap on a bit of straw. No one bothered about them.

On May 7th, we were at Neu Sandec and on the eighth, we got off at Biezc. From Neu Sandec to Biezc the train proceeded very cautiously, because the Russians had torn up some of the tracks during their retreat.

In the depot at Biezc we saw huge piles of ammunition, machine guns and a considerable amount of other material, which the Russians had abandoned in their retreat. Then we understood why we had been given Russian guns. Biezc was in ruins. War was to begin again for us.

Our trip across Germany and Austria had lasted five days.

The 56th Division was to assemble here and await orders.

Now we knew that we were to pull the chestnuts out of the fire for our dear allies, the Austrians, many of whom, as we shall see later on, did not themselves wish to fire on the Russians.

20

In Galicia

We of the staff could not take a moment's rest, for we had to study maps and receive orders. We were going to take up quarters at Jablonica. We went ahead to prepare them. Our maps were not bad, but as the Russians had built new roads during the war, we lost our way twice. People of whom we asked directions would not open their mouths, and looked as though they were making fun of us. Our dear allies even refused to give us water. The roads were wretched. We had to carry our bicycles, sinking up to our knees in sand.

Because a battalion of the 118th Infantry and a hospital unit had preceded us, we could find no quarters for our men. It was all we could do to hunt out a place to house Eger who did not like to sleep in the open. The place we found for him was an unbelievably filthy hovel, where about ten persons, men, women and children, slept in a single room, all jumbled together in two beds filled with straw.

A frightful, musty odour greeted us. A number of chickens ran unmolested around the room. We opened doors and windows, and began to clean up a bit, and chased the chickens out. A woman brought us sheets and fresh straw, and sent the family away. She only consented to this on the condition that she would be well paid; but she is still waiting for her money. Eger made a face when he saw his quarters. In spite of the airing the smell was awful. These people were accustomed to live on dung heaps, and this explains why there were not more epidemics. Moreover, wherever we went in Galicia it was the same; the people were repulsively dirty, and covered with lice.

Eger, Rickert, Loffelhardt and I had to sleep in this hovel. When we went in we found a young man and woman sleeping in our bed. Eger chased them out. The rest of the family were lying on tables. Two old women slept on straw mattresses in front of the fireplaces.

We could not close an eye all night for lack of air and because of the "cooties," which did not give us a moment's peace. On the following day we saw one of the women carefully inspecting the head of another woman. In answer to our question, she said she was looking for lice. We had obtained permanent guests during that night in the hovel. These new companions did not leave us during our entire stay on the Eastern front.

At ten o'clock we left for Jaslo. The battalion's march was very fatiguing, for the men were continually sinking into the sand. Rickert, Loffelhardt and I, who had gone ahead on horseback, met the famous General Mackensen, whose quarters were about two kilometres away. All the troops along the road cheered him. He passed by without saying anything, as though he were weary of hearing soldiers shout.

The Russians had blown up the great railroad bridge at the southern entrance of the village. The troops crossed the Wistoka over a pontoon bridge, built by our engineers. In order to proceed more rapidly we found a ford which our horses could cross easily enough.

The Jaslo station was completely destroyed, we could not tell whether by the Russians or the Austrians themselves. In any case it had not been done by those Russians who had just evacuated the town about four days ago because we could see that the work had been done long, long before.

The Galicians who stayed behind did not speak very badly of the Russians, except the Jews, who told frightful tales but at the same time seized the opportunity to cheat us terribly whenever we bought anything of them.

As the inhabitants did not understand German, we talked to them by means of signs. Rickert got down on all fours to show that he wanted a stable.

On May 10th we rejoined the rest of the division.

The 188th led, followed by the 88th Infantry, and the 111th and 112th Artillery; the 35th Infantry brought up the rear.

An Austrian regiment was marching alongside of us. Some of these men shouted insults at us in Polish.

"Cowards!" answered our soldiers. "You've gotten a good licking from the Russians, and now we've had to come to your help in this dirty country, full of lice."

The officers forbade the men quarrelling with the Austrians.

Columns of Russian prisoners were also going along the same road. Rogge, upon seeing them, said to his men: "Do me the favour of letting those pigs carry your knapsacks, and you take their tobacco and cigarettes." In an instant the soldiers had obeyed his order. There were many wounded among the Russian prisoners.

Everywhere the roads were in a terrible state, and the men, weighed down by their knapsacks, advanced painfully slowly, sinking in the sand. Eger spoke harshly to them, saying that they weren't making rapid enough progress. He even threatened to cut down their rations. Howls of protest and cries of anger were heard among the soldiers. "Pack of thieves," they all yelled at once, "as it is we've got almost nothing to eat, because you take all the best stuff, and now you're shooting off your mouths, because you're on horseback and we've got to carry our knapsacks, while we trudge along in the sand. But one day the war'll be over and then we'll see who'll be the boss—who'll be the bravest then!"

Eger was furious and spurred his horse on the men, holding his crop aloft and wounding one man with it. Nevertheless, and although they all hated him no one dared move to give Eger a lesson. Rogge, whom he told about the whole affair, approved of it and said: "Those pigs need a bullet in their hides, it's a regular mutiny. The beasts don't even deserve to fall in battle." On hearing this we wondered who *did* deserve to fall in battle, for it was a well known fact that Rogge never ventured in a place where he might be under fire.

German newspapers reported that the Galicians had been maltreated by the Russians. We saw that this was absolutely false. During the six months of the Russian occupation everything was peaceful. The fields were cultivated and everything was ready for the harvest. It was the Germans, the so-called liberators, who on the contrary destroyed everything. And so the Galicians were very displeased that we had come to rid them of the Russians. Soldiers offered women rings and jewellery stolen in France, if they would give themselves up to them. Rogge himself ordered a good looking young woman to be brought to him for the night, saying: "What has been done by the Russians can be done over again by the Germans." Eger was certainly a tyrant and a brute, but he never showed himself to be the coward and satyr that Rogge was. Such conduct only served to spur on the soldiers who followed women into the churches where they had taken refuge. The Galicians will never forget their liberators.

The Jews never missed a chance to rob us and always asked exorbitant prices for the goods they offered. In order to trick us the better they began by flattering us, saying: "Oh, what brave and generous soldiers the Germans are—oh, how great and good your emperor is! How happy we are that you've delivered us from the Russians. The whole world admires the Germans...."

But some soldiers who wanted a certain object did not hesitate to take it without paying, if the Jews asked too big a price. In such cases, Eger always sided with his men.

"You damned dirty Jews," he said to the merchants who complained to him, "how dare you cheat Prussian soldiers?"

The Jews had the cheek to answer:

"Captain, the Russians have robbed us so that we must sell our goods a little higher in order not to go bankrupt."

Eger was furious, and ordered them to be off at once, or he would have them beaten by the soldiers. The children of Abraham departed hurriedly. Eger formally authorized his soldiers to take anything they wished without paying for it, if they thought the Jews were asking exorbitant prices. One can easily understand that the soldiers no longer refrained from stealing.

21

First Battles in Galicia

On June 15th, 1915, we were quartered at Albigowa where we were to stay two days to make our final preparations for going into the first line trenches.

But at 4 a. m. we were ordered to leave immediately for Markowa, where we would find the general staff of the division.

Four hours later we found there the following order signed by the lieutenant general commanding the 56th Division:

"The 88th Infantry will march at the head of the 56th Division. No precautions must be neglected because the regiment is about to meet the enemy. I hope that the regiment will do its duty here as it has done it in France. I count absolutely on the brave and heroic soldiers of the 88th. This order is to be read to the troops."

The horrors of war were to begin again for us.

We left in the direction of the San and passed through the village of Przeworsk, where there were a great many wounded, for a fierce struggle had just taken place.

Since most of our German horses had fallen owing to the heat and the bad roads, we had replaced them by little Russian ponies which were much hardier.

In spite of the battle the inhabitants had chosen to remain behind. The Russians, during the entire time of their occupation of Galicia, had devastated nothing and had scrupulously respected persons and property. But we and the Austrians were now laying waste all the country. Dr. Meiniecke said to us:

"It's not surprising that these people hate us. Just consider! The Russians did not touch their houses, their gardens or their fields. We, on the contrary, destroy everything. In the houses and villages from which the Russians had just retired I did not see any trace of pillage as in France and Belgium. After all these people have a right to complain about us."

But Eger answered him:

"Doctor, we're going to show these Slavish pigs, these lice-infested peasants, what stuff war is made of. We who have fought the Russians and French will force them to go down on their knees to us for a piece of bread. If I ask one of these brutes for a drink and get no response, I strike him across the face with my crop. I'll show them what a Prussian soldier is!"

No one said a word because Eger could brook no contradiction. He was a real Prussian, after Kaiser Wilhelm's own heart.

At six o'clock we were eighteen kilometres to the north of Jaroslav and on the banks of the San. The day before, the Russians had retreated, leaving their unburied dead behind. The struggle must have been desperate, and no mercy shown for the skulls of many of the dead had been smashed by musket blows.

We crossed the San on a bridge built by our engineers. Hardly had we reached the other side, when Rogge ordered us to form in skirmish line. That was foolish, for as yet we had no idea where the enemy was and we didn't even know if we were to attack him.

Rogge assembled the officers in back of a little hill and addressed them as follows;

> At last we are going to match ourselves against the Russians. I hope, gentlemen, that you will exert yourselves to the utmost, to spare us the shame of defeat. During the combat I ask you to keep in close touch with me, so that I can from time to time give you the divisional orders. Captain Eger with the 2nd Battalion will advance against the enemy, about six or seven metres in front of the rest. The 1st Battalion will be on his right and the 118th on his left. Captain Radke with the 3rd Battalion will remain with me in reserve. Now, gentlemen, good luck to you!

Loffelhardt and I handed our horses to our orderlies and took our bicycles, in order to carry orders of which the soldiers were to know nothing.

It was 7 p.m. We were advancing on the village of Wiazownica, which we were to attack from the left. Hardly had we arrived within three metres of the village, when we were greeted by machine gun fire which did us no harm, however, because the aim was very bad. Eger ordered a rest and telephoned Rogge for instructions, but got no answer. So he had us advance again and many of us were killed and wounded. Seeing that we would gain nothing, Eger again stopped our advance. I stayed with him, Rickert and Loffelhardt in a sand pit, to which some soldiers a little later brought Lieutenant Daucher of the 8th Company. He had a bullet in his abdomen and seemed to be suffering intensely. He begged us to kill him. We had no means of affording him any relief. He died a little while afterwards. When the battle was over Eger had him buried on the banks of the river.

Eger, not knowing what to do, sent me with Loffelhardt and a first class private to Rogge, for instructions. Bullets whizzed all around us, we started to crawl, and finally landed in the midst of the 2nd Company. They had been without a word from their battalion for four hours. A young reserve officer said boldly that Rogge had shown himself absolutely incapable of commanding his regiment. Finally we found Rogge's adjutant, Lieutenant von Stein, who, without listening to us, said that the orders were to take Wiazownica at two o'clock.

We extracted a written and signed order from him, because this young fellow was quite capable of issuing such instructions on his own responsibility to distinguish himself and so get the Iron Cross of the first class. We promptly returned to Eger, who immediately ordered the battalion to hold itself in readiness to attack.

We advanced without a single shot being fired at us. A patrol that had gone ahead returned to say that the town was heavily fortified. We told Rogge of this, and he said nothing. Eger then ordered us to attack and to our great surprise we entered the town without a single shot being fired at us and without finding a single Russian soldier there. The enemy had retreated. Such was the capture of Wiazownica which was the subject of a magnificent *communiqué* and which all the German newspapers celebrated as a great victory of the 56th Division. The soldiers all laughed and made fun of us and above all of Rogge, who had not even yet arrived on the scene, so afraid and distrustful was he of the Russians.

Toward ten o'clock we took possession of the Russian trenches, which led from the town to the river Lubaczawka. Hardly were we settled there when we were ordered to return to the town: every one thought that our officers did not know what to do, and were embarrassed. Suddenly the first Russian shell hit us, killing about six men. As Rogge had announced that we would not resume our march for another hour we had time to bury our dead.

"Give no quarter," said Eger in the speech that he made on this occasion; "this band of beasts deserves no pity. If you let yourselves be captured you will have to work in the mines of Siberia, with your feet in chains."

Punctually at one o'clock, our artillery opened fire. Our gunners aimed well and we were able to advance, pipes in our mouths and arms shouldered, without the slightest difficulty. Lieutenant Schaller, who was a forester by profession, advanced calmly, gun slung over his shoulder as if he were off for a hunt. The Russians were massacred in these woods by our shells and later we found their dead and wounded. It had been a veritable carnage.

The battle was now practically won, but we still had to capture Radawa to prevent the enemy from attacking our flank. Lieutenant Knell, at the head of a patrol that had only to fire a few shots, took the town. Its only defenders were a few Cossacks who retreated at a gallop.

22

Radawa

Eger, who was in command, had chosen the best house in the town for us. As we were settling ourselves there in his absence an officer of the Uhlans who was adjutant of the 35th Infantry, came in and addressing himself to Loffelhardt asked us to get out and make room for him. Loffelhardt explained to him that these were Eger's quarters and that the latter was in command of the town.

"Shut your damned mouth," cried the trooper, "you fool, a one year volunteer. You think I'm going to sleep in a hovel full of peasants while you lounge about this beautiful house? Get out; away with you, and the quicker the better."

But Loffelhardt shook his head at the Uhlan who disappeared, furious, only to return a few moments later accompanied by an elderly colonel.

"Where is that blackguard," said he on entering, and his eyes sought Loffelhardt. I took a hand. "What do *you* want," roared the old colonel. I tried to explain to him that we had been the first to arrive and that it was our place because the battalion was actually in the town while the 35th had only reached its outskirts.

"I see," said the colonel, "you are in league with this wretch."

Things were beginning to look serious for us when Eger arrived on the scene. As he never was afraid of anything, he explained the affair to the colonel, who went away leaving his adjutant to disentangle himself as best he could. Hardly had he gone when Eger, who did not have too much patience, said to him:

"What are you doing here and why did you make so much noise in my house? Do you think that you are in your stable? Get out of here and quickly or I'll have you put out by my men!"

The brave Uhlan did not dare answer Eger and left like a whipped dog. Eger told us that we should have kicked him out ourselves and showed him what proper treatment was.

We had a good meal with Eger, but could not close an eye all night because of the cooties. The suffering those creatures caused us while we were in Galicia was perfectly incredible.

The next day we repaired to the woods called Radawa, leaving the town of that name behind. We wandered about, first to the right then to the left. Apparently our officers did not know what to do. In the evening we returned to the town for food. Then the battalion encamped at the edge of the woods.

During this time the 35th threw up defences along the Lubaczawka to prevent the Russians from crossing. The Lubaczawka is a little river that empties into the San at Monasterz. We were to stay in this position for several days without advancing.

On the twentieth we began to dig trenches in the woods. Our men cut down great quantities of trees for dugouts. They were officially forbidden to destroy things wantonly in Galicia, but the truth is that the German officers did exactly what they liked in Galicia and to the Galicians and all the Austrians in general.

During the night of May 21st we left the woods to occupy an excellent position between Radawa and Monasterz. We were well sheltered there, and only about twenty metres from the river where the soldiers could bathe.

Unfortunately, and it was the case during our entire sojourn on the Eastern front, the provisioning of the soldiers was badly managed, and the soldiers often complained of not having enough to eat. Where were the chickens and the good wines of France?

Rickert, who had charge of provisioning the battalion, came to Eger one day and said:

"I noticed some cattle on a farm five hundred metres from here. The owners refuse to sell them. How shall I get meat?"

Eger, delighted, immediately gave orders to seize the cattle. Lieutenant Bortger, Loffelhardt and I were ordered to accompany Rickert with several men on this very noble errand. We went into the backyard of the farm, where several women and children were gathered. With tears in their eyes they implored us to leave them their cattle which constituted their entire fortune. Without them, they said, they would surely all die of hunger.

"What nonsense!" cried Lieutenant Bortger, "We'll take four cows, one for each company, and a fifth for the regimental staff. Come, men, hurry and be sure 'to choose the fattest ones."

The soldiers hastened to obey, but the poor women fell on their cows as if they were their children threatened by danger. It was impossible to loosen their hold. It became a veritable battle. The frightened cows ran into their backyard, dragging the clinging women along with them. The angry soldiers, encouraged by us, bullied the women and kicked them about.

One of the latter held her hand clasped to her breast, as though trying to hide something in her blouse. Bortger, perceiving this, commanded us to search her. We were scarcely able to make her let go of the beast, one of whose horns she was holding with her other hand. Bortger and Rickert[1] drew their revolvers and threatened to kill her.

By Lieutenant Nolte's order, he having also joined our expedition, the soldiers tore every stitch from the unfortunate woman, and there she stood quite naked before us all.

Then we saw that it was a crucifix that she held, clasped fiercely to her breast. The soldiers on seeing a naked woman let go the cattle and came to amuse themselves about the hapless creature who was crying from shame. Bortger and Nolte *then began to spit on this woman's body*, while Adjutant Hoffman of the 8th Company and several soldiers closed round her and touched her with their dirty hands.

It was only at the end of an interval that the woman was permitted to dress.

"What say you, Nolte?" said Bortger. "It certainly was funny. What a lovely picture! I shall never forget it. I nearly died laughing."

"Too bad all the soldiers were there," answered Nolte. "Otherwise I should have . . ."

Bortger was to forget that scene sooner than he thought, as he was killed on the next day. May 23rd, 1915. He was buried behind the trenches without a single word of regret being spoken over his grave. At the moment that the body was being lowered. First Class Private Bender took off Bortger's leggings because the latter owed him some money.

On the twenty-fourth, between six and seven o'clock we suddenly heard the Russians "hurrahing" in their trenches. Thinking that they were about to attack us, our artillery sent them a shower of shells. They still continued their yelling and even began to sing. We did not understand what was happening, when suddenly the singing stopped and in the midst of the silence a loud voice shouted:

---

1. This Rickert had been a theological student.

"Brothers, Italy has declared war on Austria. You had better surrender, as all resistance is henceforth useless."

This was not joyful news for the German soldiers. They said it was a diplomatic failure, etc. But Eger told them to have no fear, because the Italians were cowards, incapable of serious fighting, and that soon the Austrians would be in Venice. To annoy the Russians, the men were ordered to sing *"Deutchland Uber Alles"* and *"Die Wacht Am Rhein."* That evening, May 23rd, was of the pleasantest of the war for us, as the Russians and Germans both sang all through it—one from joy, the other out of spite.

On the twenty-fourth, Captain Lindwurm, who had been slightly wounded at Lenglier and had since succeeded in staying in hiding in Mayence, returned to his regiment, and being older than Eger, took command of the 2nd Battalion. The latter took command of the 10th Company. No one regretted his departure. But his successor was one of the greatest cowards in the army.

Lindwurm, who had not yet been in the trenches, was horribly afraid of catching the "cooties." He did not dare eat with us nor touch anything that we had handled. He always spoke to us from a distance of live or six feet. He made fun of us, called us lousy fellows, and was ever so proud of being clean himself. Loffelhardt and I tried our best to make him catch some of the dirty little creatures but always in vain as we could not get near him. But at last Loffelhardt had an ingenious idea. We put a few of these insects into a match box, and during his absence put it, half opened, into his bed, and awaited the result. By the next day we knew that we had succeeded. Lindwurm asked us to dinner with him, a new and unheard of thing.

"There is no use in isolating myself any longer, because some day I'll catch these fleas anyway," said he; "it seems to be quite inevitable." It was funny to see him scratching first his arms, then his throat and legs all during the meal. "Gentlemen," said he at last, "I think that I have caught the damned things, though I don't know how it could have happened, I've been so careful to use insect powder all the time."

Then we showed him why the powder was of no use at all. A flea buried under a speck of powder would emerge from it as fresh and gay as ever. After that evening we always dined with Lindwurm.

We occupied this position until June 4th.

At our left was the 98th Imperial and Royal Austrian Regiment. One day a soldier from this regiment came to our staff and asked permission to speak to the commander of the battalion about a matter of importance. Eger was then in command during Lindwurm's absence. Here is what the soldier said to him.

> Some Russian prisoners of ours told us that their regiments are going to attack us this evening in order to retake the town. However, all of my comrades, who are mostly Bohemians and Czechs, have decided to make no resistance but to surrender as they have had enough of war. The officers have also decided to give themselves up for they know what's going on although they have said nothing. But I am a German-Austrian from Vienna and I don't want to see it all end this way. That is why I come to warn you what those dirty Slovaks are planning to do.

Eger immediately telephoned for reinforcements. The 92nd Brunswicks were immediately sent to us. Our artillery was ordered to fire on the Austrians if they retreated. The 92nd was to do the same.

The Russians attacked at the hour that our informant had promised and as they advanced the Austrians began their retreat. But we were prepared for that very contingency. While Lieutenant Huck of the 5th Company of our regiment advanced against the Russians our artillery and the 92nd Brunswicks started shooting at the Austrians, who on finding themselves between two fires, began to advance again.

If the Russians had been able to hold their town our entire battalion would have been captured. On the following day, the Austrians were replaced by German troops at the request of the commandant of our division. Our officers spat in disgust at the Austrians and the men did likewise.

23
Last Battles in Galicia and Our Return to France

During the night of June 3rd we abandoned our position to go to a bend in the Lubaczawka to the right of Radawa. On the fourth at eight o'clock we were to open the general offensive which was to put us in possession of the other bank of the river and drive the Russians out of Galicia. Everything was ready. We had an excellent bomb thrower in our trenches and a captain of the 111th Artillery who was with us to time the firing, thanks to his telephonic instructions (too far to the right, too far to the left, too near, too far), helped marvellously. This bomb thrower was a small cannon, about the size of a German machine gun. The gunner aimed, pushed the lever and the bomb mounted into the air with a sort of grumbling sound.

It carried in the neighbourhood of four hundred metres, and on bursting destroyed everything within a radius of about thirty metres. The explosion was accompanied by a cloud of heavy black smoke which took several moments to disappear. The Russians, demoralized by our artillery, surrendered themselves in a body. The captain told us that had we had the French to fight, things might have turned out differently for us, and that many of us would have fallen, as the latter were good fighters and knew how to defend themselves.

Toward ten o'clock the Russians had to draw on their reserves.

The 6th Company was isolated for a while and might easily enough have been captured.

During the fight, Lindwurm, scared silly, had hidden in his dugout. When it became necessary for him to rejoin us, he had himself surrounded by six soldiers who served as a shield. This cowardliness did not prevent him from shortly becoming commander.

A little later we had to attack in order to get possession of the hill in front of us and so continue to drive back the Russians. We also captured the woods to the right of the hill. During all this time no one saw Lindwurm. Rickert, Loffelhardt and I had all the responsibility. Without too great loss the battalion rapidly obtained all its objectives.

Until June 7th we occupied the line from Gaydy to Zaradawa, and then we continued our advance. During all this time food reached us irregularly and in insufficient quantities.

On the tenth we were in Dobra. The famished soldiers began to pillage the houses. Lindwurm was the first to approve of this.

On the eleventh we were the reserves in a wood north of Rudka. On the twelfth we were relieved; we then went to Rudka for our next orders. Our march was very painful. At Rudka we received bread, eggs, milk, butter and cheese. We sat down to eat without waiting for Lindwurm who was never about. He had spent the night in a hole that a child could hardly have crept into. Just imagine a man with a paunch sleeping in a cradle! Such was the spectacle that the brave Prussian captain presented. It was hard for us not to burst out laughing when we saw him.

As the Russians were still retreating, we dug a sufficiently large shelter and asked Lindwurm to join us. But he was paralysed with fright and would not move but remained where he was, occasionally scratching himself on account of the fleas. Out of pity for him we dug a trench between his hole and ours so that he could join us without exposing himself. He almost wanted to kiss us and could not thank us enough.

On the next day we went to Dobza. The Russian artillery fire was intense. Lindwurm commanded the sections to advance on the run, but far from setting the example himself he remained on his belly in a trench. How could the soldiers be brave when their commander was such a coward? At Dobza, he had the impertinence to rebuke Lieutenant Schaller for having exposed us all to the enemy's fire by crossing the open field with his company. Schaller answered with some irony that he had quite forgotten to ask the Russians not to fire while Commander Lindwurm passed.

At Dobza there was a Bavarian division. One of these regiments, the 19th Infantry, joined our division. On June 13th we passed Kawale, where a desperate battle had taken place two days before, apparently between the Russians and Bavarians. No quarter had been given and we found many Russians with throats cut and skulls smashed by blows from the butts of rifles. The Bavarians said quite frankly that it was far better for all the Russians to die than not to have enough to eat. Every one knew that our own rations were in truth insufficient. Anyway, the Bavarians made a practice of butchering their wounded and prisoners. A Bavarian lieutenant himself said that he gave no quarter. "It is serious warfare, war to the knife," said he, "and I want to see blood flow."

From Kawale we proceeded to Cisplice. We spent a bad half hour ascending a little hill where the Russians bombarded us heavily. The 7th and 8th companies had many casualties and lost nearly all of their privates. Sergeant-Major Heer was wounded in the neck and lost his right arm.

We were now under a general who commanded a Bavarian army corps. We were ordered to take the village of Wolezasby. Lindwurm, following his usual custom, stayed behind with the telephone and it was up to us to lead the battalion. We took the village without very great difficulty or heavy losses. In the evening Rickert and I went to look for Lindwurm, who as I have said had been out of sight the entire day. When we told him that we were in possession of the town he had the audacity to say to us proudly:

"I am happy to be in command of so noble a battalion and I thank you, my friends, for assisting me so splendidly in the execution of my orders." When we were alone again we burst out laughing.

On entering the village we noticed a Russian captain at the edge of the road. He was wounded and apparently in agony. We went up to him to see whether we could do anything for him. He had several bayonet wounds and had almost lost consciousness. As we raised his head he opened his eyes and said:

"Away with you, assassins! Why do your men commit such awful crimes? I was no longer an enemy when I surrendered with my company. Unarmed, we were all massacred. At least blow out my brains so that I may no longer suffer." We called the nurses and left him. Afterwards the nurses told us that they had ended his sufferings as it had been impossible to move him. In any event we knew that he had spoken the truth because we saw the Russian muskets piled up fifty metres behind the place where we had found him and his butchered men.

We occupied the Russian trenches until June 19th. Our staff was magnificently installed in a church where we had had fresh straw brought. A telephone installed in the sacristy enabled us to keep informed of all that happened in the trenches.

On June 20th we were ordered to seize the village of Dornach, scarcely fifteen kilometres from the Russian frontier. Lindwurm made a wry face on hearing this; he told us that it was very easy for those gentlemen in the rear, well protected as they were, to give like orders.

"Captain," we said to him, "Why do you not have yourself placed on the general's staff? Haven't you proved that you can direct a battle lying hidden in a wheatfield? You've been an adjutant for twelve years and know quite as much as a colonel."

Lindwurm answered, shrugging his shoulders: "I've tried everything. But it's no use; they don't want me."

The taking of Dornach was easier than we had thought. We found many dead there, besides dying horses and a lot of damaged material. One man had had his chest run through by a wagon pole. We also found three Russian soldiers killed by bayonet thrusts and stripped naked. Even their boots had been carried off. The inhabitants of the village had fled and numbers of frightened cattle were running all over the place.

Rickert seized eight calves and had them killed for our battalion (just the members of the staff). Dirrig, our cook, was delighted. The extraordinary thing was that we ate the eight calves in two days. There were only about fourteen of us, including the cook and the orderlies. It is true that we kept eating it all day long and without bread and that it was a long time since we had had anything so delicious. But still I never would have believed that one could eat so much meat.

On June 22nd the rumour was about that we would soon be replaced by a division of the 11th Army Corps. That very same evening indeed, we were relieved by the 44th Brigade of this corps. We left for Céwkaw, then for Oleszyu, where we were quartered. The city was full of Jews who sold vodka, an alcoholic beverage so strong that all the soldiers became drunk.

On the twenty-fourth we reached Polank, which had been almost completely destroyed by the Germans. Rogge installed himself in a house that happened not to have been damaged, putting its inmates, including an old woman who was ill and in her bed, into the street. In the evening he had the regiment's band play.

On the twenty-sixth we went to Jaraslaw where we were to entrain to be killed elsewhere. We changed all of our wagons, but kept our little Russian ponies, which we were to take to France. For it was to France that we were returning after two months' absence. Our train went through Lancut and Cracow where we were given food. At last, on a Sunday, at five o'clock we reached the German frontier of Poland. A disinfecting plant had been put up so that we could at last get rid of our vermin. Everything had to pass through this establishment: men, horses, wagons, even the kitchens.

Each man made separate packages of his cloth and of his leather clothing. These packages were numbered for identification and handed in to be returned to us later. There we stood in our shirts. Then they took us to tanks in which we plunged into hot water up to our necks. We soaped and scrubbed one another with a special soap which killed the lice and their eggs. Only then could we realize the damage these dirty little beasts had done. Some of the men's bodies looked like open sores. Then we had cold showers, and each of us got a fresh shirt and a pair of drawers and socks. These had been requisitioned in France and Belgium.

They were of every imaginable colour: one man wore a pair of blue drawers, a red shirt and yellow socks; another had on a pink shirt, green drawers and black or white socks. In this outfit we went into a room where a meal was served us. It looked more like a masquerade than war and all the soldiers were very gay. Then we received back our clothes and leather garments which had all been submitted to a high temperature in a special furnace. Naturally they were in a frightful condition, but we were happy to be rid of our vermin.

24

Hérin

Our journey from Galicia to France lasted five days. July 1st, 1915, we reached Brussels where we stayed for several hours. When we were crossing Germany the people had cheered us everywhere, but here no one noticed us.

July 2nd we were at Valenciennes, four kilometres from the town. Our battalion was quartered at Hérin, where we rested for quite a while from the effects of the campaign in Galicia. Lindwurm and Rickert were lodged in a castle. Loffelhardt and I found a place for ourselves in a small house where a woman and two children lived. All the 7th and 8th Companies were billeted, the 5th and 6th were quartered in the big breweries (those of Sauvage and Giran). The men behaved themselves well and there were no complaints.

The entire 56th Division was at Valenciennes and in the vicinity. The staff-office of the division was at Saint-Saulve with a motorcycle company. The staff-office of the regiment and of the 3rd Battalion was at Valenciennes itself. A company of machine guns was encamped between Hérin and Aubry continually on the watch for French and English aviators flying over the town. The 111th Artillery Corps with its ammunition train was at Aubry. All the cannon had been sent to Douai where there was a huge repair shop.

We had few duties, for the division was there to recuperate. On the ninth our general held a big review and distributed the decorations awarded by Emperor Francis Joseph to our soldiers who had fought in Galicia. Lindwurm was decorated by the general who congratulated him on his excellent leadership in Austria.

The soldiers grumbled and Sansler, a non-commissioned officer of the 6th Company, said, in a loud voice, "We—we are the ones who did the fighting, we carry the scars of battle, but the cowards are decorated!"

After the review Lindwurm had Sansler brought to him and asked him how he could talk that way. Sansler replied that he had refused to be a reserve officer, that he had fought at Roye, at Champagne and in Galicia and that he had been wounded twice, but he had received no decorations. Two days later Sansler was made a sergeant-major and immediately received the Iron Cross which he put in his pocket. He did not care to wear it "like a coachman," he said.

On July 10th, our brave Rogge was made a lieutenant-colonel and Nolte received the Iron Cross of the first class. Everybody hoped that Rogge would be transferred to another regiment where he would be made a colonel.

On the eleventh an order was issued allowing fifty soldiers from each company leave of absence. At this news everybody was happy and all the suffering and injustices were forgotten. I had my leave and was preparing to start off at seven o'clock to see my mother when I got an order to report to headquarters at Valenciennes to act as interpreter. All my efforts to go into Germany were futile, and Lindwurm in tearing up my leave, said, "After all aren't you in your own country just the same, since you said while you were studying to be a reserve officer, that those who have once lived in France wish to remain there always?" It was true, and it was this very fact that had prevented my being made a reserve officer.

What answer could I make to this coward who owed so much to Loffelhardt and me?

25
Headquarters at Valenciennes

In July, 1915, military headquarters at Valenciennes were installed in the town hall. The mayor was authorized to keep several small rooms for himself and his assistants. The Germans turned the court house, where the water and fire departments had been located before the war, into a storehouse for revolvers, guns, munitions, bicycles, harness and other articles which they had confiscated. On the second floor was a civil prison and one for German soldiers.

In charge of headquarters was Lieutenant Colonel Spiers, who was a member of one of the Uhlan regiments of the 13th Army Corps. His adjutant who represented him when necessary was Captain Kolb. Reserve Lieutenant Korneman, a coffee salesman in civil life, was also connected with headquarters. The court martial was composed of the Imperial Adviser Dr. Wunder (an attorney at Karlsruhe in civil life). Dr. Lewin, who represented him when necessary, and Sergeant-Major Sohn, interpreter and secretary. The last named was not always present for they distrusted him; but they were afraid to get rid of him because of the many secrets he knew which he might disclose to avenge himself.

In the right wing was the office where the French and Belgians who had charge of the food supply of the civilians received their passports.

The Food Commission was composed of a captain in the reserves, a lieutenant of the *landwehr*, several Americans, and a certain number of French citizens. Among the last I commend M. Dreyfus who did his best for his people and his country.

During the little while that I stayed at Valenciennes—that is to say until the 56th Division left for the front—I learned and I saw some very interesting things concerning the regulations which the captured peoples were subjected to in this conquered village.

The civilians were allowed to be about the streets, frequent the *cafés* and restaurants and the public buildings from six o'clock in the morning till eight o'clock at night. The stores and the *cafés* were open from eight o'clock in the morning till seven o'clock at night.

Soldiers were quartered in almost every house.

The band of the 88th played every day in front of headquarters from twelve until one. On the door of the town hall hung the imperial flag of Germany and the royal flag of Bavaria. On a large shield were the words:

ETAPPEN KOMMANDATUR

During the day there was considerable traffic in the streets.

A German canteen sold only to German soldiers.

The officers and the men of these troops on the staff lived a great deal better than they did in Germany.

In addition to their salary or advanced pay, the commander received an indemnity paid by the town of thirty-five *francs* per day; the other officers received ten *francs* a day; the sergeant-majors six *francs* and the non-commissioned officers and soldiers four *francs*. Over and above this they enjoyed free lodging in the hotels for which they paid in four-*franc* checks issued by the town. In theory the indemnity was levied for food because their duties hindered them from eating as usual or at mess. But in reality everybody ate where it cost him nothing and pocketed the indemnity. They all ate at the Saint-Vincent barracks in Rue de Lille. Briefly one can say that the troops on the staff were maintained at the expense of the population.

Up to the present time the war had lasted for more than a year and everything that we had had been stolen; the requisitions always were excessive. We took everything that could have the least possible value. All the bicycles for example had been sent to Germany but we kept on finding more every day.

The mines and the factories at Anzin were operated by the Germans. Many civilians were forced to work in the mines at a pitiful wage. The fields were cultivated by their owners or by the peasants but the German government requisitioned all the crops and left to the owners barely enough to supply themselves with absolutely necessary food and with seed for planting the following spring. The grain was sent to a large mill at Valenciennes under the direction of a non-commissioned officer. The needs of the army were supplied and the surplus sent into Germany.

Many difficulties could have been avoided by the civilians if they had remained on good terms among themselves. But they often did not agree and complained of one another.

Fines were payable in German money and since the town had only paper money, the people were obliged to go to a money changer; this was very expensive.

The police at headquarters were veritable brutes, especially one called Ruff.

My duties were to act as interpreter for the court martial, especially for Dr. Wunder, and to requisition throughout the town and its vicinity, motors, and certain implements, machines and tools for harvesting. It was thus that I frequently had an opportunity to communicate with the French awaiting court martial. The majority of the detained civil prisoners were charged with smuggling either letters or goods from France into Belgium or vice versa.

Thus a china manufacturer from Saint-Amand who often came to Valenciennes with a permit was arrested and accused of being an agent for smuggling letters between France and Belgium.

When arrested, they found no evidence on him and he swore that he was innocent. Nevertheless, he was fined five hundred *marks* and forbidden to leave Saint-Amand where his factory was.

Another curious affair was that of M—— and L——. A certain M——, a Belgian but a resident of Valenciennes, was arrested and accused of selling French newspapers which came from Holland through Belgium. Here is the way this little game was played: some civilian members of the Food Commission were ordered to report at the Dutch frontier to purchase provisions. There the Dutch easily gave them some French newspapers. L——, editor of the *Gazette de Valenciennes*, sold these papers at fifteen *francs* apiece to M—— who lent them to the people for three to five *francs* an hour. When his customers had read them, he sold them at Douai. When he was arrested they found at his house several verses making fun of the *Kaiser*; this was another offence. During the prosecution Sergeant-Major Sohn never stopped annoying Mme. M——, who was very pretty, with his attentions, assuring her that if she would be agreeable he would do all he could to help her husband. L—— and M—— were fined one thousand *marks* each for selling French papers. M—— went to prison for three months for his verses about Wilhelm II.

The mayor of Marly, M. Druy, was imprisoned for travelling to

France by way of Holland and England to see his son who was at Brest. He had then returned. This trip was possible, for there was in France and Belgium a secret organization for people who wished to escape. Everything was ready so that the fugitives could cross the electrically charged barrier; they did this by means of a double ladder. Naturally that was rather expensive. Sometimes also the sentry was bribed. M. Dreyfus, member of the Food Commission of Valenciennes, thus provided for the escape of fifteen hundred young men. He was sentenced to three years at hard labour, about the same time that Miss Edith Cavell[1] was condemned. As for the mayor of Marly, I don't know what his sentence was since I left Valenciennes before his trial.

Two women who struck some policemen were fined one thousand *marks* each and sentenced to three months in jail.

In the prison at headquarters there were quite a number of German soldiers awaiting court martial for overstaying their leave or for being absent without leave. There were some also who had refused to obey orders and had said things against their officers. If their former conduct had been good, they were punished lightly, but they were always sent to the front line trenches and the actual infliction of their punishment suspended until the end of the war. If they behaved themselves they would then be pardoned. One wonders if many soldiers did not commit offences purposely so that they would be sentenced, hoping in this way to escape the war.

When Prussians and Bavarians were in the same locality, there would often be quarrels. In August, 1915, there was a veritable battle at Douai between the troops of these two countries; eight officers were killed and a great many men; there were also many wounded. Four hundred men were sentenced by the court martial at Lille to from one to twelve years in prison at hard labour. This affair was never mentioned by the German press.

Every Tuesday a trainload of soldiers, convicted citizens and persons sentenced to deportation, left for Germany. A great many inhabitants were deported without having been tried,—simply by administrative act.

Every one at headquarters from Lieutenant-Colonel Spiers down to the police had had quantities of shoes made for themselves from

---

1. *Nurse Edith Cavell* by William Thomson Hill and Jacqueline Van Til, *Two Accounts of a Notable British Nurse of the First World War*, *The Martyrdom of Nurse Cavell* by William Thomson Hill and *With Edith Cavell in Belgium* by Jacqueline Van Til is also published by Leonaur.

leather requisitioned for the needs of the army. They sent these shoes into Germany. Dr. Wunder ordered the non-commissioned officers to act cautiously so that this trick should not be discovered and he himself would mark the cases "*Soiled Clothes*" with the headquarters seal.

The following, however, is by all odds the most interesting story I can tell of my experiences in Valenciennes:

At the automobile station at Valenciennes, there was a boy, from a Munich family, who was a chauffeur and who, although he had not done his year's service as a volunteer, went about with the officers: a young slacker of high birth. This young fellow who passed his time agreeably behind the lines had noticed a very pretty girl, about eighteen years old. Her mother kept an inn between Marly and Saultain. The young chauffeur often came to the inn, always ordering the costliest wines and brandies, and trying in all kinds of ways to enter upon friendly relations with the girl. But the latter had such a violent dislike to him that she always left the room as soon as he entered it. Not to be discouraged, he followed her several times into the street but she always found a way to evade him.

One day she met him in the market at Valenciennes. He had a scheme, and coming up to her orders her to follow him immediately. The young girl, very much frightened, follows him obediently, for as soon as a German soldier tells a civilian that he arrests him, the latter must follow without protest, even though he might later, after examination, be set free. The chauffeur leads the young girl to his house, pushes her into his room, turns the key and goes out again to perform his duties. At night he comes home to find his prisoner. A little while later he goes out again and gives himself up at headquarters where he says that he has just accidentally killed a young French girl. They find the body of the young girl in his room; she had been shot through the forehead.

The chauffeur's story—absurd—is as follows:

The young girl had consented to give herself to him. As he was undressing, his revolver which he was in the habit of placing every night on the table next to his bed, went off accidentally and killed her.

The girl's parents accused the chauffeur of murdering their daughter whom he had entrapped because she had refused to give herself up to him. The medical examination showed that the girl had not been outraged.

The man was condemned to six months' imprisonment for arbitrarily imprisoning a person. The apparent fact of murder was overlooked. As he had spent five months in prison before his court martial, he was released a few weeks afterwards.

On hearing this wicked judgment pronounced, the girl's father protested violently, saying that the Germans were acquitting the murderer of his daughter, that there was no such thing as German justice, etc. The poor man was immediately arrested and a few days later deported to Germany.

The old woman in mourning is now all alone in the inn on the Marly road grieving for her husband and daughter, (as at 1919). This story was confirmed to me by Sergeant-Major Sohn who was at the trial. The entire headquarters staff, one and all, confirmed it. The murder and sentence made a deep impression on all the village but could not possibly cause more hatred than already existed for everything German.

My stay at Valenciennes ended on September 20th. That day I was ordered to report at Saverne, in Alsace, where my regiment was located.

26

The Battle of Champagne
(September, 1915)

On September 11th, I arrived at Saverne (Alsace), where my battalion was quartered. I was going to board with my friend Loffelhardt who lived with an Alsatian woman whose husband was a lieutenant in the reserves at the front. This woman told us that all citizens of Saverne (she spoke of the Alsatians) were positive that the war would give them back to France. All the Alsatians hated the Prussians cordially, especially since the Reuter and Forsner affair and had but one desire—to become French citizens once again. After dinner we took a walk through the town and talked with a few of the inhabitants. They all spoke French and pretended not to understand German. All of them told us that after the war Alsace would again become French. They complained a good deal of the severe German administration which treated them like the French and Belgians of the invaded districts.

We were expecting to spend a little more time at Saverne when we were suddenly ordered to leave immediately for Champagne where the French were making a big offensive.

We broke camp that night in a disorder and haste that cannot be described. Many men took this occasion to desert. They were court-martialled later.

On the twenty-fourth at six o'clock in the morning we left for Savigny by way of Sarreguemines, Thionville, Longuyon and Vouziers. The train made very good time and we hardly stopped long enough at Longuyon to eat. Automobiles were awaiting at Savigny to carry us to the front in great haste. The road from Savigny to Séchault resembled the great boulevards of Paris, there was so much traffic. We could already hear the roaring of the guns and soon we passed the artillery positions at high speed. Never have I seen so many cannon so close to each other. We all understood that the French armies were making a huge effort to pierce the German line.

Before arriving at Séchault our automobiles had to slow down, so badly was the road encumbered. The French shells began falling in this region and of course did considerable damage.

For the first time we heard the terrifying noise of the aerial bombs. All the soldiers of the battalion, so happy only two days before, were now sad and discouraged for they believed they were going to their death.

At Séchault we left our automobiles and reached Ripont by a forced march. We were at the identical spot near the famous "Devil's Hole" where we had suffered so during May, 1915. The ground cut up by numerous shell holes was covered with carcasses of men and horses.

At Ripont we waited till night before going into our trenches. During the journey we had suffered several losses. Reserve Lieutenant Abraham had been killed and all of us felt that we would never return from that hell alive.

We finally took possession of our trenches. They had been half destroyed by the French artillery and we had to get to work immediately right under the enemy's infernal fire, to put them in condition.

At daybreak the French attacked us after a terrific bombardment which had lasted three hours. If the French had not attacked so soon our positions would certainly have been wiped out. However, they were a little premature and the first of them to come at us were shot down or captured. The fire was fierce; we sheltered ourselves behind piles of corpses and we looked around us like madmen thinking our last hour had come. Never expecting to come out alive, we prayed for death to finish us off once and for all. We were not exactly nervous but we were dully resigned to the inevitable. The soldiers acted mechanically. We gazed stupidly at our comrades who fell beside us and we lay quietly down beside them as if we did not understand.

Naturally our brave battalion chief, Lindwurm, had, in accordance with his noble habit, preferred not to go into the trenches. He hid himself in a cave between Ripont and Gratreuil, and all of the responsibility of leading the battalion fell upon Rickert, Loffelhardt and myself. Greatly annoyed, we asked First Lieutenant Zietz, commander of the 6th Company, if he would take command of the battalion. He told us that he was not able to take such a responsibility upon himself, that he was not in action and that he had had enough, and that he would be delighted when this dirty business which consisted of killing and of being killed would be over. Then we found Lieutenant Dehes, who was on active service. He said he preferred to die at the head of his company and that he would carry out all the orders he received from us.

On September 26th hell was let loose. The artillery fire reached the height of violence, the earth trembled and many soldiers lost their minds, becoming living corpses. To stay in an underground shelter was to expose yourself to being buried alive. The men wandered like mad through the trenches seeking shelter from death. All at once the French broke through on our right. Passing by our position, which could offer no resistance, and piercing our rear on the run they completely surprised our second line. The French continued doggedly toward Ripont. A few minutes later we saw their cavalry advance. Instinctively, our men began firing at this living target and a number of French troopers fell victims of their bravery. The frightened horses bounded at a gallop over the dead and wounded. Some dragged their riders along with them.

Our artillery had immediately concentrated its fire on the French cavalry without concerning themselves about us, so that we were obliged to abandon our lines on the run, lest every man of us be killed by our own guns. We did not know where we were or what we were to do. We were surrounded on all sides by the French. Furthermore, it was impossible for us to surrender, as the German artillery swept the position, which wais; as untenable for the French as for us. At last we arrived at the second line without knowing what we were doing. There we found heaps of dead and wounded Germans and several crazy soldiers, who were singing and laughing at the uproar. All the rest had been thrown into confusion by the French, who had taken Ripont and passing that place had pushed forward.

These brave men had to stop before a ravine between Ripont and Gratreuil, where the German reserves, waiting for them, opened fire on them. But in their dash, they would probably have overcome this new obstacle if unfortunately they had not found themselves just at this critical moment within the range of their own guns. There was nothing left for them to do but to surrender. Many of our soldiers told me afterwards that they were sorry for this for if it had not happened they themselves would have had a chance to surrender to the French and so be finished with the war.

Rickert asked Loffelhardt if we could not take advantage of this and retake our front line. All our companies except the 5th, commanded by Dehes, had lost their officers. There only remained as leaders in all the ten battalions, Dehes, Rickert, Loffelhardt and I. We told Dehes to attack and we retook our front line, where we found only a few French soldiers, who surrendered, but were instantly killed at Dehes' orders, for the excitement was so great that no one showed any mercy. Dehes received the Iron Cross, first class, for this brave deed. After all it was only our 5th Company which advanced. The others refused on the pretext that they had no officers. Lieutenant Zietz was killed and his orderly, on his knees before him for half an hour, kept begging him to get up. The poor boy had gone mad.

Back in our first position we were able to get an idea of the awful massacre which had taken place. We literally walked over piles of dead and wounded, French and German mixed promiscuously. Cries, groans, the death rattle, veritable shrieks of pain arose from this field of slaughter. For a moment I thought I was going mad like all the rest, for my mind seemed to ramble and my senses were benumbed. A great many men had become stone deaf and remained sitting on the ground, oblivious of everything. If you spoke to them they just stared at you with a stupid expression.

Naturally, on this day there had been no distribution of rations and we found our food by searching through the packs of the dead. The men preferred to search the French, who had white bread, boxes of sardines, chocolate and coffee in their canteens, but no spirits. Luckily, the canteens of the German dead were full of rum. Sitting in our ruined trenches we ate and drank mechanically, thinking of nothing and without bothering about the battle which was still raging on our right towards Somme-Py, where it must have been frightful, for the shells burst by the thousand, darkening the sky with a huge cloud of black smoke. The ground trembled as if there was an earthquake.

At last on September 28th there was a comparative lull and we were relieved in the middle of the night.

Thus ended as far as I was concerned, that horrible Battle of Champagne, through which I did not expect to live.

On the twenty-ninth, we bivouacked at camp Number Three, between Gratreuil and Ripont. Who had taken our places in the front line? We never knew, everything happened so rapidly, and the soldiers had taken off their epaulets, on which were the numbers of their regiments.

We were now able to count our losses. They were terrible. We lost more than two thirds of our force. Only three hundred of us remained in a battalion which, completely reorganized before we left Saverne, had counted a thousand men at that time.

Our battalion chief, Captain Lindwurm, who, as I have related, had refrained from taking command during the battle and had left us to our own resources, had the effrontery to assemble us and to speak to us in this manner:

"Dear comrades, I thank you for your courage and for your heroism. You bravely retook the positions captured by the enemy. I am proud to be your leader. You have obeyed all my orders and have covered the 2nd Battalion with glory."

Such words as these were quite incredible, coming from such a coward as he who, now that danger was over, acted as if he had saved the German Empire. Janecke, a first class private, at headquarters told Rickert and me what Lindwurm had done during the fight. On September 25th, Lieutenant-Colonel Rogge, through a non-commissioned officer, Zentgroff of the headquarters company, ordered Lindwurm to report immediately to him. Lindwurm promised to come, but didn't and instead hid himself in a dugout at Ardeuil. The next day Rogge came himself to find him and said to him:

"Captain, I am sorry to have to tell you that I have proved that the officers of your battalion do not do their duty and do not obey the orders of their superiors. Before you, an officer of this company disobeyed my orders and I had to complain about him" (he was speaking of Schmidt), "and yet he was not a coward. You, you seem to be afflicted with the same disease. I want you to note that I hold you responsible if the discipline of your company does not come up to what is expected and demanded of Prussian troops. I command you for the last time to rejoin your battalion and to lead it."

Lindwurm started out with First-Class Private Bastian, but he stopped at Séchault and Bastian reached us by himself. He transferred the orders signed by Lindwurm to us and warned us that all communications with the regiment would have to be sent to Lindwurm first for his signature.

All this did not prevent Lindwurm's taking command a few days later. He made us another speech at this time in which he had the nerve to speak of the awful battle of Champagne, which he would never forget. What he has certainly not forgotten was the fright he had had.

On October 8th we returned to the trenches with new recruits which made up for our losses and enabled us to reform our units. Seeing these new men one would think that Germany was at the end of her man power, for there were boys scarcely eighteen years old and grey haired men from forty to forty-five. Amongst them there were even cripples, the lame and some poor devils who had already lost a leg or an arm and were being sent to the front just the same.

On October 4th, General von Einem, in his order of the day, thanked us for our bravery. This order ought to have been read to the soldiers, but Lindwurm thought that unnecessary.

"Those whom it would interest," he said, "are dead, wounded or missing; those who are left have not enough sense to understand it. As to the new recruits, it is none of their business."

27
Douai—in Champagne

On November 6th we left our Champagne trenches for the last time and started towards Arras. On the ninth we arrived at Mouchy and on the tenth we were before Arras, where we stayed as reserves.

Our men were quartered on the citizens. We were forbidden to have anything to do with the Bavarian soldiers, so as to avoid quarrels and disputes. We were also forbidden to hold communication with the natives, for it seemed that most of the allied spies were at Douai and Lille. This order did not, however, prevent *monsieurs* the officers from running after the women and trying by every means—almost always by force—to find mistresses. I can mention for example an awful scandal about our own battalion chief, the heroic Lindwurm.

He boarded with a respectable woman who lived alone with her daughter, a girl about twenty-four years old.

Lindwurm decided to become this young girl's lover and he told us of his intention. Rickert, who was a theological student in civilian life, gave him a good lecture and told him he was not conducting himself as a gentleman should. But the fine Lindwurm would not listen to him and straightway entered the young girl's bedroom. The latter told him that Monsieur the Commander must have made a mistake and that he was in a young woman's bedroom.

"My dear young lady," answered Lindwurm gallantly, "believe what you want but let me tell you that I have decided that you are going to be my mistress. Also please take note that all resistance will be futile. If you do not consent I will have you deported to Germany."

Rickert and I, who were in the hall, could hear everything until Lindwurm closed the door.

Rickert, disgusted, went to Lieutenant-Colonel Rogge's headquarters and asked to be relieved from duty as adjutant of the 3rd Battalion. Rogge demanded an explanation and Rickert told him about Lindwurm's behaviour.

"Don't get so hot, my friend," answered Rogge. "These little affairs happen in the best society, you know. Don't get excited. If every one had your scruples it would have been better for Germany never to have gone to war. Maybe you are a little jealous, my dear Rickert, but there are so many women in the streets that assuredly you can find some one to your liking."

Meanwhile, Lindwurm ordered all kinds of food taken to the old lady's house, chiefly dainties, old wines and liquors. When we returned he said:

"Gentlemen, I am your commander and the master of this house. I ordered these provisions and I invite you—no, *I order you* to help celebrate tonight my marriage with this young girl."

A few minutes later, I found myself alone with the girl who, weeping, said to me:

"He threatened to have me deported to Germany like all the rest. What would happen to my poor mother if she were left alone here."

Before dinner we again remonstrated with Lindwurm for uselessly making two women unhappy. But he answered:

"You go to the devil. That's the custom of the staff and I intend to follow it."

Loffelhardt, who sometimes spoke frankly, was indignant and did not hesitate to answer him roughly:

"Sir, if everything went according to custom, how are there the many slackers and cowards at the front, that these gentlemen and I are well acquainted with?"

Lindwurm paled but did not answer.

The bridal dinner was funereal; no one ate and no one knew how to act. The two poor women could hardly keep from crying and Lindwurm, crestfallen, did not know what to say and realized what a ridiculous and beastly part he was playing in this very sad comedy.

The atmosphere became so strained that he could not maintain his position. At dessert he spoke to Rickert and said he was sorry for all this childishness and he begged the ladies to forget it all. We all congratulated him on his virtuous resolution.

On November 23rd we returned to Champagne for the third time. There was now a relative lull on this front in comparison with the horrible battle of September and we were not so miserable. We occupied the same positions as before.

During our absence the engineers had stubbornly laboured at burying mines which were to explode under the French trenches. Our battalion was chosen to attack right after the explosion of one of these mines during the night of December 4th and 5th, 1916, at exactly half-past eleven o'clock. At the given time, a frightful report resounded and in front of us we saw a huge red flame suddenly cover the whole sky and rise upward in the midst of an eruption of earth and black smoke. One clearly saw as if on a luminous screen several human bodies hurled to a great height by the force of the explosion.

Lindwurm, as I said before, gave his orders for half-past eleven. But no one moved except a few new men recently arrived in the battalion. Lieutenant Becker, only nineteen years old, immediately sent word that his company refused to leave the trenches, unless Lindwurm himself came to the front line to lead the attack at the head of his battalion. Lindwurm replied by repeating the order to attack immediately and said that he had to stay behind to direct all stages of the attack. One must admit that in principle he was right, but his cowardice in the past had exasperated the soldiers.

The delay caused by this incident made us lose all the benefits of the confusion brought about by the explosion of the mine. The whole affair was a failure and it was we who were the object of a furious attack from the French, who immediately seized their opportunity. We had to defend ourselves, and it was only through hard work and with great loss that we held our positions. The engineer who had exploded the mine and who wanted to win the Iron Cross of the first class, made a brave counter attack with his fifteen men. He was killed and all his men, except two who came back, were killed, wounded or taken prisoners.

At the close of the affair the regiment was severely reprimanded by the general commanding the army corps.

"It is an act of cowardice and a crime," said the general, " to refuse to obey. It is not the soldier's business what his superior does. He has only to obey and to execute the orders given him. If this happens again, the severest measures will be taken."

Rogge added his remarks to this reproach, accusing the regiment of mutiny.

As punishment the battalion had to stay in the trenches several extra days, but the soldiers made light of it, for existence was even more disagreeable when off duty than on. We were not relieved till the 13th of December. When we were sent to the rear, Rogge assembled the battalion and made a speech in which he said he was ashamed to be in command of such cowards. He announced that sanction had been given for a certain number of men to be chosen from each company and sent to another regiment. When the men had withdrawn, hissing and grumbling, it was the turn of the officers and the non-coms whom he had detained.

"You have heard me, gentlemen. I have kept you to tell you that this disobedience is the result of your indulgence of these peasants, who do only what they want. You treat them as equals and they make fun of you and your orders. You must never speak to them in a friendly way, but on the contrary, treat them severely. The disgrace of the 2nd Battalion rests on me. I trust that a like occurrence will not take place again."

When Rogge was gone, Harnishmacher, who was serving as an officer, said:

"Rogge is great on making speeches but he never comes within the lines himself and prefers to soak himself with wine and in the company of the biggest drunkards of the regiment. I would like to be selected to leave this regiment, which is nothing but a society of antiquated fighters and cowards."

Lindwurm listened to all of this without saying a word.

During the seven hours that the battalion was resting, they tortured the men by prolonged drills as punishment. Many became ill, but Major Fisher of the medical corps said to them: "As long as you can stand on your feet I'll pay no attention to you."

One day a man of the 7th Company, who was in great pain and whom he had just sent away in this manner, took a gun by the barrel and struck him a terrible blow. Dr. Fisher, almost beaten to death, fell fainting and had to be sent to the hospital. The man was arrested and put in prison, where he hung himself during the night. This accident made the officers a little more careful during the next few days.

On December 21st, we returned to the trenches. We had not been relieved when our turn came after the explosion of the mine, so the 3rd Battalion spent Christmas in the front line trenches. Christmas Eve, Lindwurm sent the men great quantities of wine and rum. There was at least one bottle for every four men. The result of this generosity could not be in doubt; everybody was drunk and if the French had attacked us then they would have captured the whole battalion without firing a shot. New Year's Day was celebrated in the same way in the trenches only they gave out less alcohol in order to avoid the general drunkenness of Christmas Eve.

When we reached our resting place behind the lines on January 4th lectures were given every day for the men on the soldier's duties, still on account of their disobedience on December 4th. The men had to repeat and memorize the twenty-nine rules of war.

The first article is as follows:

> I swear before God Almighty, to be faithful to His Majesty Wilhelm II, King of Prussia, Emperor of Germany, never to desert him, to help him and defend him under all circumstances on land and sea, in peace and in war.

On January 15th, 1916, after another sojourn in the front line we were relieved by the 81st Reserve Regiment of the 18th Corps, and sent before Verdun to take part in the Crown Prince's big attack on this fortress. It was there that I was severely wounded at the beginning of the attack.

28

Verdun—Frankfort—Mayence

From January 16th to February 18th, 1916, we rested at Savigny without once going into the trenches. Without a doubt they wanted us to recover our strength for the big drive against Verdun.

On February 18th we left for Thionville, where we spent the night in barracks located near the station. The nineteenth we were at Stenay, where the Crown Prince had his headquarters, then at Réville, where we rested for several hours. During the night we went into the trenches between Brabant and Beaumont. We were placed between the 35th and 118th regiments of the 56th Division.

On February 21st, 1916, toward five o'clock in the morning a heavy artillery fire began such as we had never heard before, even in Champagne. From the whizzing of the shells we could tell at once that only the heavy pieces were being fired.

At nine o'clock we were ordered to attack and take the fort of Bras on our right. The French put up a strong resistance and we advanced very slowly. The battle of Champagne had certainly been terrible, but it was nothing compared to what was going on here in the thick of the fighting. One felt that the methods used were of such magnitude that it was beyond the power of the imagination to grasp it. The fire of the heavy German artillery was something terrific; the sensation was as though every conceivable kind of engine of war had been gathered together. We were engaged in a huge battle in which one regiment was nothing at all.

It was no longer a question of giving and obeying orders (I am speaking of what concerns a battalion); that was impossible. We ran forward, for to retreat was just as dangerous as to advance. We were between two fires: the German artillery firing before us and the French on the site which we had just left. At last we arrived at the first French trench. We thought we could take it easily, but we were wrong, for the few soldiers who were holding it fought desperately. In several places the wounded kept on fighting furiously before they fell under our blows. Not a section surrendered; such were the orders given the small detachments and even isolated individuals.

At last we were in possession of the trench, which had been completely ruined by the heavy German artillery. It was a, frightful chaos of human wreckage. One heard groans which seemed to rise from the very bowels of the earth—the cries of the unfortunates buried alive in their shelters. We were forced to install ourselves in these positions and lie down to escape the fire of the French artillery. On the twenty-second we had to search through the packs of the dead for food. We were not exactly hungry but we did not know what to do, and we ate mechanically.

The following day, the twenty-third, Lindwurm ordered me to go to the rear with a soldier to report to the head of the regiment that the battalion had been entirely broken up and that many soldiers belonging to other regiments were mixed in with us.

We left the trenches. The shells were bursting everywhere. We had not gone quite sixty metres behind the line when suddenly I saw my companion fighting like mad while I felt a blow on my right side. I fell—I remembered afterwards—screaming "Help" like a fool. Then I fainted, and I have never learned how long I remained unconscious.

When I opened my eyes I was in a bed in the field-hospital at Stenay. It was February 26th. The orderly told me that I had been brought to the hospital during the night of the twenty-fourth and twenty-fifth.

I had a wound in my right side. At my request the head surgeon promised me to do his best to send me to the hospital at Frankfort-on-Main, the headquarters of the 18th Army Corps. He kept his promise.

The twenty-eighth I was sent away by automobile to Longuyon and was taken at once to Frankfort in a Red Cross train, a wonderful hospital on wheels, very comfortable, and well organized. There was in my compartment a French lieutenant and an Arabian officer, both wounded at Verdun. The doctor gave each of us an injection of morphine and we fell asleep.

I woke up in the hospital at Frankfort, installed in a comfortable room together with the French lieutenant.

I was extremely well taken care of by the doctors. Concerning the ladies of the German Red Cross, I wish to say that they make life very hard for the English and the Germans but pet and spoil the French like little children. I had the proof of this at Frankfort. The lady who looked after the French officer and myself was the wife of Dr. S——, who was at the front. She gave the lieutenant absolutely everything he wanted, even what the doctor forbade. To me she refused almost everything. As she spoke a little French she would come when her patient was not asleep to chat with him.

The Frenchman, who had noticed that she refused me everything, told me that he would ask her for whatever I needed as if it were for himself. As a result all my desires were gratified without her knowing it. She did not know that I spoke French, and did not bother about what she said to her lieutenant in front of me. She asked him questions about Parisian life, especially about the women. "Don't you miss your sweethearts? It must be very sad for a young man like you to be separated from his little friend," etc., she would say simperingly. I who heard all this and saw her little intrigue enjoyed myself immensely where I lay and made a great effort not to laugh on account of my wound. Sometimes when she got too tender the French officer politely begged her to let him sleep a while, because he felt tired.

As soon as she left the room we laughed so hard that we forgot our sorrows.

One day while we were dozing she came in softly. I made believe I was sound asleep but watched her out of the corner of my eye. She gazed lovingly on the slumbering French officer and then bending over him she kissed him on the forehead.

On March 20th I had the joy of kissing my mother. Our hospital nurse, Mme. S——, having discovered that I understood French had me removed to another section, where I was taken care of by an orderly. I stayed at the hospital till June 26th. I had a fifteen day furlough, which I planned to spend at Fulda with my mother. I was not entirely well, for my mother was opposed to a dangerous operation which the doctor wished to make and which he told me would either completely cure me or prove fatal.

During my fifteen days of convalescence I was able to see the suffering of the civilian population of Germany.

On July 10th I reported at Mayence where I found our battalion of young recruits whom I drilled for about twenty days.

At last on August 1st I rejoined my battalion at the front which was not far from Verdun, between Neuvilly and Aubréville. Lindwurm,

Rickert and Loffelhardt were still there. All the other officers were dead, wounded or missing. They were all sad for the big drive against Verdun had failed and our position was anything but agreeable. Loffelhardt and I were thoroughly disgusted with this war in which, however, we had done our duty and risked our lives so often for more than two years.

On October 20th my wound which had not healed well gave me so much pain that I went to the hospital at Valenciennes whither my battalion had returned. I was sent back a second time to the hospital at Frankfort where they dismissed me in two days telling me that I would not have to return to the front. On the twenty-eighth I received my ticket at Hanau for Ober Jersdal in the north of Schleswig on the Danish border.

29

At the Danish Border

I was enrolled at Ober Jersdal in an auxiliary corps assigned to the duty of building defences on the Danish frontier. Captain Kopp, my chief, gave me permission to live in the town.

In crossing Germany I was able to notice the many precautions taken to prevent espionage and indiscretions. Travelling officers had to remove their epaulets so that no one would know to what regiment they belonged or where they had come from.

I went on duty with my new battalion on November 10th. Almost all the soldiers were war cripples.

We had to dig trenches from Hadersleben to Tondern in case of an English attack by way of Denmark. Our sector extended from Nieder Jersdal to Aokaer and Skovby where tunnels had been excavated, regular catacombs and deep concrete trenches fortified by hidden cannon and machine guns. At Skovby I counted in a small space six of the heaviest guns and twenty-four machine guns placed in concrete shelters. At Nieder Jersdal a family were forced to leave their house so that the basement might be mined. A barrier of wires heavily charged with electricity was stretched from Nieder Jersdal to Ober Jersdal. The source of the current was underground. Countless wagons were bringing the materials necessary for the fortifications to Flensbourg. All the inhabitants of this country with whom I had occasion to speak talked Danish and considered themselves Danish. They did not like to speak German.

(Here end Feldwebel C——'s Memoirs)

ALSO FROM LEONAUR
AVAILABLE IN SOFTCOVER OR HARDCOVER WITH DUST JACKET

DOING OUR 'BIT' by *Ian Hay*—Two Classic Accounts of the Men of Kitchener's 'New Army' During the Great War including *The First 100,000* & *All In It*.

AN EYE IN THE STORM by *Arthur Ruhl*—An American War Correspondent's Experiences of the First World War from the Western Front to Gallipoli and Beyond.

STAND & FALL by *Joe Cassells*—A Soldier's Recollections of the 'Contemptible Little Army' and the Retreat from Mons to the Marne, 1914.

RIFLEMAN MACGILL'S WAR by *Patrick MacGill*—A Soldier of the London Irish During the Great War in Europe including *The Amateur Army, The Red Horizon* & *The Great Push*.

WITH THE GUNS by *C. A. Rose & Hugh Dalton*—Two First Hand Accounts of British Gunners at War in Europe During World War 1- Three Years in France with the Guns and With the British Guns in Italy.

EAGLES OVER THE TRENCHES by *James R. McConnell & William B. Perry*—Two First Hand Accounts of the American Escadrille at War in the Air During World War 1-Flying For France: With the American Escadrille at Verdun and Our Pilots in the Air.

THE BUSH WAR DOCTOR by *Robert V. Dolbey*—The Experiences of a British Army Doctor During the East African Campaign of the First World War.

THE 9TH—THE KING'S (LIVERPOOL REGIMENT) IN THE GREAT WAR 1914 - 1918 by *Enos H. G. Roberts*—Like many large cities, Liverpool raised a number of battalions in the Great War. Notable among them were the Pals, the Liverpool Irish and Scottish, but this book concerns the wartime history of the 9th Battalion – The Kings.

THE GAMBARDIER by *Mark Severn*—The experiences of a battery of Heavy artillery on the Western Front during the First World War.

FROM MESSINES TO THIRD YPRES by *Thomas Floyd*—A personal account of the First World War on the Western front by a 2/5th Lancashire Fusilier.

THE IRISH GUARDS IN THE GREAT WAR - VOLUME 1 by *Rudyard Kipling*—Edited and Compiled from Their Diaries and Papers Volume 1 The First Battalion.

THE IRISH GUARDS IN THE GREAT WAR - VOLUME 2 by *Rudyard Kipling*—Edited and Compiled from Their Diaries and Papers Volume 2 The Second Battalion.

AVAILABLE ONLINE AT **www.leonaur.com**
AND FROM ALL GOOD BOOK STORES

ALSO FROM LEONAUR
AVAILABLE IN SOFTCOVER OR HARDCOVER WITH DUST JACKET

ARMOURED CARS IN EDEN by *K. Roosevelt*—An American President's son serving in Rolls Royce armoured cars with the British in Mesopatamia & with the American Artillery in France during the First World War.

CHASSEUR OF 1914 by *Marcel Dupont*—Experiences of the twilight of the French Light Cavalry by a young officer during the early battles of the great war in Europe.

TROOP HORSE & TRENCH by *R. A. Lloyd*—The experiences of a British Lifeguardsman of the household cavalry fighting on the western front during the First World War 1914-18.

THE LONG PATROL by *George Berrie*—A Novel of Light Horsemen from Gallipoli to the Palestine campaign of the First World War.

THE EAST AFRICAN MOUNTED RIFLES by *C.J. Wilson*—Experiences of the campaign in the East African bush during the First World War

THE FIGHTING CAMELIERS by *Frank Reid*—The exploits of the Imperial Camel Corps in the desert and Palestine campaigns of the First World War.

WITH THE IMPERIAL CAMEL CORPS IN THE GREAT WAR by *Geoffrey Inchbald*—The story of a serving officer with the British 2nd battalion against the Senussi and during the Palestine campaign.

STEEL CHARIOTS IN THE DESERT by *S.C. Rolls*—The first world war experiences of a Rolls Royce armoured car driver with the Duke of Westminster in Libya and in Arabia with T.E. Lawrence.

INFANTRY BRIGADE: 1914 by *Edward Gleichen*—The Diary of a Commander of the 15th Infantry Brigade, 5th Division, British Army, During the Retreat from Mons

HEARTS & DRAGONS by *Charles R. M. F. Crutwell*—The 4th Royal Berkshire Regiment in France and Italy During the Great War, 1914-1918.

TIGERS ALONG THE TIGRIS by *E. J. Thompson*—The Leicestershire Regiment in Mesopotamia During the First World War.

DESPATCH RIDER by *W. H. L. Watson*—The Experiences of a British Army Motorcycle Despatch Rider During the Opening Battles of the Great War in Europe.

AVAILABLE ONLINE AT **www.leonaur.com**
AND FROM ALL GOOD BOOK STORES

ALSO FROM LEONAUR
AVAILABLE IN SOFTCOVER OR HARDCOVER WITH DUST JACKET

OFFICERS & GENTLEMEN *by Peter Hawker & William Graham*—Two Accounts of British Officers During the Peninsula War: Officer of Light Dragoons by Peter Hawker & Campaign in Portugal and Spain by William Graham .

THE WALCHEREN EXPEDITION *by Anonymous*—The Experiences of a British Officer of the 81st Regt. During the Campaign in the Low Countries of 1809.

LADIES OF WATERLOO *by Charlotte A. Eaton, Magdalene de Lancey & Juana Smith*—The Experiences of Three Women During the Campaign of 1815: Waterloo Days by Charlotte A. Eaton, A Week at Waterloo by Magdalene de Lancey & Juana's Story by Juana Smith.

JOURNAL OF AN OFFICER IN THE KING'S GERMAN LEGION *by John Frederick Hering*—Recollections of Campaigning During the Napoleonic Wars.

JOURNAL OF AN ARMY SURGEON IN THE PENINSULAR WAR *by Charles Boutflower*—The Recollections of a British Army Medical Man on Campaign During the Napoleonic Wars.

ON CAMPAIGN WITH MOORE AND WELLINGTON *by Anthony Hamilton*—The Experiences of a Soldier of the 43rd Regiment During the Peninsular War.

THE ROAD TO AUSTERLITZ *by R. G. Burton*—Napoleon's Campaign of 1805.

SOLDIERS OF NAPOLEON *by A. J. Doisy De Villargennes & Arthur Chuquet*—The Experiences of the Men of the French First Empire: Under the Eagles by A. J. Doisy De Villargennes & Voices of 1812 by Arthur Chuquet .

INVASION OF FRANCE, 1814 *by F. W. O. Maycock*—The Final Battles of the Napoleonic First Empire.

LEIPZIG—A CONFLICT OF TITANS *by Frederic Shoberl*—A Personal Experience of the 'Battle of the Nations' During the Napoleonic Wars, October 14th-19th, 1813.

SLASHERS *by Charles Cadell*—The Campaigns of the 28th Regiment of Foot During the Napoleonic Wars by a Serving Officer.

BATTLE IMPERIAL *by Charles William Vane*—The Campaigns in Germany & France for the Defeat of Napoleon 1813-1814.

SWIFT & BOLD *by Gibbes Rigaud*—The 60th Rifles During the Peninsula War.

AVAILABLE ONLINE AT **www.leonaur.com**
AND FROM ALL GOOD BOOK STORES